A DELICIOUS SLICE OF
JOHNNERS

A DELICIOUS SLICE OF JOHNNERS

Brian Johnston
Edited by Barry Johnston

For Olivia and Sam,
Nicholas, Rupert and Sophie,
Harry, Emily and Georgia

This edition first published in this form in Great Britain in
2001 by Virgin Publishing Ltd
Thames Wharf Studios
Rainville Road
London W6 9HA

First published in this form in Great Britain in 2000

A catalogue record for the book is available
from the British Library.

ISBN 978 0 7535 4071 8

Phototypeset by Intype London Ltd

The Random House Group Limited supports The Forest Stewardship
Council (FSC®), the leading international forest certification organisation.
Our books carrying the FSC label are printed on FSC® certified paper.
FSC is the only forest certification scheme endorsed by the leading
environmental organisations, including Greenpeace. Our
paper procurement policy can be found at
www.randomhouse.co.uk/environment

www.randomhouse.co.uk

Printed and bound in Great Britain by Clays Ltd, St Ives PLC

Contents

PART III: RAIN STOPS PLAY

Acknowledgements

My grateful thanks to all of the following:

Les Bailey for his streaker poem; *The Times* for the reproduction of an article by Michael Leapman; Mrs Alan Hamilton for her late husband's poem, *The Cricketer's If*; and an unknown lady for her parody of the Crispin Day speech from Shakespeare's *Henry V*.

Introduction

IN SEPTEMBER 1972 my father, Brian Johnston, went off to his holiday home at Swanage in Dorset to relax and to write his autobiography, *It's Been a Lot of Fun*. He had just retired after twenty-six years as a member of staff at the BBC. He was sixty years old and it seemed likely that his broadcasting career was coming to the end of a long and successful innings. But at an age when most people are contemplating a quiet retirement, Brian went on to achieve his greatest popularity and over the next twenty-one years he became a national institution on radio programmes such as *Down Your Way* and *Test Match Special*.

When Brian died in January 1994 at the age of eighty-one, the Prime Minister, John Major, spoke for millions of radio listeners when he said: 'Summers will never be the same.' In the *Daily Telegraph* Christopher Martin-Jenkins wrote: 'It is hard to believe that anyone in the history of broadcasting has induced such widespread affection.'

Brian Johnston was born on 24 June 1912, the youngest of four children, in the Old Rectory at Little Berkhamsted, Hertfordshire. When he mentioned it to one of his friends in later life, he thought it was highly appropriate. 'After all,' he told Brian, 'you *are* a bit of a wreck and we all know what your politics are!' His father worked in the Johnston family coffee business in the City and his grandfather had been Governor of the Bank of England in 1909 and 1910, so the family was well established and, to use Brian's words, 'moderately well-off.'

Then in 1922, when Brian was ten years old, he saw his father drown in a tragic swimming accident while the family were on holiday at Bude in Cornwall. His mother had to sell their house and the family fortunes took a turn for the worse. There was enough money, however, to send Brian and his two brothers to boarding school. Brian went to Temple Grove Preparatory School in Eastbourne and then to Eton College. He always said that his Eton schooldays were among the happiest times of his life. He was good at sports and played rugby for the school, although he only made the cricket Second XI, much to his eternal disappointment.

He also discovered an ability to make people laugh and for the rest of his life he was unable to resist telling jokes and making the most awful puns. His humour remained firmly of the schoolboy variety. But his theory was that making jokes is rather like batting at cricket. If you hit *every* half-volley, you are bound to score the occasional boundary. 'However obvious or corny,' he would say, 'have a bash and sooner or later you will get a laugh!'

On leaving Eton, Brian went up to New College, Oxford, where he read history and P. G. Wodehouse and played cricket, although not necessarily in that order. He wanted to go into the theatre, but after pressure from his family he reluctantly joined the family coffee business in the City. He was shipped out to Brazil to learn more about coffee beans, but after eighteen months he became so seriously ill that he nearly died and was sent home.

When war was declared in 1939 Brian joined the 2nd Battalion Grenadier Guards and became a Technical Adjutant. After D-Day he went to Normandy with the Guards Armoured Division and was responsible for the rescue of battle casualties, often from blazing vehicles, and the recovery and repair of the battalion's tanks. At the end of the war he was awarded the Military Cross for his inspirational leadership and his 'untiring determination and cheerfulness under fire'. Brian was so modest that he never mentioned it in any of his books.

In the summer of 1945 he was promoted to major and put in charge of organising an army revue called *The Eyes*

Have It, which toured all the units of the Guards Armoured Division in Germany with great success. Brian took part in several sketches and performed a comedy double-act. By now he was adamant that he would never return to his former office job in the City. He wanted to do something – *anything* – in the entertainment business. In November he was demobbed and he arrived back in London. And that is where our story begins.

Here are the highlights of an extraordinary broadcasting career. The great state occasions such as the funeral of King George VI and the Coronation, the royal weddings of Princess Margaret and Princess Anne, and the Queen's Silver Jubilee. From his early radio success in the forties on *In Town Tonight* to the final critical and public acclaim on *Test Match Special*. Here too are all the famous gaffes, practical jokes and leg-pulls.

After the success of *It's Been a Lot of Fun*, Brian wrote a second volume of autobiography called *It's a Funny Game*. This was followed by *Rain Stops Play*, a collection of his favourite anecdotes, jokes and stories. Now for the first time all three books have been edited together and condensed into one volume. So why not sit back and treat yourself to *A Delicious Slice of Johnners* and I hope you will agree that it really *was* a lot of fun!

Barry Johnston
July 2000

PART I:
IT'S BEEN A LOT OF FUN

1 I meet 'Auntie'

THE AUTUMN OF 1945 was a series of leaving parties for the British soldiers still serving in Germany, as wartime-only officers and men were gradually demobbed and sent home. In November it was my turn. Pleased as I was to be going back to civilian life, it was also with great regret that I said my goodbyes to all my friends in the 2nd Battalion Grenadier Guards – both officers and men. For five years they had given me their friendship and in spite of all the unpleasant things we went through together, it is the fun and laughter that I always try to remember. I have kept up with many of them and thirty years later I still receive at least ten cards every Christmas from various members of my technical staff.

And so I returned to England, drew my blue pin-stripe demob suit from Olympia, and went down to my mother's thatched cottage in the village of Chearsley in Buckinghamshire, to sort myself out and decide exactly what I was going to do with my future.

Now that I had time to sit back and think, I was more determined than ever to escape from my old job in the Johnston family coffee business – the Brazilian Warrant Co. Ltd – and to do something in the entertainment world. But I realised only too well all my limitations and how inexperienced I was. I had a slick way of telling a story and after performing in the Guards' wartime revues I could now put over a cross-talk act. But that was about all and if I wanted to become an actor it would mean learning the business from the bottom either in repertory or in drama school. I was now aged thirty-three and felt that it was too late in life to start. So I decided to try for the management or production side of the business.

I came up to London and stayed in the Guards Club, which was then in Brooks Street. First of all I went to the Brazilian Warrant offices in the City, to say goodbye to everyone and to apologise for leaving them in the lurch. I then set about seeing some theatrical managers and producers who were all very kind and sympathetic. But it soon became obvious that they had nothing to offer me, which was not really surprising, because I really had nothing in the way of experience or ability to offer them.

I trailed around for about a fortnight and began to get very depressed. What *was* I going to do? And then luck – of which I freely admit I have had more than my fair share – came to my aid. I was sitting rather gloomily reading a paper in the Guards Club when an old officer friend asked me whether I would like to have dinner and help entertain two BBC types whom he gathered I already knew. They were the former BBC war reporters Stewart Macpherson and Wynford Vaughan-Thomas, whom I had met in 1943 while on manoeuvres with the Guards in Norfolk. It was this dinner party with them that was to decide my future.

During conversation I casually mentioned that I was looking for a job in the entertainment world, but could not think of exactly what to do. At that time I never gave a thought to the BBC which I regarded with a mixture of respect and tolerant amusement at its 'Auntie' image.

Stewart said nothing that evening but next day rang to say that there was a vacancy in the Outside Broadcast Department and would I like to come up to their office in Portland Place for an interview with the Head of 'OBs', Seymour de Lotbinière. Even then I was only mildly enthusiastic but had the sense and good manners to say thank you and yes of course I would come.

I vaguely knew de Lotbinière or 'Lobby', as he was always called, from before the war. He was an old Etonian, about 6 feet 8 inches tall and had been a keen member of the Toc H movement. Its founder, Rev. 'Tubby' Clayton, used to tell how he had once been staying with the Provost of Eton, and was going up to bed when a tall figure opened a bedroom door to put his shoes out to be cleaned. (I believe it is considered terribly non-U to do this in a private house and of course is a waste of time nowadays in an hotel.) Tubby did not know who it was but in typical fashion said: 'Good evening. And what do you know about Toc H?' To which the tall figure replied: 'Nothing, thank God,' and slammed the door. Tubby was never defeated however and it was not long before he had converted Lobby, and he later said of him, 'Lobby came to us as proud as Lucifer, but we made him scrub floors.'

So I went to see Lobby without honestly thinking there was much in it for me. His secretary had told me the wrong time for the interview, so although I arrived in true Guards' fashion five minutes early for parade, I nearly missed it altogether. In the time available Lobby quizzed me about my knowledge of entertainment and sport, and seemed particularly keen to discover whether I was interested in people. At the end of the interview he said he would give me two tests and if I passed them he could then offer me a job. It might only be temporary and in any case would be pretty poorly paid. I told him that neither of these things worried me as I did not expect to make broadcasting my career and I still had a bit of my army gratuity left.

Nothing like being honest! Anyway I said I would like to have a crack at the tests. The first was to go down to Piccadilly Circus and write a five-minute report on what I saw there – just as if I was going to give a radio talk. And here again luck or fate took a hand. As I was walking down Regent Street wondering what on earth I was going to say I passed one of those shops where you can record a birthday or Christmas greeting. 'Why not record your message?' it said in gold letters in the window and that's just what I decided to do. I went to Piccadilly Circus, made some notes and then went back to the shop to record my five-minute message. I played it back and it sounded ghastly. It was the first time I had heard my voice recorded and like most people in similar circumstances I could not believe that it was my voice. It sounded far too low. Anyhow the nice girl in the shop was very sweet and said it sounded 'smashing', and I left the record at Broadcasting House for Lobby to hear. He was I learnt later, surprised and moderately impressed at finding a record instead of a piece of paper, so that my chance look into the record shop turned out to be a lucky one.

The other test was more difficult. Wynford was due to do some street interviews outside the old Monseigneur News Theatre in Oxford Street in a programme called *Saturday Night Out*. His interviews would be live but when he had finished I was to record some interviews of my own with passers-by.

I must admit I was scared stiff as I was now beginning to be bitten by the broadcasting bug, fired by the obvious enthusiasm and happiness of those working in OBs. Wynford was a great help and gave me tips on how and how not to do an interview. First and foremost, if you have the time make friends with your 'victims' beforehand and gain their confidence. Chat them up in fact. Never start (as so many people do these days) 'Now tell me . . .' Never frame a question so that the only answer left is yes or no. Always *listen* to the answers in case you can follow them up. Many interviewers are so busy thinking of their next question that they often fail to do this. Unless the answer is not clear or is inaudible never repeat it. Be courteous, don't hector, don't lose your temper. But if the answer is evasive press on politely until you get something definite.

Finally, always remember that you are only the link between the listener and the person being interviewed. They want to hear him or her, not you. So keep your own opinions to yourself, your questions as short as possible, and try not to swamp your victim with your personality.

These and many other tips Wynford passed on to me and they have proved a valuable basis to work on throughout my broadcasting career. They do not apply of course to the type of hard political interview that you hear so often nowadays on television or on radio programmes like the *World at One*. But thank goodness I have never been caught up in those.

On this occasion I watched Wynford's technique carefully while he was doing his interviews, then with butterflies in my stomach stepped out on to the pavement to do mine. I asked passers-by what they thought of the present rations and as you can imagine got quite a few earthy replies. But I got through it somehow and as Wynford said afterwards at least I kept going and did not dry up, an invaluable asset in a broadcaster.

Lobby must have thought roughly the same as, after I had waited anxiously for a few days, his secretary rang to say that I had 'passed' and that I was to report to OBs on 13 January 1946. So I was in the BBC, although I had been warned it might only be temporary. When as frequently happens, people ask me, 'How *does* one get into the BBC?' I can truthfully answer that in my case it was largely due to luck. I *happened* to meet Stew and Wynford during the war. I *happened* to be demobilised early when the BBC was short of staff. I *happened* to be in the club to receive that dinner invitation to meet Stew and Wynford again. I *happened* to have looked up as I passed that record shop. And I suppose I ought to add in fairness that I *happened* to have been born with the gift of the gab.

Once started it had all happened very quickly and I only had a few days in which to find myself some rooms before I was due to report to the BBC. I found some in Gloucester Place, which was very handy being only ten minutes' walk away from Portland Place. Neither before the war nor since have I ever commuted to work. I have always felt it an awful waste of two hours or so a day to spend them dashing to and from stations and sitting or standing in trains. What I have done with the time saved I am not sure but at least I have been spared the strain and tension of having to catch the 8.14 am train each morning or the 6.11 pm in the evening. In my job at the BBC it would in fact have been doubly difficult as I often worked up to late hours at the theatres or had to come in early for programmes such as *Today*. Later when I became BBC Cricket Correspondent I was frequently rung up at my home in St John's Wood at all hours of the day and sometimes at night, asking me to pop in to Broadcasting House to do a two-minute report on some cricket news, such as the announcement of a Test team or death of a famous cricketer. Had I not lived near my work this would have been impossible.

I was to be in rooms on my own, as I had lost touch with my old friend William Douglas-Home for the time being. We had been at Eton and Oxford together and before the war we had shared rooms in a house at No. 35 South Eaton Place in London, but it had been wrecked by a bomb during the Blitz. William had had rather an unhappy war, ending up in prison after being court-martialled for disobeying an order on active service. This sounds bad and at the time we all felt indignant and unsympathetic about it, and thought it served him right. There were we fighting the Germans not approving of it nor enjoying it any more than he did. But if everyone had behaved like him Hitler would presumably have won the war and then what would have happened to our families and homes and our way of life in England.

That's what we thought at the time but when it was all over and everyone had cooled down it was easier to see his side of the whole thing. At heart he had always been a conscientious objector or a pacifist in the sense of wanting to abolish war – we are all of us pacifists in its other sense of liking peace. He had started the war in the fire service and when conscripted accepted without protest but with the proviso that he would not make a very good soldier. He went to the Buffs as a private and was then sent to the OCTU at Sandhurst from where he passed out as an officer. Then comes the incredible part.

He was posted back to the same battalion to command men with whom he had served as a private. On one rifle inspection he told a man his rifle was dirty. 'Not half as dirty as yours used to be, Bill,' was the retort. An impossible position, especially as William was still loud in his criticism of the war and the way it was being run, and even stood in a by-election at Windsor as an anti-Churchill candidate.

Then came the invasion of Europe and the Buffs were part of a force ordered to take the port of Le Havre, which in spite of repeated demands the Germans refused to surrender, although it was full of civilians, mostly women and children. The only way left to take it was by shelling and it was at this point that William told his Commanding Officer that he could not obey an order to attack which meant endangering the lives of these women and children. His Commanding Officer knew and liked William and understood how strongly he felt. He overlooked this refusal to fight and gave William instead a more non-combative job with the transport. But William also refused this and wrote a letter to the local paper in Maidenhead, where the Buffs had been stationed, explaining exactly what had happened. Now that it was public, the Commanding Officer was left with no alternative but to put him under close arrest and have him court-martialled.

William was sentenced to a year's imprisonment, which he spent in Wormwood Scrubs and Wakefield, serving eight months of his sentence. Needless to say he was visited by his parents, Lord and Lady Home. The 'wee Lordie', as Lord Home was known, was as near to being a saint as any man I have ever met. To him, everyone was good and I never heard him say an unkind word about anyone. At the end of their visit Lady Home was sitting in the taxi outside the prison gates when she saw Lord Home going down the street to another entrance. She called out to him that the taxi was waiting for him. 'I know,' he said, 'but I must just go and thank the Governor for having dear Willie!'

Based on his experiences in prison, William wrote his first really successful play called *Now Barrabas*. I attended the first night and in the audience were some of his old prison friends, with whom of course he had been extremely popular. At the reception afterwards Lord Home greeted them and chatted as if they had been fellow peers at some Scottish gathering.

From all this you will have gathered that I had got in touch with William again. I have gone into his case in some detail because I have always felt guilty and ashamed that at a time when he was in trouble I had been too proud or superior to try to help him or even to write to him. My only excuse is that war seemed to make one intolerant of anyone who did not conform. But I am still deeply sorry that I behaved as I did.

Some years later his second brother, Henry, was gaoled for a short time for some motoring offence. William wanted to go to see him but could not get permission. So he asked his brother Alec, who was a Conservative MP and of course later became Prime Minister, if he could use his influence to arrange a visit. Alec refused, so William went and called on the Governor of the prison where Henry was. He asked for and was given permission to see Henry. In triumph he went back and told Alec how he had managed to get in to see Henry. Alec said, 'All I can say is, that it must have been Old Boys' Day!'

2 My OB apprenticeship

THE OUTSIDE BROADCAST DEPARTMENT, or OBs as they are always called, is responsible for all broadcasts which take place outside a studio. These include all sport, ceremonials, relays from the opera and theatre, church services and events from places like the Royal Albert Hall.

During and just after the war most of the now-famous commentators were on the staff, but by the time I arrived some of them were beginning to become freelances. The basic difference here is that on the staff you get a fixed salary and of course a pension. You get paid the same no matter how many or how few broadcasts you may do. The freelance on the other hand is paid for each broadcast so that his income depends on the amount of work he does. With some of the freelances the BBC gives a short-term contract of three or five years. This guarantees them a fixed amount but also leaves them free to do other outside work as well.

The BBC has always been very generous in allowing staff to accept outside work so long as it does not interfere with BBC duties. For instance, for years I have given talks at dinners or luncheon clubs, or done commentaries for films, but always with the rider that if a BBC job crops up at the last moment it must have preference. This has worked very well, though of course I was never able to do any advertising for commercials while on the staff.

Every Monday, Lobby used to hold a meeting to discuss past programmes and to plan future ones. At my first meeting I felt very much the new boy as I sat down to join such household names as Raymond Glendenning, Stewart Macpherson, Freddy Grisewood, Rex Alston,

Audrey Russell, Wynford Vaughan-Thomas, John Ellison and even Gilbert Harding before he left the department.

My confidence was soon restored as I saw these famous broadcasters waiting humbly for Lobby's verdict on their particular efforts of the week before. Lobby was a perfectionist and the architect of all commentary technique which remains basically unchanged today (or should do if it is a good commentary).

He tried to listen to every OB and had a little black notebook in which he jotted down all the good and bad things in a broadcast. He was extremely fair but never over-fulsome with his praise. 'Not bad' or 'On the whole a brave effort' meant you had done pretty well. But if he began to beat his clenched right hand into the palm of his left, and say: 'Brian, I was a bit puzzled . . !' you could be sure that your commentary was about to be pulled to bits. But no one ever resented it, and at these weekly meetings we all used to chip in and say exactly what we thought of each other's efforts. No holds were barred. It was always perfectly friendly and the helpful criticism kept everyone up to the mark.

For as long as he was Head of OBs most of us used to ring Lobby up at home after every broadcast, and ask anxiously for his verdict. It was quite a tense moment as one waited to hear if that fist would start beating, something incidentally which he seemed able to do with a telephone receiver in his hand.

The OB Department was divided into various sections such as events and ceremonials, sport, and entertainment, and I was allotted to poor John Ellison as his assistant in the latter. I could not have wished for a better person to teach me my job. He had been in the BBC for six years after being invalided out of the RAF as the result of a car accident. He had also been an actor in repertory and the West End and knew everyone in the entertainment world, both performers and management.

John and I had a big office without any carpet on the

floor. In those days one's status at the BBC was reflected by the amount of carpet one was entitled to. The top people had wall-to-wall carpeting, and the lower down the scale you were the smaller was your carpet. So you can see how highly we were rated!

At that time there were a lot of live relays from theatres and music halls and we had to go and vet all the West End shows to see if they were suitable for broadcasting. Normally we did a half-hour excerpt, usually from a musical or a farce. Straight comedies or dramas were too visual and difficult to understand. Once we had found a suitable show we had to check whether the management wanted a broadcast. If the show was doing well they usually preferred to wait, but if it was at all shaky they leapt at the chance of getting it on the air.

They all remembered the famous example of *Me and My Girl*, which had been doing badly at the Victoria Palace. By chance a programme fell through and at the last moment an OB from *Me and My Girl* was hurriedly arranged. There were some bright tunes in it by Noel Gay, and though the knockabout humour of Lupino Lane was largely visual, the radio listeners heard the theatre audience roaring their heads off with laughter.

Even before the broadcast was over the box office telephone began to ring and *Me and My Girl* was saved. It ran for another three and a half years, and proved what a wonderful shop-window radio could be.

So long as the music was good and there were plenty of laughs the listener at home would then pay to go and see the show. John and I had to choose the best bits to broadcast and if necessary had to persuade the management to change the running order about a little in order to include a particular hit song or a strong piece of comedy in our excerpt. They usually agreed to do this so long as it did not interfere with the story line. But in one pantomime both the management and we slipped up badly. We had brought forward into the broadcast a dramatic scene in which the Wicked Robbers were finally killed off. After the broadcast we were watching the rest of the show when to our horror and to the puzzlement of the audience, the Robbers came back live and well in a scene which normally preceded the one in which they had been killed.

The most important thing we had to do was to write and speak the linking commentary from one of the boxes. We had to fill in all the visual gaps, describe the scenery and action and explain the story up to date, also mentioning the names of the actors and actresses playing the various parts. We had to be as unobtrusive as possible so as not to interfere with what was going on on the stage. It required perfect timing and crisp, clean delivery. To get everything right we had to see the show two or three times before the broadcast, not only to perfect our commentary but to give our engineers a chance to place the microphones in the right places.

So there I was, slap in the middle of the entertainment world to which I had so badly wanted to belong. I was meeting all the stars and leading players and, what was more important, was working with them. I was also seeing all the shows in the West End free! We broadcast such shows as *Song of Norway, Oklahoma, South Pacific, Annie Get Your Gun, Carousel, The King and I*, plus a lot of farces. I know I saw *Carousel* fifteen times because we did separate broadcasts from it – and I cried each time! I had certainly fallen on my feet.

Another chore – and a very pleasant one – was a weekly half-hour broadcast called *Round the Halls*, which came from one of the many music halls which then existed all over the country. So I was back with my old love – variety – and visited all the big music halls to choose suitable acts. On the day of the broadcast I would then rehearse and time the three acts chosen, usually made up of a singer or singers, a stand-up comic or cross-talk act, and some sort of speciality which would make good radio. This could be an impressionist, instrumentalist or animal impersonator.

The timing was difficult because the broadcast took place direct from the theatre during one of the two evening performances. The running order often had to be adjusted to include our three acts, who in turn had to adapt their own timing and material for the radio. What went well at the New Cross Empire was not always suitable for the front parlour in a spinster's home in Bournemouth!

First of all the whole broadcast had to last a maximum of twenty-nine minutes to allow time for the studio announcements. Singers and instrumentalists were easy – if they were any good their songs or pieces which they played lasted exactly the same time at each performance. But comics were more difficult. One had to gauge the amount of time to allow for the laughs, which varied from audience to audience. Also if they knew they had a hidden audience of several millions they used to try to 'milk' the laughs with a lot of extra visual effects so that people at home would say, 'He *must* be funny. We must go and see him.'

And then of course there was censorship. In those days the BBC was very strict and there was a long list of things that could not be the basis of a joke – sex (naturally), physical disabilities, politics, religion and of course any innuendos. Even mother-in-law jokes were frowned on as they might be embarrassing to a family sitting at home with ma-in-law present. It's difficult to believe now but I was given a rocket for passing the following:

'Have you seen the PT instructress?'

'Oh yes, she's stripped for gym.'

'Lucky Jim.'

Just think what gets by today! It was not always easy to make some comics cut their material. After some outrageous double entendre they would look at you with great big innocent eyes and say: 'What's filthy about that? It's all in your mind.' Or they would say: 'Oh, I did that one in *Henry Hall's Guest Night* last week and he did not object.'

But we soon got to know the form and most of them played ball, though occasionally one would slip a joke in which we had taken out. One of these was a 'drunk' comic who took a drink out of a glass on the table and spat it out with the words, 'I'll kill that ruddy cat.' Note too the word ruddy which was just allowed, whereas bloody was definitely out. The BBC's solution to any joke was: 'If in doubt – out,' which did not make the comedian's job any easier. It was a wonder that they had anything left to be funny about.

But they were fabulous people to meet and I was made welcome in all their dressing-rooms. They were all extremely kind to me and there was a wonderful feeling of camaraderie back-stage. For the first time I met and made friends with people like Arthur Askey, Ted Ray, Tommy Trinder, Hutch, Terry-Thomas, Jimmy Edwards and two promising newcomers whom I first met when they were unknowns in a Jack Payne show in 1947 – Frankie Howerd and Max Bygraves.

In the summer *Round the Halls* was given a rest and instead we used to broadcast concert parties from the seaside. What fun they were! Some were in the open air, some in winter gardens or floral halls. There was always a lovely holiday atmosphere with everyone out to enjoy themselves. If the weather was fine I must admit that John and I sometimes took more time than we should have done to rehearse and broadcast the shows. By this time we knew pretty well every gag in the business and when a comic started a story or a joke we used to have a competition to see who knew the finish. In the end if we thought a concert party needed a bit more humour we would suggest gags ourselves. We 'sold' one to an outdoor concert party at Eastbourne and were rewarded by hearing the roar of laughter from the audience in their deck-chairs. It was as corny as they come.

Comic I was walking along the beach here the other day and saw a girl bathing, and she was calling for help as she slowly drifted out to sea.
Stooge Really. What did you do? Dive in and save her?
Comic Nothing of the sort. I threw her a cake of soap.
Stooge Whatever for?
Comic To wash her back of course.

There was one famous producer who used to star in his own show and after every broadcast used to write and tell us what a wonderful reaction he had had from the listeners – 'hundreds of telegrams of appreciation old boy'. John and I suspected he sent these telegrams to himself and were proved right after one broadcast, which due to a technical hitch had not gone out over the air. We did not know this until the end of the show and went round behind to break the news to our friend. But before we could get a word in edgeways he greeted us at the door of his dressing-room with: 'Wonderful broadcast. It's gone over a treat. The telephone hasn't stopped ringing with people from all over the country sending their congratulations.' We hadn't got the heart to tell him the truth.

I was also made responsible for an amateur show which had started in the war and carried on for a few years afterwards. It was called *Work's Wonders* and was a variety show put on by workers of a factory with their own talent. I used to go down and audition them, choose the best (or least worst!) and then produce and introduce the show. Some were quite good but naturally lacked the professional touch. One exception was certainly George Martin, the casual comedian, who at that time was working in an ordnance factory in Aldershot.

We sometimes used professionals to entertain the audiences before the shows began and two young comics who were especially popular were called Bob Monkhouse and Benny Hill.

The other celebrity of today whom I met in very

different guise was the chairman of an RAF Old Tyme Music Hall which we broadcast from the RAF station at Henlow. He was tall and very funny and spoke with a slight lisp and a drawl. He kept his RAF audience in fits of laughter and was down in the programme as Aircraftsman Frank Muir.

But my very first broadcast for the BBC had nothing to do with entertainment.

Early in 1946 the authorities drained the lake in St James' Park so that the sappers could blow up an unexploded bomb that lay on the bottom. At the last moment it was decided to do a live broadcast of the blowing up and Lobby thought he would throw me in the deep end without any preparation or warning. He kindly came down to hold my hand and we took up our position with a microphone on one of the bridges. But the police told us that this was too dangerous and advised us to go inside the nearby ladies' lavatory. By standing on one of the loo seats I managed to look out of one of the small windows and could just see enough of what was going on to give my first commentary. I described the explosion and its after-effects and Lobby has told me since that I got very excited and finished the broadcast by promising the listeners to bring them a bigger and better bomb next week! All I know is that I was very nervous and came out of that ladies' loo looking very flushed!

In spite of the fact that we all seemed to work very long hours there was plenty of time for fun and games in the office. There was a marvellously happy spirit in the department and it was a great joy to be working in it. At our weekly meetings we used to play a game with the OB Manager, Frank Anderson. He was a dear person who pretended to be crotchety and we nicknamed him 'the crusty old faggot'.

One of his jobs was to see that billings of programmes for *Radio Times* were handed in to his office in good time for publication. If any of us were late in sending them in he used to read out our names from a book when requested to do so by Lobby. He loved to catch us out but his book was not always up to date. So we played it like tennis, everyone shouting out the score after each announcement. If he was right he would start fifteen love and then if we could prove him wrong the next time we would call out fifteen all, and so on. Just before one meeting John and I realised that we had not sent a billing for *Round the Halls* to his office, so as we entered the meeting we slipped it into his pocket without him knowing.

There were a lot of entries in his book that day, some right, some wrong and the score had reached advantage in his favour, and he only needed one more success for game. With a gleam of triumph in his eye he announced that Ellison and Johnston had failed to give him the billing which was due for Lewisham Hippodrome. 'Oh no we haven't,' we shouted. 'What's that sticking out of your pocket?' Frank sheepishly put his hand in his pocket and withdrew our billing. 'Deuce,' roared the meeting. Childish but great fun.

We also used to ring each other up pretending to be someone else and it got so bad that no one was ever quite certain whether any call was genuine or not. It all started soon after I had joined when at the weekly meeting Geoffrey Peck brought up the question of commentators for Wimbledon in the summer of 1946. He explained that he had written to the former French tennis champion Jean Borotra to see if he would be interested in being one of the summarisers. Since then, however, our European Service had heard about it and were not entirely happy. At that time evidently there were some queries about Borotra's co-operation with the Germans, though these were subsequently satisfactorily cleared up. But meanwhile the European Service felt he should not be used.

Geoffrey asked Lobby what he should do and was advised to write to Borotra and regretfully cancel his offer without giving any reason. After the meeting I went round to my room and dialled Geoffrey's number and when his secretary answered I said in a very phoney French accent that I was Borotra and could I speak to Mr Peck. Geoffrey came on and began to say that he was just about to write to me. But I did not let him get any further and went on to say how much I was looking forward to broadcasting at Wimbledon, how much it would mean to me after six years of war and how nice it would be to meet all my old English tennis friends again.

I then let Geoffrey get a word in, as he had been spluttering in the background for some time, trying to interrupt. He just managed to say that he was very sorry but his offer was cancelled and then I let fly, pretending to be very excited and angry. I called him an 'English pig-dog' and that I would make 'the big sue' of the BBC for breaking a contract, and demand 'ze big money' in compensation. I could hear Geoffrey saying, 'Please, please Mr Borotra, let me explain.' But after a few more expletives I rang off.

I then wandered out of my office and saw Geoffrey looking very harassed and upset as he rushed round to Lobby's room. I gave them a minute or so and then walked in to hear Lobby saying that he had better telephone the BBC solicitor at once to warn him what might happen. I let Lobby ask for the number and then quickly started off at Geoffrey in my phoney accent: 'Ah, you English pig-dog, you make to ring *your* solicitor . . .' Lobby slowly put down the receiver and a look of doubt came into his eyes. Had he been right after all to give this chap a job?

On another occasion I had Frank Anderson rushing off to meet the Dean of Westminster in the Crypt of the Abbey as a result of a fake call from me complaining about some BBC broadcast of one of the services from there. I managed to stop him as he was going down in the lift. But not all my leg-pulls were so successful. We had a marvellous little man called Spud Moody who was the number two in charge of engineering in the department. We had been playing around and I locked him up in his room. I returned to my desk and after a few minutes looked up as a shadow fell on the desk from the window. There to my horror was Spud. He had walked along a narrow ledge of about two feet and our offices were six storeys up. Had he slipped or fallen backwards he would have plunged sixty feet or so to his death. I hurriedly opened the window and let him in and never locked anyone else in their office again.

3 Start of a long innings

SOON AFTER I HAD JOINED, the department was a bit short of soccer commentators and we were all encouraged to have a test to see if we were any good. Geoffrey Peck and I thought we might as well have a go. He was the producer in charge of sports like racing, boxing and football so knew something about it. I knew very little except what I had learnt from watching the Arsenal before the war.

Anyway we went down with a recording car to Loftus Road where Queen's Park Rangers were playing a mid-week fixture. We read up all that we could about the two teams and found that the QPR centre-forward McGibbon had scored three goals on the previous Saturday. The Press had labelled him '3 Goal McGibbon' and there he was No. 9 in the programme. During our tests of about fifteen minutes each we both gave him the full treatment with phrases like: 'There goes "3–Goal" again, a typical dribble, would recognise his style anywhere, easy to pick out with his balding head, anyone could see that he's an England prospect, etc, etc.'

It was not until we read the evening papers that we discovered McGibbon had withdrawn at the last moment and that the No. 9 whom we had been praising was a substitute. That was my first and *last* soccer commentary!

But my wonderful luck held, so far as cricket was concerned. When I joined the department there was no mention of cricket and it never entered my head that I would ever get the chance to be a commentator. There was already Rex Alston, a promising newcomer with a burry Hampshire accent called John Arlott, and Jim

Swanton recently returned from being a prisoner of war under the Japs.

So I just could not believe my luck when my telephone rang one day and the voice at the other end was Ian Orr-Ewing recently out of the RAF and now Head of Outside Broadcasts Television. He and I had played a lot of cricket together before the war, and he knew how much I loved it and perhaps gave me some credit for knowing something about it, too. Anyway he said that television was starting up again after the war and would be doing some cricket matches from Lord's and the Oval during the summer. Would I like to have a shot at doing the commentary?

You can guess what my answer was though I had no idea of how to do a television commentary. Luckily, so far as cricket was concerned, no one else knew much either. There had only been four Tests ever televised, two in 1938 and two in 1939, so everyone including producers, commentators and cameramen would be learners. But once again fortune had been very kind to me. I *happened* to have played cricket with Ian Orr-Ewing who *happened* to be the man chosen to restart cricket on TV after the war. By such a small turn of fate was I destined to do the television cricket commentaries for the next twenty-four years.

The 1946 cricket season was excellent training for a new commentator. First of all, it was a wet summer, so right from the start I learnt to live with the frustrations of 'bad light stopped play' or 'no play today because of rain'. Cricket commentating must be one of the few arts which can be so interrupted. Imagine an actor having to stop in the middle of Hamlet's soliloquy because of bad light from one of the spots. Or a concert pianist being prevented from completing a concerto because of a leak from the roof on to his piano.

People often ask what commentators do when rain has

stopped play. I don't know why, but unlike most of the players we don't play cards. Some have their writing to do for newspapers, so get on with that. Others help sort out the hundreds of letters which we receive during every Test. On radio we now have a fixed spot for answering these during the lunch interval on Saturdays. But sometimes if there is a long delay we have an unscheduled answering session to fill in the time, though those who have sent in questions may of course not be listening. Otherwise we do what all cricketers do when two or three are gathered together – just talk cricket.

The touring team came from India, the first tourists since the West Indies in 1939. Asians are usually very difficult to tell apart so this offered quite a challenge to a new commentator. When a touring team first arrives, we usually meet them at dinners or receptions and get to know them personally, so that we can recognise them easily by sight. But of course it's much harder once they take the field, especially if they are wearing caps with big peaks, or worse still the now fashionable floppy white hats. These completely obscure their faces, so I personally have always tried to study the walks and mannerisms of every cricketer.

Sometimes, if a ball is hit to the far corner of the ground and the fieldsman is running away from you, the only way to tell who it is is by the way he runs, the slope of his shoulders or perhaps even by the size of his bottom! It is the same with batsmen at the wicket, who from a distance, if they are both wearing caps, often look alike until they start to make their strokes. So one looks for their particular habits, such as the way they prod the pitch or touch the peak of their cap when waiting for the bowler.

The other difficulty with Asian sides is the formation and pronunciation of their names, more so with the Pakistanis than the Indians. It is quite possible to have a Mohammad Ali and an Ali Mohammad in the same side. The second time Pakistan toured England in 1962 Rex

Alston got into an awful mess over one of their names. They had a player called Afaq Hussain – try to pronounce it at your peril! We were all naturally very nervous about it and dreaded having to commentate when he was playing. Luckily he was not much good and was seldom selected.

When the Pakistanis were playing MCC at Lord's I was doing the television commentary and Rex as usual was on the radio. I walked into the radio box during one of the intervals and said to Rex, 'Thank goodness this chap Afaq is not playing.' 'For goodness sake,' replied Rex, 'don't mention his name or I shall get it into my head.' So somewhat mischievously I murmured 'Afaq, Afaq, Afaq' and left the box. Alan Gibson was the other commentator and swears that about an hour later it was obvious from consultations going on out on the field that there was to be a change of bowling. Barry Knight was the batsman waiting to take strike and Rex presumably as a result of my visit said: 'I think there is going to be a change of bowling. We are about to see Afaq to Knight at the Nursery End.' He quickly realised what he had said and added: 'Oh, what am I saying – he's not even playing!' I felt a bit of a cad when told about it afterwards but I am glad to say that none of our bosses spotted it.

There is a golden rule for any broadcaster who has said something outrageous by mistake. Never stop, nor apologise, nor try to explain what you *meant* to say. This can be fatal. Just carry on and the listeners will probably think that they have heard wrongly. A famous example of how an attempted explanation only makes matters worse was the American golf commentator talking about Arnold Palmer's wife. He was saying how very superstitious she was and that 'before every championship match she used to take Arnold's balls in her hand and kiss them.' All might have been well had he not realised what he had said and hastily added '. . . his golf balls of course I mean.' It is sadly but not surprisingly reported that he got the sack!

In 1946 and 1947 my fellow TV commentators – all new

boys like myself – included Aidan Crawley, Percy Fender, Walter Franklin and R. C. (Crusoe) Robertson-Glasgow. Our first task was to learn to live with the 'dirty talk-back'. Let me explain.

On TV the commentators use a lip microphone which has to be held close to the mouth and is specially designed to cut out all noise except the commentator's voice. This means that in the TV box everyone can talk in a normal voice to each other so long as the commentator is either speaking into the mike or has his hand over the business end of it if he is not talking. (The noise of ball on bat and the applause of the crowd is picked up on an effects mike outside the box.)

Each commentator also wears headphones through which the producer can talk to him from his control van or scanner parked somewhere behind the pavilion. The producer gives instructions such as when to start or return to the studio; or he may want to report that one of the cameras is temporarily out of action; or suggest that the score should be given at the end of the over, or perhaps that he has a good picture of the three slips talking to each other and that he will be showing it after the next ball.

All the time, remember, the commentator may be commentating on what is going on out in the middle or worse still be trying to give a summary of what has happened so far. At the same time he must learn to take in what the producer is saying. One of the hardest things for a beginner to avoid is acknowledging the producer's instructions or making a counter-suggestion if he does not agree. Viewers may sometimes have been puzzled to hear in the middle of a commentary a commentator say something like: 'Right ho, thanks,' or 'I've only just given the score.'

In addition to talking to the commentator the producer can also be heard giving instructions to his three or four cameramen about what pictures he wants or possibly discussing some technical detail such as the light or quality of the picture. You cannot become a TV commentator or introduce a programme until you have learnt the art of simultaneously talking *and* listening.

You will notice that 'front' men like David Coleman and Robin Day all have a small ear-piece behind their ear like a hearing aid. While talking to you they are getting instructions such as what to do next or a warning that the next piece of film is not yet ready.

All this was of course new to us and naturally we all reacted differently. Once Percy Fender was reminiscing about Tom Hayward the old Surrey batsman, and so missed something going on out on the field. 'Stick to the play, Percy, and keep that sort of chat for between the overs,' said the producer into his headphones. This irritated Percy, who put his hand over his microphone (thank goodness he remembered), turned to me and said: 'If he thinks he can do any better why doesn't he come up here and do it himself?' A natural reaction you might think. So was Crusoe's when just after he had given the score, he heard the producer say: 'I think it's about time we had the score, Crusoe.' To which Crusoe with slight venom in his voice said over the air: 'For those of you who were not paying attention when I gave the score just now, may I repeat . . .'

We televised three matches that year: MCC against Indians at Lord's, and the two Tests at Lord's and the Oval. We could not do the other one at Old Trafford because the transmitters only covered the London area. It was not in fact until 1950 that we were able to televise Tests from Trent Bridge and Edgbaston and 1952 before we were able to go to Old Trafford and Headingley.

There was nothing remarkable about the 1946 season except the rain. England won the first Test, and the other two were drawn, thanks to bad weather. Players were still flexing their muscles and trying to regain their form after the long lay-off during the war. Even so seven batsmen, including Washbrook and Compton, scored over 2,000 runs while Hammond sat proudly at the top of the averages, making 1,783 runs in only twenty-six innings for an average of 84.90.

Although aged forty-three, Hammond seemed to be batting as well as ever and scored seven hundreds, all for Gloucestershire. This made his failure in Australia the following winter all the more sad and surprising. But I expect the truth is that the standard of English bowling in 1946 was pretty low compared with that in Australia. Bowlers like batsmen get rusty. The one new star was A. V. Bedser, already aged twenty-eight. He bowled brilliantly in the Tests, taking twenty-four wickets in the short series, and finished with 128 wickets in his first season.

The year 1947 was a complete contrast to 1946. This was the golden summer for cricket when the sun and Denis Compton both shone consistently and brilliantly throughout the season. The crowds – so long starved of first-class cricket – flocked to the grounds to bask in the sun and enjoy the sparkling cricket. Many of them were just out of the forces with their gratuities and with so few goods in the shops there was little to spend their money on. So cricket benefited and the players gave the huge crowds their money's worth. Nearly three million people paid to watch cricket that summer. The South Africans led by Alan Melville were the visitors, but as good a side as they were, they found a revived England too much for them and lost the series 0–3. How they must have cursed the Middlesex twins Edrich and Compton who scored 1,305 runs between them in the Tests and then went on to help Middlesex win the County Championship. The debonair Compton, especially, played cavalier cricket and danced his way down the pitches of England to make 18 hundreds and score 3,816 runs in the season. Both are still records and likely to remain so, now that the number of county championship matches has been cut to twenty.

I shared all the TV commentaries except for the last afternoon of the Oval Test when I went off to the show-jumping at the White City to commentate for radio on the

King George V Cup. I had never done it before and never understood why I was chosen. They must have thought that I knew something about horses. But they were dead wrong. However, I soon learnt about double-oxers, five-bar gates and triple bars, and had as my expert alongside me the announcer Lionel Marson, an old cavalry officer who did know what he was talking about. He was very horsey and used to commentate in a bowler-hat. He loved horses and got terribly emotional. When Foxhunter won the King George V Cup for the third time tears streamed down his cheeks. I'm not saying that I did not have a lump in my throat – there was something special about that horse.

This dual loyalty between TV and radio became quite a problem in the years ahead, and in the early days there were one or two clashes. But we came to an amicable agreement, which existed right into the late sixties. TV had complete priority over me for cricket, radio for everything else. Although I was always administered by radio OBs and had my office there, TV paid a percentage of my salary and everyone seemed happy. It was nice to be wanted! But I got no more money over and above my salary for appearing on TV – only a minute dress allowance of about £25 a year for appearing in front of the cameras.

However in those early days cricket occupied only a small percentage of my time. I was chiefly involved in broadcasts from theatres and music halls. My very first broadcast from a theatre was from the *Song of Norway* at the Palace Theatre presented by that king of pantomimes, Emile Littler. We made quite a big OB out of it, including some backstage interviews.

My first theatre commentary was from *Under the Counter*, the first of many such broadcasts with that wonderful couple, Cicely Courtneidge and Jack Hulbert. Looking through my 1946 and 1947 diaries I am amazed at the number of famous names that figured in our relays from variety theatres.

What a marvellous music-hall bill they would make up, though alas some of them are no longer with us. But their names make one's mouth water in these days of largely synthetic entertainment. Here are some of them: Arthur Askey, Max Bacon, Max Bygraves, Clapham and Dwyer, Peter Cavanagh, G. H. Elliott, Cyril Fletcher, Frankie Howerd, Hutch, Nosmo King, Charlie Kunz, Murray and Mooney, Cavan O'Connor, Ted Ray, Terry-Thomas, Nellie Wallace, Robb Wilton and Anona Winn.

There was also a husband and wife team – Ted and Barbara Andrews. He was a tenor and she played the piano and they had just begun to include in their act their ten-year-old daughter. She sang quite beautifully with a wonderful top note. We all thought it wrong at the time, thinking it would damage her young voice. But it didn't seem to do any harm and as Julie Andrews she is still singing as beautifully as ever.

Behind the scenes I met all the people who make the entertainment world tick – the impresarios, producers, agents and so on. Lew and Leslie Grade, and Bernard Delfont – those three astonishingly successful brothers were just starting in those days. John Ellison and I often used to ring them up to arrange our broadcasts and agree on the three acts for *Round the Halls*. They are probably all millionaires now and it's amusing to think that they used to concern themselves personally with finding us an impressionist who could fill a six and a half minute spot in our broadcast.

The secret of their success is hard work and Lew and Leslie were always at their desks an hour or so before any of us had had breakfast, and would often be visiting theatres in the West End or suburbs up to late at night. Lew and Leslie soon became the largest and most powerful agents with numerous artists on their books. There's a good story of Lew Grade spotting a promising young artist at one of the outlying music halls. He went round to see him afterwards and suggested he should handle him in future. Lew said he would get the young man X pounds a week more than he was getting now. Was he tied up with another agent, if so what was his name? 'Lew Grade,' was the surprising reply. The young artist was already on their books!

One of the most amusing men was Charlie Henry, Chief of Productions at Moss Empires. He was a great variety director and first under George Black and then Val Parnell was the power behind the scenes at the London Palladium and was really responsible for staging many of the Royal Variety Shows.

Charlie's special forte was comedy and for the whole of their life he directed and advised the Crazy Gang in all their comedy routines. He had a marvellous sense of humour and pulled everyone's leg with a deadpan face, but was a martinet when it came to producing a show. He demanded the best and got it, because he knew the business backwards and was respected and loved by artists and stage staff alike.

Charlie had been a song and dance man himself and was full of stories of funny things that had happened on stage. One of my favourites was of the two actors in a repertory company who were acting a scene together when the telephone on stage started to ring and went on ringing. There was no call for this to happen in the script and obviously someone back-stage had accidentally pushed the wrong button. Neither actor wanted to answer the phone as it would have meant improvising an imaginary conversation quite out of context from the plot of the play. But as they manfully tried to carry on their conversation the bell went on ringing and ringing. Obviously something had to be done as the audience were beginning to roar with laughter, and there were a few shouts of 'you're wanted on the phone' from the back of the stalls. So one of the actors got up from the sofa where they were sitting, picked up the receiver and said, 'Hello?' He paused for a few seconds, then put his hand over the mouth piece and shouted across to his colleague, 'It's for you!'

I have always been a glutton for theatrical stories and Dulcie Gray told me one once which she swears was true. It happened when she was with the open-air theatre in Regent's Park in the days of Robert Atkins. When the weather was fine the audience used to sit outside in deck-chairs and watch the performance on the open stage. In the event of wet weather there was a large marquee with another stage. If it was wet the performance would start there, or if rain began during the play then actors and audience would hurriedly repair to the marquee. The snag of the marquee was that it became stiflingly hot and not only were the seats hard and upright but there were not as many of them as there were deck-chairs. So if it was a full house outside and it started to rain conditions inside the marquee became hopelessly overcrowded and the heat unbearable.

It was during a heatwave, and the outside auditorium was packed at every performance with the audiences lounging comfortably in their deck-chairs under the hot sun. Robert Atkins had had occasion to sack a young actor for some reason at short notice and the afternoon matinée was to be his last performance. It was blazing hot and there was a full house. The actor only had a few lines to say such as: 'His Majesty requires your presence, sir' and would then normally have made his exit. But he was determined to get his own back for what he must have considered to have been an unjust dismissal. So with the temperature in the eighties, and glorious blue sky overhead, the young man walked down to the front of the stage and said in an authoritative voice: 'In view of the inclement weather this performance will now be continued inside the marquee!'

Dulcie swears that the audience, typically British and

obedient to any order from authority, quietly rose from their deck-chairs, gathered up their things and disappeared into the marquee before the damage could be repaired.

I was also lucky enough to meet Ivor Novello but not because of any broadcast. He was appearing in *Perchance to Dream* and one evening I went along to see it with Nico Llewelyn-Davies, one of J. M. Barrie's wards. He was an ex-Grenadier and had been with me in our wartime revue, *The Eyes Have It*, in which he did a lifelike impersonation of Ted Lewis, singing *On the Sunny Side of the Street*.

Nico and I were friends of Zena Dare's daughter, Angela Thornton. We went with her and her husband to see the show and she arranged for us to meet Ivor at supper afterwards in the Savoy Grill. We were naturally thrilled to meet him and he was as charming and friendly as we had been led to expect. What is more, he appeared to listen and be interested in everything we said, not a very usual trait in a great artist. Naturally we told him how much we had enjoyed the show, but were audacious or cheeky enough to offer a slight criticism – and even then he went on listening.

Our complaint was that the hit song of the show, that lovely number, *We'll Gather Lilacs*, had been largely wasted in the show. You could not have a much more romantic song and it cried aloud for a duet between a handsome young tenor and a beautiful young girl. But in the show, so far as I remember, Ivor as a composer, said to some ladies at a party, 'Have you heard my new song? Would you like to sing it?' Olive Gilbert and Muriel Barron then picked up the music, stood by the piano and sang a duet between a contralto and a soprano. They sang it beautifully of course, but it largely lost its impact being sung by two ladies. This worried me right to the end of the show. I felt the song had been thrown away. So I had the audacity to suggest to Ivor that he had a reprise just before the final curtain.

As the show stood, Ivor was sitting playing some chords

at the piano as Roma Beaumont walked slowly up the stairs. Just before she disappeared from our sight, she turned and blew Ivor a kiss and the curtain slowly fell on this quiet and rather sad note. Why, I suggested, could Ivor not be playing *We'll Gather Lilacs* and when Roma Beaumont reached halfway up the stairs could she not turn and softly sing to him the words of the song, disappearing as the last note died away. Ivor said nothing at the time but I must say took it very well from two inexperienced strangers. But to my surprise and delight about a fortnight later the change was made and from then on *Perchance to Dream* ended with the lovely melody of *We'll Gather Lilacs*.

4 Climbing the ladder

NINETEEN FORTY-EIGHT was one of the most eventful years of my life. I got engaged and married, I was auditioned for and offered my first film part, I commentated for the first time at an England–Australia Test match, and I started my series *Let's Go Somewhere* in *In Town Tonight*, which was to be my big breakthrough in radio. I will take them in order.

It started on Monday, 1 December 1947, when the telephone in my office rang and a girl's attractive voice said, 'This is Pauline Tozer. I am working in the photographic section of the BBC and my brother Gordon told me to give you a ring.' I immediately realised who she was, as Gordon Tozer had been my Assistant Technical Adjutant in the Grenadiers from 1942 to 1945.

My normal reaction would have been rather a cool one as I was quite happy leading a busy bachelor life plus working long and varied hours in the BBC. As a result I had not had much time or inclination for the opposite sex. In fact I learnt later from Pauline that Gordon *had* told her that I would not be interested in her but that I might introduce her to some of my younger BBC colleagues. Certainly at that time most of my friends looked on me as a confirmed bachelor or thought that no woman would ever be brave enough to take me on. But there must have been something in that voice. Anyway I whipped out my diary and asked her to lunch with me two days later.

I went to pick Pauline up at her department in the old Langham Hotel and to my delight found that she was a very attractive blonde with blue eyes. We then had lunch in the Bolivar restaurant, now the BBC club. We got on well and laughed a lot, and the next night I took her along to the Chelsea Palace where I was doing a broadcast of a variety show. When I introduced her to Dorothy Squires and Billy Reid, Dorothy asked: 'Are you two engaged?'

We weren't then, but ten days after our first meeting I proposed. Pauline played for time a bit before giving her answer and I don't blame her. However, she finally accepted me on 6 January, just over a month since we had first met. My mother was delighted and the Tozers, though slightly taken aback by the speed of the whole thing, seemed quite happy and gave their approval. I did the old-fashioned thing of asking her father Colonel Tozer for his permission.

I invited myself to lunch with the Colonel in the City and was so nervous that I talked about everything except the engagement. He knew exactly why I had come and was as relieved as I was when after the cheese and biscuits I plucked up courage to introduce the subject. Afterwards he told me that Mrs Tozer was waiting for him by the telephone to hear the result of the lunch. They wanted us to get married in June but I pointed out that this might mean me missing the Lord's Test against Australia. So in the end we were married at St Paul's, Knightsbridge on 22 April. As a wedding present the OB department recorded the whole ceremony and some interviews by Stewart, Wynford and Raymond as we emerged from the church under an archway of microphones.

The first week of our honeymoon we spent at the Grand Hotel, Eastbourne. It was an old haunt of mine from my early schooldays, when I was at Temple Grove Preparatory School in Eastbourne. My parents used to take me there for lunch and we listened to Leslie Jefferies and his Orchestra – the original orchestra from the radio programme, *Grand Hotel*, which used to be broadcast from the lounge in the hotel. There was one amusing coincidence. We had shared the cost of the flowers with another couple called Tetley who were being married at St Paul's on the morning of the 22nd. We had never met them though I knew he had been at Sandhurst with me during the war. When we staggered down to lunch on the first day there was a couple sitting at the next table to ours, and I recognised him. It was the Tetleys!

After a very happy week we flew off to Locarno to stay at a small hotel by the lake for a fortnight. But this was not a success, due to my catching some kind of barber's rash on my face. I could not shave so grew a beard and had to go to a doctor who prescribed a course of injections. These had to be administered twice a day by Pauline in my bottom. Luckily she had been a naval VAD in the war so handled a pretty nifty needle. But it was not exactly romantic, and the injections made me feel very low and dispirited.

Furthermore, in those days we were only allowed £25 of currency each and with the extra cost of the injections on top of the hotel charges we had no money to spend on ourselves. All we did was to sit around the hotel and wait for the 4 pm steamer, which took us across the lake to a tea-house. We were just able to afford one meringue each a day, oozing with cream, an unheard-of luxury in England in 1948.

When we came back to London, we set up in a small flat in Bayswater, which was singularly devoid of furniture. I had my beard shaved off and returned to work, while Pauline set about finding us a home. I left it entirely to her, with only one stipulation. It must be in St John's Wood, near Lord's.

In the month before our marriage I had been asked by film director Terence Young whether I would like to appear in a film he had written about the Guard's Armoured Division. He had been one of the intelligence officers and the film was to be called *They Were Not Divided*. Some of his characters were based on officers whom he had known in the Division. He had the idea of getting them to play themselves in the film. He had written a part for me and

37

for some reason, I can't think why, the character was nicknamed 'Nosey'! With one or two other officers I went down to Denham studios to do a film test. We were made up, put into battle-dress and had to wear one of those awful berets again.

The test took place in a hay-loft as we were meant to be hiding from the Germans. All went well and I was offered the part at £50 a day whenever I was needed, with an option on my services of up to six weeks. The BBC had agreed to give me leave without salary but I was suspicious of film-makers, and suspected that the six weeks would stretch into several months, and that I would have to make myself available if this were so. It would mean that I would definitely miss the Lord's Test. So to make it worth my while I decided to ask for £100 a day.

Somewhat naturally perhaps, the casting director, who was a lady, turned down this demand from an unknown 'actor'. So I said 'Right that's it' and somewhat relieved rang Terence to tell him the sad news and also to thank him for having given me the opportunity in the first place. He seemed disappointed and tried to get me to change my mind, saying he might be able to get me the extra money. But by now I had realised how much BBC work I would be missing, so regretfully but definitely said no. My part was then slightly rewritten and given to David Niven's friend Michael Trubshawe with the mutton-chop whiskers. Nosey became Bushy and as it turned out the filming did take far longer than six weeks. But it was a jolly good film and I saw it again recently on TV.

In the cricket world there was great excitement at the arrival of Don Bradman's Australian team. It was exactly ten years since the last Australian tour, which had ended so disastrously for them in the 5th Test at the Oval, when England made a record 903–7 declared and Len Hutton his 364. This 1948 team was probably the best team Australia has ever sent to England. It had everything and was full of great and exciting cricketers. There was Bradman himself, Arthur Morris, Sid Barnes, Ray Lindwall, Keith Miller, Don Tallon and Neil Harvey. England were still recovering from the war years and except for Alec Bedser were woefully weak in bowling, and had to rely too much on Hutton and Compton for the batting.

With their powerful attack of fast bowlers Australia also gained a tremendous advantage from the current law of a new ball after only fifty-five overs. The tour was full of drama and excitement, and more important still the big crowds saw some splendid cricket. Don Bradman made his usual hundred at Worcester and in spite of being in his fortieth year still looked the master batsman except for a certain fallibility against Bedser's in-swinger. On three occasions he was caught at short leg by Hutton.

Lindwall and Miller provided one of the fiercest and fastest opening attacks in the history of cricket, and this made Compton's two hundreds against them an even greater achievement. His 184 at Trent Bridge only ended when he trod on his wicket defending himself from a Miller bouncer, and his 145 at Old Trafford was a gallant effort after being carried off with a nasty cut over his eye.

Then there was that incredible Australian victory at Headingley where they scored 404 to win on the last day in the fourth innings. Unfortunately TV could not be there but I remember listening on the radio to Alston, Arlott and McGilvray as first Morris and then Bradman thrashed the England bowlers all over the ground. And then the final drama of Bradman's last Test innings at the Oval, after England had been dismissed for a miserable 52. He only had to make four runs to average exactly 100 for all his Test innings and was cheered by the huge crowd who stood up as he made his usual slow way to the wicket.

As he approached the square, Norman Yardley called for three cheers from the England side. This was the best cricket moment on TV so far, and there was a complete hush as he played his first ball from Hollies. But the next ball was fatal. It was Hollies' googly, Bradman pushed slowly and uncharacteristically forward, missed it and was bowled. Possibly he had been affected by the emotional reception which he had received. Anyway once again the crowd rose and applauded him all the way back until he finally disappeared into the pavilion and out of Test cricket for ever, but with a batting average of only 99.94! A great moment both for TV and cricket.

It was about the Headingley Test that one of cricket's best-ever stories was told. It was probably apocryphal but I hope not. The England team had assembled at the Queen's Hotel in Leeds on the Wednesday afternoon before the match, but Alec Bedser and Jack Crapp were late arriving. Surrey had been playing Gloucestershire and they had travelled up to Leeds together. Jack went into the hotel first ahead of Alec and approached the girl receptionist, who did not recognise him as one of the England team.

'Bed, sir?' she said.

'No, Crapp,' replied Jack, thinking she had mistaken him for Alec.

'Second door on the left,' said the receptionist as she returned to her books.

One of the luckiest breaks of my career came in March 1948. For some time John Ellison had taken over the outside interview spot every Saturday in *In Town Tonight* on the Home Service. It had originally started with Michael Standing's *Standing on the Corner* and then became *Man in the Street* with Harold Warrender and Stewart Macpherson as the interviewers. John took over from them and changed the spot to *On the Job* where he went and talked to people at their work.

One Saturday in March he was to interview an air-hostess in a BOAC plane on its flight from London to Prestwick. In case the ground-to-air contact failed, he asked me to stand by with another air-hostess at London Airport. Once again I was lucky. The engineers could not contact John in his plane, so I did my interview instead. Peter Duncan, the producer of *In Town Tonight*, must have thought it was not too bad. At any rate a few weeks later John became the studio interviewer and I was asked to take over *On the Job*. This was just another instance of how lucky I have been throughout my career at being in the right place at the right time.

Except for a break for my honeymoon I did *On the Job* throughout the spring and summer, but somehow it did not seem to amount to very much. It was all talk and too similar to what was taking place in the studio. Peter Duncan thought the same and asked Lobby and me whether it would be possible to do something with more movement and excitement and even with the occasional bit of humour – in complete contrast to the scripted interviews in the studio. So we decided to revive a feature called *Let's Go Somewhere*, which John Snagge had done in the thirties.

Let's Go Somewhere was to start in October and we immediately set about thinking up some ideas. Little did I think then that I would do 150 of these broadcasts and that, except for the summer break which *In Town Tonight* always took, Saturday nights would not be my own for the next four years.

I could never have done the series without the help and skill of our engineers in OBs. Spud Moody, a dynamic little grey-haired man, was to be my 'Svengali'. He was responsible for many of the ideas, and worked out how they could be done technically. This was not always easy if I was riding a horse round a circus ring or being rescued from the sea by a helicopter. Without his cheerful support I could never have gone on week after week. People of course sent in ideas but many of them were impossible to do and others I just did not fancy. Like the listener who suggested that I jump off Nelson's Column with an open umbrella as a parachute!

The spot was always live, not recorded, and lasted from

three and a half to four minutes. This meant that each Saturday became a 'first night' and one either got it right or wrong. There could be no re-takes. As a result we had our failures and I hope our successes. But it was always hit or miss. I had no producer to help me and I even had to carry and keep an eye on my own stopwatch, no matter what I was doing. My team just consisted of myself and our engineer, Nogs Newman who, with occasional relief from Oggie Lomas, gave up all his Saturday nights. He never complained and remained cheerful, wet or fine, failure or success. I owe these backroom boys a deep debt of gratitude for all their skill and loyalty. But like me they seemed to enjoy it. It was a challenge with plenty of variety and the skills required by both engineers and commentator in order to produce a good broadcast were really what broadcasting is all about.

5 Let's Go Somewhere

I WON'T BORE YOU with a complete list of all the things I did during the course of our show, but will select a few from each category – exciting, funnies, musical, theatrical and so on.

The very first came from the Chamber of Horrors in Madame Tussaud's. There was a story going about that they would pay £100 to anyone who would spend the night there alone. It was rumoured that one or two people had tried and had gone off their heads. We checked with Tussaud's PRO, Reg Edds, who denied the story completely. He added that no member of the public had in fact ever been there alone after the section closed at 7 pm. He offered to let me be the first person to do this and that after *In Town Tonight* I could stay on until 11 o'clock for a later broadcast, but definitely *not* all night.

I was secretly very relieved at this and we agreed to do *Let's Go Somewhere* at about 7.30 pm and then a later broadcast before the Home Service closed down at 11 pm. Just before 7 pm I somewhat apprehensively went down the twisty stone staircase into the Chamber, and through the iron gate which clanged shut behind me. Nogs had left a microphone and a pair of headphones by a chair under the only light in the Chamber – a very dim bulb rather like those in a wartime railway carriage. The leads from the mike disappeared through the iron gate, and were my only link with the outside world.

Reg had had the chair placed in front of a group of murderers consisting of Crippen, Smith of the brides in the bath, and Mahon the Eastbourne trunk murderer. These figures were tremendously lifelike and were dressed in the actual clothes they had worn when alive – Madame

Tussaud's used to buy them off the widows. In addition to all the murderers, there were instruments of torture like the rack, a guillotine and the actual bath used by Smith. Definitely not a place for the squeamish. I had brought the evening papers with me and while waiting sat down to read the football results. I had the uncanny feeling that Crippen was looking over my shoulder to see how Arsenal had got on.

Then I tried walking round the dark Chamber. But it was too eerie and I felt that all the staring eyes of the figures were following me around. So I hurried back to my chair and something soft brushed against my head – it was the noose of a hangman's rope! Even worse when I sat down, there was a low rumbling noise and all the figures began to sway slightly. It shook me for a moment but I then remembered we were directly over the Bakerloo line and that this must be the trains passing by underneath.

I was in quite a state by the time I put on my headphones to get my cue from John Ellison, and my voice was unusually shaky as I greeted listeners for my first *Let's Go Somewhere*. I described the Chamber to them and tried to give a picture of what it was like down there alone in the semi-dark with all those terrible people. I said goodbye with great reluctance when my time was up, as it was the last time I would be speaking to anyone for the next three and a half hours. Home Service were to come back before they closed down to check up if I was still sane.

I must say it seemed a very long wait. Pauline had provided me with some food, but when I took my first bite at an apple it echoed round and round the Chamber. I did not dare walk round again so just sat and got colder and stiffer. And for those of you who, like me, are interested in that sort of thing, I can reveal that there was a bucket available should the call of nature make it necessary. But in fact it wasn't. Anyway I was extremely relieved when Home Service called me up just before 11 pm and Reg Edds unlocked the iron gate to let me out. It was not an experience I want to go through again, and although I think I just managed to keep my sanity, I have never been down there since.

As a boy I had often read thrillers in which the hero was trapped on the railway, and had to lie down between the rails and let the express roar over him. He always emerged none the worse for the experience, so we thought we would try it in real life.

Southern Region gave me permission to do the broadcast from a stretch of line about a mile out of Victoria Station. It was not as dangerous as it sounds, as at that spot there was a deepish pit between the lines where it was possible to crouch as the trains roared by overhead. We ran out the microphone cable under the lines but had to be very careful as they were of course electrified and my heart was in my mouth each step I took over one. A man from the SR and myself took up our position in the pit and it was hoped to time my broadcast to coincide with the arrival of the *Golden Arrow*. Unfortunately it was late and when they cued over to me I had to make do with an electric train. It was quite a frightening sight as it thundered towards me in the dark, sparks flying everywhere. When it was about thirty yards away I ducked down and I must say got a terrific shaking as it sped over me. It made quite an exciting broadcast with my build-up of the approaching train and the sound effects when it finally arrived.

The SR man told me to stay where I was, as the *Golden Arrow* was now due on the same line, and when it had passed we should have more time to negotiate the live rails in the dark. It was jolly lucky we were not on the air when the *Golden Arrow* did eventually come as, when it passed over me, someone was washing their hands – at least I hope they were! I got absolutely soused and my subsequent language would not have enhanced my BBC career had it gone out over the air.

One Christmas I went to the circus at Harringay Arena and tried my hand at riding bareback (the horse not me!)

round the ring during a performance before a packed audience. This involved some rather tricky technical arrangements as I was suspended on the end of a pulley so that if I fell off I would be landed gently into the middle of the ring. The idea was to canter round once or twice in the normal position, then try kneeling and finally standing up.

I just managed the kneeling part but as soon as I tried to stand up lost my balance and was swung across the ring. I breathlessly described my efforts into the microphone tied across my chest. But for good fun I had added one extra ingredient. One of the clowns lent me his 'quick-release' trousers and as I felt myself falling I pulled a tape and the trousers fell down to my ankles as I landed with a plop in the middle of the ring. The audience had been told that I was broadcasting in *In Town Tonight* and the sight of 'the man from Auntie' with no trousers brought the house down.

There was a sequel to this. A few weeks later a friend of mine went to the same circus when my clown friend came on disguised as a member of the audience to try his hand at riding the horse. He always did this at the end after everyone else had tried, and in fact I had filled his spot. He did what I had done, though of course far more skilfully and at the end down came his trousers. Two people sitting behind my friend said: 'What a shame. He must have been listening to *In Town Tonight* and he has pinched Brian Johnston's idea.'

Something rather more frightening was when we decided to see how effective a police or guard dog could be in chasing and catching a criminal. A broadcaster called Trevor Hill owned an Alsatian called Rustler who was trained to do almost anything and had in fact played himself in a radio series *Riders of the Range*. I was given a special coat with heavy padding on the left arm and was assured that Rustler had been trained to go for this, and no other part of me. For the broadcast I got Pauline to walk across the BBC cricket ground and I crept up behind her and snatched her bag, and ran off. As rehearsed, she let out a piercing scream and Trevor was soon on the scene with Rustler on a lead. After hearing Pauline's explanation of what had happened he released Rustler and ordered him to 'get' me. By this time I had gone about eighty yards and was quite out of breath trying to talk and run at the same time.

I could hear Rustler padding up behind me and it reminded me of the Hound of the Baskervilles, as he got closer and closer. When he reached me he leaped through the air and seized me by my padded left arm, and his weight knocked me to the ground. I could just feel his teeth through the padding, but as soon as I was down he let go and stood on guard wagging his tail as he waited for Trevor to arrive. But when I tried to get up and escape he bared his teeth and seized me once again. So I thought it wiser to lie still until Trevor arrived and put him on his lead. It had been an impressive performance and I hope acted as a deterrent to any potential bag-snatcher who happened to be listening – especially as they would not have the benefit of the padded arm.

I was several times challenged to be the target for a knife-throwing act but always refused, making the excuse that there was bound to be an element of risk of serious injury and that it would not be fair to Pauline. Actually of course I was scared stiff at the prospect. I reckoned that even knife-throwers are human and can make mistakes, just as a great batsman is clean bowled or an expert shot misses the bull's-eye.

But I did accept a similar challenge and looking back, I was a fool even to do that. There was a darts champion called Joe Hitchcock who in his spare time used to visit pubs and give demonstrations of nail-throwing in aid of charity. He had a stooge who stood sideways about ten feet away and Joe would then throw four-inch nails with specially sharpened points. The stooge would start with a cigarette in his mouth. Joe would knock this out with a nail. The cigarette was then replaced with a matchstick, with the same result. The stooge then turned his back on Joe and stuck a cigarette in each ear and whizz would come the nails and knock them out – usually but not always first throw. Then the stooge would again stand sideways, fling his head back and balance a penny on the end of his nose. This time Joe took one or two 'sighters' but always just above the penny not under, as otherwise the nail would have gone slap through the stooge's nose.

Then, as if that were not enough, came the climax. The penny was replaced by a pin of all things, and once again Joe knocked that off. I felt an awful coward but all I would agree to Joe doing was the cigarette stuck in the mouth and ears. Even so I was frightened and let the listeners hear the pounding of my heart as I held my mike over it. It was a horrid moment waiting for those nails realising that the slightest mistake and one of my eardrums could be punctured. He missed once or twice – deliberately I am sure to build up the tension – and each time the nails whizzed by my head. That was a broadcast I did not enjoy. About two years later I had another challenge from Joe. He said he was now doing the act blindfolded! You can guess what my answer was!

Equally frightening was riding on the pillion of a motorbike through a wall of empty beer barrels. This was a stunt done by a character called 'Mad' Johnny Davies. He also used to ride through burning hoops or even through a sheet of glass. He did this stripped to the waist and afterwards had to pluck bits of glass splinters out of his body. I decided to play safe and chose the barrels as being the least dangerous. But in all these stunts I always made sure first of the skill and safety record of those with whom I was working. In the same way that Joe Hitchcock's stooge was apparently unharmed, Johnny Davies was still in one piece.

So I strapped a mike to my chest, got on the pillion and

prepared to take a two-hundred yard run at the barrels which were piled in a pyramid fifteen feet high. We were on a large recreation ground and it was a bit greasy from rain. But we soon got up speed and by the time we reached the barrels were going at a good 50 mph. I really was scared at what lay ahead but I tried to keep talking as we roared across the ground. I must confess that I was hugging Johnny as if he had been my girlfriend. I had worked it out that I would be the third thing to hit the barrels, first the front wheel of the bike, then Johnny, then me.

There was a terrific bang as we hit the barrels, piles of debris shot into the air and the bike slithered and skidded all over the place. But Johnny managed to keep it upright and we came to a welcome halt. Except for the impact as the bike struck the barrels I had not felt anything except a few bits of barrel landing on my head. But it's not a way I would like to earn my living.

Another test of my nerves was when I lay on a table on the ice rink at the Empress Hall and was jumped over by a speed skater. Once again I made sure he was an expert but even so the flash of the skates as they passed inches over my body was a fairly forbidding sight. Some years later on TV I was jumped over by four horses as I sat drinking a cup of tea at an army trestle table. This was during a rehearsal for a Military Tattoo and I think that I preferred the skates to those hooves. Just suppose one of the horses had made a mistake and landed on the tea-table or me.

At the start of the series we had been asked to get some movement into the programme and we did our best to carry out our brief. I piloted a light aircraft, drove a steam train, launched a lifeboat, rode on the Big Dipper, and tried to keep talking as I was hurled round and round the Rotor at the Olympia side-shows. I also challenged the Brighton police to catch me in my car after doing a smash and grab and needless to say I lost.

One of the coldest jobs was when I went out in a boat

five miles off Folkestone with Sam Rockett the Channel swimmer. We wanted to see what it was like for a swimmer to be fed while in the water. I trod water by the boat as Sam lent out and fed me with nuts, dates and grapes and gave me orange juice to drink. This I understand was the staple diet for such occasions, but I found it almost impossible to talk and eat and avoid swallowing oceans of sea water. It was also freezing cold so far out and I was frozen and exhausted when lifted back into the boat. I had only been in the water for about five minutes. Channel swimmers stay in for fourteen hours or more. Rather them than me.

One of the most painful things I did was to try out the ejector seat which pilots use to escape from the cockpits of jet planes. In the old days a pilot could clamber over the side and drop with his parachute. But now the jets go so fast that if a pilot stuck his head out it would be like hitting it against a brick wall at 500 mph. So now he slides back the canopy of his cockpit and pulls a small canvas screen over his face. This fires two charges which eject the seat at great speed, sixty feet into the air clear of the plane. The seat has its own little parachute which opens and gives the pilot time to get out of the seat, drop off and open his own individual parachute.

The purpose of the screen over the face is to prevent burning and blast on the face when it meets the air at speed. It also pulls the head and neck down. Otherwise they might be thrown back and the neck possibly broken. The seat was invented by Sir Martin Baker and is made at a factory at Denham where they have a test seat, which shoots sixty feet up a vertical tower and is halted when it reaches the top. I broadcast from this seat and had a nasty few seconds before pulling the face screen down. I shot up into the night. The acceleration was phenomenal and I had no time to say a word before I reached the top. It is a wonderful invention and has saved hundreds of lives all over the world. The only snag from my point of view was that I had a terrible pain up my backside for a few days, as a result of the tremendous boost when the charges went off. I wonder if other people who have ejected have experienced the same thing.

Just before Christmas 1950 we did the first-ever live broadcast from the actual face of a coal-mine. It was at Snowdon Colliery in Kent, one of the deepest mines in the country. We went down over three thousand feet in a cage at what seemed a terrific pace. I believe it was 40 mph but we got the impression of greater speed as we shot down through the hot, dust-laden air which blew up the shaft. At the bottom we walked a few hundred yards and then travelled over a mile in a paddy – the miners' name for an underground truck. Finally we had to crawl on our hands and knees along the coal face, only three feet high. I broadcast, half-kneeling, half-lying, in a temperature of 90°F trying to hew some coal with a pick. It was back-aching and nearly impossible and I only managed to loosen a few measly lumps. I was only at the face for half an hour and down the mine altogether for about two hours, but it seemed a lifetime to me. I felt trapped, shut in and completely at the mercy of nature.

I couldn't help thinking of the three thousand feet which lay between me and the surface. It seemed that the only things which prevented the coal above from crushing us were the wooden pit props. These have been replaced in some pits I believe by aluminium props. But the miners told me that they preferred wood as they could tell by their creaks when danger was near.

After this experience, I have always believed that miners were entitled to a special high wage. I certainly won't take any criticism of them from people who have not been down a mine, as they can have no idea what the job is like. The long journey to the coal face, working in cramped conditions for hours on end, the dust and the heat. No smoking, no telephoning girlfriends, no popping out to get a haircut or a breath of fresh air. Plus of course the ever-present sense of danger.

One Saturday I became a fireman with the London Fire Brigade. In uniform and helmet I sat playing cards with the crew at Chiltern Street Station as we waited for the alarm to go. Peter Duncan had organised a fire on some waste ground behind Broadcasting House and then dialled 999 during the programme. When the alarm rang in the station we made a dash for the hole in the floor and slid down the shining steel pole to the ground twenty feet below. Within twelve seconds the doors had been flung open, the engine started up and we had all scrambled aboard. The Station Commander shouted where to go as we shot out into the street.

It was a tremendous thrill to commentate as we raced through the streets, bell clanging and cars and people dashing for safety. These drivers really are terrific and are allowed to go through red lights and pass the wrong side of traffic islands. But if they have an accident they are treated like any other motorist. They do a grand job.

One broadcast which I hope did some good was when I became a blood donor (for the first time). In those days people knew very little about it and as a result everyone – including myself – was a bit scared of giving their blood. But while on the air I was able to describe the actual insertion of the needle and the blood running off into the bottle. Except for a slight wince when the needle went into the vein, I hope I made it all sound as easy and painless as it undoubtedly is, and possibly secured some badly-needed recruits for the Blood Transfusion Service.

I have always been fond of music, mostly of the sort you can whistle or hum. I had had piano lessons up to the age of sixteen and then rather stupidly gave them up as I was not allowed to learn what would now be called 'pop'. But as a result I am able to read sheet music of popular numbers, though my rhythm is not much good. I had always envied the cinema organist as the spotlight turned on him and he slowly rose up on the console of the organ from the depth of the orchestra pit.

So one Saturday night I went along to the Granada Tooting to try out my skill on the mighty organ in front of a full house. A notice was flashed on the screen saying that Brian Johnston, the famous BBC organist, would be broadcasting a short recital on the organ. On my cue from John I pressed a button and slowly ascended as I played a few chords. As the organ reached the top I swung round and bowed to the applauding audience. They must have thought that they were in for something good. I announced in a serious voice that for my first piece I would play part of Tchaikovsky's Piano Concerto in B Flat Minor.

There was a murmur of approval as I turned round and pulled out some of the stops which Johnny Madin, the regular organist had shown me. I started to play and after a few notes there was a roar of laughter, and no wonder. Instead of Tchaikovsky I was playing the Harry Lime theme, and then went straight into *We'll Gather Lilacs*, interrupted by sounds of trains, birds and galloping horses, which it was possible to produce by pulling out various stops. The audience had a good laugh and I had achieved one of my ambitions.

A few months later I achieved something which I would never have believed possible. I played a street piano in a side street near the Victoria Palace and, wait for it, I actually sang *Underneath the Arches* with Bud Flanagan. When I had first heard Bud and Chesney Allen sing it together in the early thirties, little did I think I would ever have the honour of actually taking Ches' place. But Bud was a real friend of mine, and to help in my spot, came out of the Victoria Palace, placed his hand on my shoulder and sang just as beautifully as if he were appearing in a Royal Variety Performance. What a lovely man he was. This really was one of the great moments in my broadcasting life.

I achieved one or two other musical ambitions. I played

a barrel organ in Camden Town and disguised myself as a French siffleur with a little pointed beard and sang at the Allegro Bar just off Jermyn Street. I was even allowed to conduct an orchestra at the Royal Academy of Music to see what would happen if they *did* follow my baton. The result was foreseeable – a ghastly cacophony of sounds ending in a tremendous race to the finish.

But I did earn some money from one of my musical broadcasts, when I sang disguised as a tramp in the Strand. I had always felt sorry for street musicians and singers and wondered what they felt like – ashamed, embarrassed, or scornful of those who either slipped them the odd penny or sixpence or pretended not to notice them as they passed by.

I put on a dirty old macintosh and hat and the oldest pair of trousers and shoes that I could find. I dirtied my face and my hands and with a microphone hidden under my scarf shuffled out into the street from under an archway where I had been waiting. I carried a small tin with some matchboxes on it and started to sing *Tipperary* in a very shaky voice. It was extremely embarrassing singing in a public street – you try it sometime and see how you feel. I had to force myself to do it and tried not to look at the various passers-by, most of whom were trying to avoid me. However, in my three and a half minutes I did collect nearly a shilling, though twopence of this was given by one of our engineers *pour encourager les autres*.

He also threw in a halfpenny at the end as a signal that my time was up, as a tramp would obviously not have a stopwatch. I was immensely relieved when it was all over and ever since then if I pass one of these singers I always try to give something – however small. I know exactly how they are feeling.

I must have tried out twenty or thirty jobs during *Let's Go Somewhere* and among these were a cowman, RAC scout, wheel tapper, bell-ringer, town crier, ice-hockey goal-keeper, salesman on an exhibition stand, a recruit in a drill squad and a toastmaster. The man who coached me in toast-mastering was himself one of the best known in the West End. He was telling me of some of the times when things had gone wrong. He was once announcing the guests at an important function when he was suddenly called away by the organiser of the banquet, who wished to discuss arrangements for the speakers. He had chosen a quiet moment when most of the guests seemed to have arrived. Unfortunately during the minute or so that he was away a guest called Sir William Orfe came up the stairs and seeing no toastmaster announced himself to his host and hostess.

'I'm Orfe,' he said, shaking hands.

'Oh, I'm so sorry,' replied his hostess, 'the party has only just begun!'

6 Let's go to the theatre

WITH MY LOVE of the stage I made sure that quite a few of my broadcasts came from theatres. For instance, during a performance of the pantomime *Puss in Boots* at the Palladium I came on as the donkey in place of the usual man. I played a short scene with Tommy Trinder but found it unbearably hot inside the skin and very difficult to breathe with the microphone inside the donkey's mouth. But as Tommy rode off on my back I could at least claim that I had 'played' the Palladium.

Another time I was challenged by a Strong Woman to see if she could lift me up and turn me upside down. Her name was Joan Rhodes and she was a young attractive blonde in a beautiful evening gown. Somewhere underneath must have been hidden some rippling muscles, but on the surface her figure was super. In her act at the Shepherd's Bush Empire she tore telephone directories in half and bent nails and iron bars. When I went up on to the stage to accept her challenge she lifted me up like a child and then held me head downwards until all the money fell out of my pocket and one of my braces burst. She got a great hand from the audience and I must admit it was a remarkable performance as I weighed fourteen and a half stone at the time.

I once sawed a woman in half and was also sawn in half myself by Robert Harbin. It was an extraordinary feeling watching the saw apparently sawing right through my stomach. But I must not reveal how it was done. The secret of a mental telepathy act in which I took part was on the other hand a little easier to fathom. I was blindfolded on the stage, while my partner held up various articles, which he borrowed from the audience.

Partner I have an article here. Tell me what it is. Take your time.
Me A watch.
Partner Quite right. And now I have a visiting card from a gentleman. Can you tell me his name. He is of Jewish extraction.
Me Is he?
Partner That's right.

That's how we did it, but I am assured that some of these acts really do pass thoughts to each other. I wonder.

I had always wanted to test out the theory that if you suck a lemon in front of a brass band they will all dry up. So one Saturday I went on stage at the Adelphi Theatre and by prearrangement interrupted Jimmy Edwards in the middle of his trombone act. I challenged him to play as I sucked. I had a very juicy lemon and as he started to play I began to suck it right in front of his face. For about half a minute he struggled bravely but what had started as *presto agitato* rapidly became *andante*. He got slower and slower and began to drool at the mouth. In the end he was just pushing the rod of his trombone backwards and forwards, and all that came out were a few phut phuts of air. He gave up and burst out laughing. He claims it had nothing to do with the lemon but that it was the sight of my face, coupled with the laughter from the audience. So I never really discovered for certain whether my theory was right or wrong.

I had always been an admirer of the way Peter Pan and the fairies in pantomimes flew unconcernedly about the stage. I was therefore delighted when I was invited to be a member of the Flying Ballet during a performance of the Ice Pantomime at the Empress Hall. I was disguised as a fantastic-looking bird, feather wings and a large yellow beak and so on. They fastened a belt round my middle, on to which were attached two very thin wires hanging down from the roof. They had to be small to be invisible

57

to the audience, but I was assured they would bear the weight of a twenty-two stone man, so I decided to take the risk. There were about six other 'birds' in the ballet and as the orchestra struck up we were hoisted into the air high above the glistening black ice fifty feet below. I did not know the steps of the ballet or whatever they are called in the air – but I flapped my wings and then held them spread out as if swooping like a bird. It was terrifying looking down at the upturned faces of the audience and realising that I was only being suspended by the two thin wires. That ice looked horribly hard. After being swung three times up and down the length of the arena I was slowly lowered on to the ice. I can understand birds enjoying flying through the air. It was a very pleasant sensation. But they don't have to worry about two thin bits of wire. And I never did discover how they knew the wires would take up to a twenty-two stone man. Had they tried a twenty-three stoner and had the wires broken? If so, that's one job I would not like – a flying ballet wire tester.

One of the most uproarious and chaotic of the broadcasts was when I was shaved and shampooed by the Crazy Gang during their show *Together Again* at the Victoria Palace. They had a barber's shop sketch and I took the place of the man who twice nightly was given the full treatment. They lent me some old clothes, a macintosh and a wig, and all I had to do was to sit in the chair and try to keep talking into the microphone. As soon as I sat down they pulled off the wig and poured bottles of coloured shampoo all over my real hair and face – green, yellow, red, any colour you can think of. They had an enormous brush, dipped it into some white lather and 'shaved' me. The lather went into my mouth and up my nose and as I tried to talk they stuffed the brush into my mouth. They were having the time of their lives, and so were the audience. Teddy Knox and Jimmy Nervo were the chief culprits, and I finished up on the floor as they poured water down my trousers and tickled me in the tummy.

It must have sounded chaotic to listeners at home. All they could have heard was my screams and the roars of the audience. But it was surprising how many people told me afterwards how much they had enjoyed it. That's one of the great things about radio. It encourages the use of one's imagination. I took over an hour to clean up and get all the colours out of my hair and skin. As I left the theatre one man came up and shook me by the hand. It was the actor who normally sat in the chair – I had spared him the ordeal for at least one performance.

The Crazy Gang were wonderful people, always friendly and cheerful, and I did quite a few broadcasts with them. They were tremendous practical jokers and I was warned never to leave my overcoat in Bud Flanagan's dressing-room. People who had done so found sewn inside a notice: 'This coat has been pinched from Bud Flanagan. Please inform the police.' Very awkward, if the owner at some posh function hands it in to a cloakroom attendant, who then spots the notice.

The Gang would go to any lengths to make a successful joke. At one time Jack Hylton used to leave his best suit in one of their dressing-rooms, so that when he came up from a day at the races, he could change into something more suitable for the theatre. The Gang hired a tailor to come in each day and take about an eighth of an inch off the bottom of the trousers and then sew it up again. For the first few times Jack did not seem to notice anything. But after a bit he began to let out his braces and could not understand why the trousers were creeping higher and higher up his legs. In the end his braces would not let out any further and he became suspicious, and finally found out. But showman that he was, he appreciated the trouble that they had taken to produce a laugh.

One of the most unusual places from which I broadcast was from inside a letterbox at Oxford. It was Christmas time and the idea was to see how people were helping the Post Office by writing clearly, putting the town in block letters, and sticking on the right stamp when posting their Christmas cards.

We went to Oxford as this was the only box the Post Office could find large enough to contain me. I crouched inside with my microphone and as the letters and cards dropped in I reported on the things that had been done right or wrong. All went well but as usual I was tempted and went a little too far. No one had any idea that I was inside so to finish I put my hand up to the slit through which the letters are posted and when a lady came up to post her card I put my hand out and took the letter. There was a loud scream and I gather she nearly fainted. You can hardly blame her. You don't expect to see a hand emerging from a letterbox and grip your letter. It was a rotten trick to play.

I also made a speech from Speaker's Corner which was not at all easy to do. It takes quite a bit of courage to get up on a soap-box and start talking about nothing in particular in front of a crowd made up largely of regulars. It is undoubtedly the best free entertainment in London and the repartee of the crowd is usually far better value than the speakers. I remember once an old favourite there called Charlie denouncing capitalists and 'their superfluous profits'. 'Was Moses one?' came immediately from the crowd.

During my broadcast one of them asked me: 'Why, with the present food shortage does the BBC waste so much tripe on the air?' It wasn't a bad question! All I could rather feebly reply on the spur of the moment was: 'Because they know their onions.'

One date in 1950 was too good to miss. The first of April happened to fall on a Saturday, so, although one is not supposed to operate after 12 noon, we decided to make an April Fool of John Ellison. I told him that I was going to do street interviews that night about 1 April. Secretly we had tried out various impersonators to see if they could copy my voice.

Funnily enough, only one of them could, and he got my rather stupid giggle off to perfection. It was Peter Sellers. On that night I hid in the studio and John quite unsuspicious cued over to Peter, thinking it was me. Peter did perfectly and I must say sounded just like me. After a few hilarious interviews he pretended he was feeling ill and that the crowd was pressing against him, so cued suddenly back to John in the studio. Peter Duncan in the control panel signalled John in the studio to take over. John, quite nonplussed said: 'We're sorry. Brian is obviously not feeling too well, so we will go on to the next item.' (He told me afterwards that he thought I was drunk!) As he said this I crept from behind a screen, went up behind him, tapped him on the shoulder and said: 'April Fool'. He turned round and looked amazed, but was decent enough to admit that we had caught him fair and square.

On two occasions I did on the radio what would have been impossible to do on the TV (in those days, anyway). I broadcast lying starkers on the slab of a Turkish bath, with all the slaps and grunts, and another time when actually having a bath in my own house. I did this because I had been going to talk to the crews after the Boat Race, but it never took place as Oxford sank. So I had to think of something at the last moment and had a boat race all of my own with some of my young son's boats in the bath. It was not one of my most exciting broadcasts!

One day late in 1950 I was sitting at my desk thinking out future stunts when I suddenly realised that I must be nearing my hundredth 'performance'. I checked up and found that all being well I would reach it on Saturday, 24 February. I puzzled my brain as to how best I could celebrate it. I thought of one or two really sensational things I might do, but discarded them pretty quickly. I did not want it to be my hundredth-and-last *Let's Go Somewhere*. So I hit on another idea.

Why not get Peter Duncan to allow me to do something I had always wanted to do on the air, but which I would obviously never do in the ordinary course of broadcasting? In fact as a birthday treat I asked for 'the freedom of the air' to do what I wanted. It was not an outrageous request, and Peter agreed to it straight away. For three and a half minutes on 24 February I could try and be a cross-talk comedian! I was lucky with my straight man. Ever since I had shared an office with John Ellison we used to try out gag routines, many of them picked up in music halls where we used to go for *Round the Halls*. So we arranged that we would do the 'act' in front of the *In Town Tonight* audience in the studio.

We spent days preparing a suitable script, and some of my most treasured gags had to go – victims of the blue pencil. But this time I was censoring myself, and however good the gag, if it was at all 'blue' I would not let myself be influenced by myself. It was out! Finally the script was ready – all taken from my file and as you can imagine as old and corny a collection of jokes as were ever heard on the BBC – and that is saying something! Our only hope was that they were so old that the younger generation of listeners might never have heard of them. We also decided to sing (rather *à la* Flanagan and Allen) the usual treacly sentimental song with which so many comics finish their acts.

We rehearsed for days as we wanted the act to go with real punch and speed – we could not afford to dawdle with some of those jokes! We eventually managed to get it off slickly enough, and the studio audience were very kind and laughed quite loud and often. And – an unheard-of thing in the somewhat austere atmosphere of the *In Town Tonight* studio – they even applauded at the end of the act. So I had my birthday wish and I think got away with it. There was an amusing sequel.

On the following Monday a well-known radio comic was walking up Shaftesbury Avenue when he was stopped by the 'funny' man of a radio cross-talk act. The conversation went as follows:

'I say, Ted, did you hear Brian Johnston in *In Town Tonight* on Saturday? He pinched all my gags from my act and I don't know what to do now. I've got *Henry Hall's Guest Night* tomorrow.'

And we thought the gags were old and corny! So that you can judge for yourself, here is the script as we did it that night. I hope you have not heard them all before, and that you get at least one laugh out of it.

J.E. Ladies and gentlemen, tonight I am going to give you a serious monologue entitled *The Orphan's Return* –

> *'Twas a dark cold night in December*
> *And the snow was falling fast,*
> *Little Nell lay in the gutter –*
> *And the rich folk by her passed.*
> *You may ask me . . .*

B.J. I say, I say!

J.E. Yes, yes, what is it?

B.J. I've just seen forty men under one umbrella, and not one of them got wet.

J.E. Forty men under one umbrella and not one of them got wet – it must have been a very large umbrella!

B.J. Certainly not, it wasn't raining.

J.E. (*Indignant and exasperated*) What d'you mean by coming on here and interrupting me while I'm reciting – now go away. I'm sorry, ladies and gentlemen, I'll begin again –

> *'Twas a . . .*

B.J. It's in all the papers tonight.

J.E. What is?

B.J. Fish and chips. We don't want London Bridge any longer.

J.E. Why not?

B.J. It's long enough already. D'you know who's in the Navy?

J.E. No, who?

B.J. Sailors. I've got a goat with no nose.

J.E. Really? How does it smell?

B.J. Terrible.

J.E. I don't want to know about that. Will you go away!

B.J. I've got a letter here. If I post it tonight, do you think it will get to Glasgow by Wednesday?

J.E. My dear fellow, of course it will.

B.J. Well, I bet it won't.

J.E. How's that?

B.J. It's addressed to Shoreditch.

J.E. It seems to me you're next door to a blithering idiot.

B.J. Well, move over and give me a chance. By the way, I *nearly* saw your brother the other day.

J.E. How do you mean, you *nearly* saw my brother?

B.J. Well, isn't your brother a policeman?

J.E. That's quite correct – he is a policeman.

B.J. Isn't he P.C. 49?

J.E. That's quite right – he is P.C. 49.

B.J. Well, I met P.C. 48.

J.E. You met P.C. 48 . . . Well, you may think you're very, very clever, but let me tell you I've got a brother who even though he was on the dole, always managed to live above his income.

B.J. That's impossible, he couldn't be on the dole and live above his income.

J.E. Oh, yes, he did. He had a flat over the Labour Exchange. By the way, what's *your* brother doing these days?

B.J. Nothing!

J.E. Nothing? I thought he applied for that job as producer of *In Town Tonight*?

B.J. Yes, he got the job. They call him Button B, you know.

J.E. Button B, why on earth do they call him that?

B.J. Well, he's always pressed for money.

J.E. Well, I must say I don't know what your wife thinks about all this.

B.J. That reminds me, here's a letter from her.

J.E. (*Reading letter*) But there's nothing written on it.

B.J. No, we're not on speaking terms. Not that it matters, I've just got six months for rocking her to sleep.

J.E. You can't get six months for rocking your wife to sleep.

B.J. Oh yes I can, you should have seen the size of the rock.

J.E. I'm sick of this, let's go into this restaurant and get something to eat. Waiter, do you serve lobsters here?

B.J. Yes, sir – sit down, we serve anybody.

J.E. I see you've got frog's legs.

B.J. Yes, sir – it's the walking about that does it.

J.E. How long will the spaghetti be?

B.J. I don't know, sir, we never measure it.

J.E. I think I'll have some soup.

B.J. Right, sir – here it is.

J.E. I say, waiter, there's a fly in my soup.

B.J. All right, sir, don't shout – all the others will want one.

J.E. Have you got any eggs?

B.J. Yes, sir.

J.E. Are they fresh?

B.J. Don't ask me, sir, I only lay the tables.

J.E. Oh! This is hopeless. I think I'll have a drink. What d'you suggest?

B.J. I'd have a mother-in-law, sir.

J.E. Mother-in-law, what's that?

B.J. Stout and bitter. Terrible weather, isn't it, sir?

J.E. Yes, terrible.

B.J. I call it Madam Butterfly weather, sir.

J.E. Madam Butterfly weather?

B.J. Yes, sir, *One Fine Day*. But cheer up – just around the corner may be sunshine for you . . .

Brian Johnston and John Ellison into song

Just around the corner may be sunshine for you,
Just around the corner skies above may be blue –
Even tho' it's dark and cloudy
Mister Sun will soon say 'How-dy'
Just around the corner from you –
We'll see you later,
Just around the corner from you.

I did my final *Let's Go Somewhere* on 17 May 1952, when I was winched out of a boat in the Solent by a Royal Naval helicopter. It was not an easy operation as the back-stream from the chopper blew the boat backwards and forwards. But of course in the safe and skilful hands of the Royal Navy it was perfectly safe and an everyday job for them. It was, however, with a sense of relief that I was safely pulled aboard the hovering helicopter and was able to say a final goodbye to the listeners of *Let's Go Somewhere*.

I would not like to be so immodest as to say I went out at the top. But I was determined to stop before everyone began to get bored with me. During the next few years people often asked me why I had stopped and could I not do some more. If I had continued they might have begun to ask why I didn't stop. As it was I was able to declare the innings closed with a final score of 150 not out.

7 A mixed bag

THERE IS NO DOUBT that at the end of *Let's Go Somewhere* I was intolerably swollen-headed. This is an occupational hazard for all broadcasters and TV personalities. They wield tremendous power because they have such a vast audience listening to what they say. You can try as hard as you like but it is not easy to hide your personal opinion about any subject being discussed. The inflection of the voice or the way of phrasing a question can reveal which side the broadcaster is on. This gives a sometimes unconscious feeling of power which is further increased by the minor flatteries, recognition and extra attention a broadcaster receives at the hands of the public.

It only requires a few appearances on the telly for people to start staring in the street. Some will greet the personality without thinking because they recognise the face and feel that he is an old friend. Others just want to be friendly and start up a conversation about the particular programme in which you have been appearing or the subject on which you are meant to be an expert. For years I have been greeted with such remarks as: 'What, no cricket today Brian?' or 'Do you think we shall beat the Australians?'

This recognition can be a great help in public places and restaurants. It's also no use denying that it is immensely satisfying to be greeted by the Immigration Authority on arriving back at London Airport with a 'Had a good trip, Mr Johnston?' All this contributes to the swollen head.

But luckily, there are antidotes. I often used to be made to look small in front of my friends. Someone would rush up to me and say: 'Oh, we do enjoy your programmes. We always listen to you.' Then as the modest smile began to play on my lips the person would go on: 'And what's in box 13 tonight, Michael?' I evidently had a certain likeness to the late Michael Miles of *Take Your Pick* fame and every time this happened I was suitably deflated.

Even better was the occasion when I had finished doing *Let's Go Somewhere* and was staying one winter's weekend down in Surrey with John Ellison. He was still introducing the programme and on the Saturday he left me by the roaring log fire and set off in his car for London. It was snowing hard and after he had gone a mile or two he skidded into a ditch full of snow. He was well and truly stuck. So he went up to a nearby cottage and knocked on the door. A man answered and John asked him if he had a spade as his car was in a ditch. The man recognised John and said: 'It's John Ellison, isn't it? Of course I'll help.'

He went off, got a spade and started to dig like mad to free the car. After about ten minutes he had not got very far so John asked if he could use his telephone to ring up a friend for help. 'Of course, Mr Ellison. You use my telephone. Anything you like. Meanwhile I'll go on digging.' He could not have been more affable. John rang me up and asked me to bring my Ford Pilot and a towing rope to pull him out, and so reluctantly I left the warm fire. John told me later that as he saw me approaching he thought he would encourage the chap who was still digging hard. 'This friend of mine coming along in the car. You'll know him. He used to do all those stunts in *In Town Tonight* – it's Brian Johnston.'

The name worked like magic on our affable friend. He put his spade down in the snow and said: 'Brian Johnston. Yap, yap, yap, yap. Can never understand a bloody word he says.' And so saying he stalked off to his cottage, leaving us to get on with it as best we could. I must say this had a very salutary effect on me, and took me down a peg or two. To think that anyone could feel so strongly about me!

During the four years of *Let's Go Somewhere* I had

become involved in a variety of programmes. It was a great experience and training ground for me but I fear the poor listeners must have suffered. They were getting as their guide a jack of all trades, who knew very little about any of them. For instance in 1949 it was decided to have an extra commentator on the Boat Race at Hammersmith Bridge and possibly because my father had been a Blue at Oxford, I was chosen. It luckily only involved describing the two crews shooting the bridge and estimating the distance between them. I did not dare to ape John Snagge and risk any 'in-outs', though I have done so more recently when I have been at the finish at Chiswick Bridge.

Again it was assumed that because of my military past I would make the ideal commentator for Trooping the Colour. It was true that I had been in the Brigade of Guards, but the one thing which I had managed to escape during the war was drill parades.

My only real experience of drill had been at the start of the war in 1939, when I was sent on an officer cadet training course at the Royal Military College in Sandhurst. Even there my inability to resist playing jokes got me into slight trouble. We were all out on a TEWT – tactical exercise without troops – where the instructors posed various military problems which they asked the cadets to solve.

We had stopped at the top of a hill and looking down at the valley below the instructor turned to me and said, 'Johnston. You and your platoon are defending this ridge. Suddenly at the bottom of the hill you see a troop of German tanks advancing. What steps would you take?'

'Bloody long ones, sir,' I replied and was deservedly 'put in the book' and had to report to the Company Commander next day for a reprimand.

So my knowledge of drill parades was therefore extremely sketchy and it was quite an ordeal commentating on such an important occasion as Trooping the Colour. I knew that the slightest mistake would bring a shoal of letters from ex-Guards colonels listening with pens poised. By doing a lot of homework and with the help of the officers from London District I just about got by. I think my most serious crime was to say that the companies were 'wheeling' instead of 'forming'.

But it was a difficult broadcast to do. It required expert explanation of what was going on, and plenty of extra titbits to fill in during some fairly lengthy pauses. The commentator also has to let the listeners hear the music of the massed bands and irate letters pour in if he speaks too much over the music. The best by far at striking the right balance is Robert Hudson, who year after year gives an impeccable commentary, a model for every budding commentator.

It was also inevitable that I should be allotted the El Alamein Reunion, although I had never been in the desert war. I did the commentary for a number of years and it was fun having a yearly meeting with Field-Marshal Viscount Montgomery. The first time we met I reminded him of the time he had inspected our Battalion, when I was a Motor Transport Officer at Parkstone in 1941, and he tactfully pretended to remember. He was always extremely helpful and co-operative, and at rehearsals the BBC were given priority over everyone else to make sure the broadcast was a success.

Sometimes Monty was there himself and would ask exactly what we wanted, and gave us the timing of his speech to which he always stuck. When he was not there we used to read aloud the copy of his speech for timing purposes, trying hard to imitate the staccato voice with the short crisp sentences. We had to make a generous allowance for applause and laughter, for he always got plenty of both. Monty was the perfect example of a world figure who knew the value of good publicity and realised that the best way to get it was to do what he was asked by the BBC – within reason!

I also used to do a late night birdsong programme from a Surrey wood with Henry Douglas-Home, who was

William's older brother and a famous ornithologist known as the 'Birdman'. Later we were joined by the bird imitator Percy Edwards and moved to Hever Castle in Kent. Henry, Percy and myself spent many happy May evenings year after year wandering round the woods and persuading the nightingales to sing. Lady Violet Astor was very kind to us and before the broadcasts we were invited into the Castle for drinks, though we were never suitably dressed for the luxurious surroundings of her beautiful home. One year we got so carried away by her hospitality that we lost count of time, and failed to notice that her house guests kept leaving the room and reappearing in evening dress, until the butler was forced to announce that 'Dinner was served', and we made our way back to the woods, feeling somewhat ashamed. We had held up the Castle dinner by half an hour.

Among the guests, Henry pointed out to me a peer of the realm, whom he said had suffered very severe shock when he had fallen off his pony as a boy. He had been so badly shocked that for the rest of his life whenever he saw a horse he started to neigh! Henry assured me that there had been complete chaos one summer at Ascot. The peer had strolled towards the paddock and on spotting the horses started to neigh loudly. All the horses parading round the ring then joined in and the peer had to be escorted hurriedly away before peace could be restored!

Cricket continued its post-war popularity in 1949. It was a fine summer and the New Zealanders under Walter Hadlee were the tourists. They were determined to show that they deserved more than only three-day Tests and succeeded in drawing all four Tests played to prove the point. They were able to do this thanks to the magnificent form of those two fine left-handers, Bert Sutcliffe and Martin Donnelly, both high on the list of Test batsmen. Of the established England stars Len Hutton had a wonderful season, scoring 3,429 runs and a new star – eighteen-year-old Brian Close – became not only the youngest player ever to play for England but also the youngest to do the double of 1,000 runs and 100 wickets in a season.

Nineteen forty-nine was an important year for Pauline and me. We had found our house in St John's Wood, 1A Cavendish Avenue, just about a hundred yards from the Nursery End at Lord's. It was possible on big match days to hear the applause and the oohs and the aahs of the crowd, and I became quite expert in guessing whether it was the fall of a wicket, a boundary or a dropped catch. Just after midnight on Easter Sunday, 17 April our eldest son, Barry, was born in the Lindo Wing of St Mary's Hospital, Paddington. He arrived a fortnight early and I am ashamed to say that I failed to carry out the traditional father's role of pacing up and down the corridors of the hospital. I was fast asleep at home and was woken by the telephone with the good news. Pauline still thinks that I should have been there by her side and I am sure she is right. I did better with the other four!

Television was still confined to the Lord's and Oval Tests but in 1950 the Sutton Coldfield Transmitter was opened and we were able to televise the Trent Bridge Test as well. It was a cold and wet summer and there was a decline in the standard of cricket played in the County Championship. But the season was saved by the brilliance and exuberance of John Goddard's West Indian touring side. They won the Test series 3–1 and won their first-ever Test in England at Lord's. This was followed by scenes of wild enthusiasm, crowds rushing across the ground to the front of the pavilion where 'Lord' Kitchener sang a Calypso especially composed for the occasion. There must have been much subterranean activity that day in the churchyards of England as old MCC members turned in their graves. A Calypso on the hallowed turf of Lord's. By gad, sir!

The tour was made memorable by the superb batting of 'the three Ws', Worrell, Weekes and Walcott, and the spin bowling of that remarkable pair, Ramadhin and Valentine. Ramadhin had only played in two first-class matches before the tour started and had a mystery leg break, which our batsmen found very difficult to detect. He bowled in a cap, which is unusual for a bowler. I remember that Ronald Colman did so in the cricket match in the film of *Raffles*, and Wally Hammond used to do so on occasions. Clarrie Grimmett also hid his bald pate under an Australian green cap. But it was a rare thing to do.

In addition to the television I was now beginning to do some radio commentary on county matches and the first one with which I was entrusted was Middlesex against Yorkshire at Lord's. Not a bad starter!

During the summer we also did a radio programme about the Hythe and Dymchurch Miniature Railway run by an enthusiast named Captain Tom Howey. On the day of our broadcast something or other was being opened by the Mayor of New Romney and as a sequel to the ceremony he was to be taken for a ride on one of the trains. In his mayoral robes and chain of office he was placed in one of the small open carriages right at the rear of the train. The guard waved his flag and blew his whistle. The engine driver gave a toot, the Mayor raised his tricorn hat as he waved to the crowd on the platform and with a slow 'chug chug' the train started on its journey. But to everyone's horror, though to our delight, the Mayor's carriage was left stranded in the station as he continued to wave vigorously. They had forgotten to hook it on to the carriage in front!

At this time I began to make quite a few journeys to Alexandra Palace. First I stood in for Leslie Mitchell as stooge for Terry-Thomas in his TV show *How Do You View?* How it ever got on the air I don't know. There were just two tiny studios for the whole of television output and the place was a mass of scenery, cables and cameras. There would be a newsreader or announcer in one corner and all the various scenes for Terry's show dotted around the place. It was all done live and he had to dash from set to set changing as he went, while someone filled in with a song.

The spot I did was an interview with him disguised as a commissionaire, lion-tamer (Captain Shaggers) or the man who hit the gong for Ranks. It was my job to put the questions and to try to keep a straight face. He had a terrible twinkle in his eye and was always trying to make me giggle. These shows were fun to do and Terry used to come and rehearse in our garden at Cavendish Avenue. Some years later he made an LP including two of these interviews and I was honoured to be chosen as the stooge. In those days the newsreaders and presenters still wore evening dress. During one of Terry's shows Macdonald Hobley, who was reading the news that night, went home as he was not feeling too well. As luck would have it a news item came in unexpectedly which had to be read. Panic stations!

However, someone spotted me and persuaded the bandleader, Eric Robinson, to lend me his dinner-jacket so that I could make the announcement, something to do with Mr Attlee at No. 10. They only showed my top half as I had a pair of check trousers on and had not got time to slip into Eric's trousers as well. Imagine that happening today with all the elaborate newsreading and presentation set-ups at Television Centre.

I also used to dub commentary on cricket film for *Television News Reel* which used to go out twice a week from Alexandra Palace. I worked from a script and was started and stopped by a chap sitting alongside me pinching my arm. He also used to produce the sound of ball on bat by actually knocking a ball against a bat into my microphone. He sometimes got it wrong and when a batsman was hit on the pad in the picture you could hear bat striking ball. This particular chap has gone quite far since then and for six years was Controller of BBC-1, before going to Yorkshire Television. It was Sir Paul Fox.

The commentator for the newsreel was Ted Halliday the famous portrait painter. He lives just up the road from me and there's a marvellous story told about him. A rich society lady called on him and the conversation went as follows:

Lady Mr Halliday. Would you do me a great favour and paint me in the nude?
Ted (*After a pause*) Well, yes I will. But on one condition.
Lady What is it?
Ted I must keep my socks on, as I have to have somewhere to stick my brushes.

Nineteen fifty was a repeat of 1949 so far as our family was concerned. Our daughter Clare was born on 14 September. This time I was present and correct which was more than our very nice gynaecologist! He arrived breathless in a morning coat and dashed up the stairs as the cries of the newborn babe came from the nursery. Pauline's mother had coped perfectly and all was well.

With two children life became even more hectic but we were lucky always to have a housekeeper who lived in our basement flat and also a nanny, or perhaps I ought to say a succession of them. They were mostly on the young side and generally quite nice. But somehow they appeared to come and go with fairly frequent regularity.

At any rate, Pauline still managed to come out on as many OBs as possible and we were also lucky in getting tickets for theatres which I had to vet. It was not only nice to have Pauline around, but being a Yorkshire girl she was very candid and always said what she thought. This meant I have always had some truthful criticism, which has been an enormous help.

Before I married Pauline, her father warned me that she had a habit of putting her foot in it unintentionally, and we have had quite a few hilarious moments as a result of this. One example was when we went out to dinner with someone we did not know too well. We were all dressed up as we had been told it was evening dress. Our hostess opened the door of her flat and I must admit did not look too glamorous. 'Oh, I'm sorry,' said Pauline, looking at her, 'I thought we were going to change.' 'I have,' replied the hostess somewhat icily.

Nineteen fifty-one brought us the South Africans, a rather dull series which England won 3–1, an undistinguished domestic season, and plenty of cold wet weather. One bright spot was the arrival of Peter May on the Test scene with a hundred in his first match. It was of course the Festival of Britain and we had many broadcasts to do in connection with this.

One of the most enjoyable was the play especially commissioned by BBC TV for the occasion. It was *The Final Test* by Terence Rattigan and I was lucky enough to be given the part of one of the commentators, which did not take a lot of acting. It was produced by Royston Morley, a rabid cricket enthusiast, so between us we were able to see that all the cricket details were accurate. Patrick Barr played the lovable professional, a part which Jack Warner was to play in the film.

Patrick had got a rowing blue at Oxford but by the end of rehearsals he had been completely converted to cricket, as were several others in the cast. It was a most moving play and it was lucky that I was not in any of the closing scenes as in rehearsals and on the actual transmission I was blubbing!

Around this time I became involved in several other activities new to me, such as the Brass Band Championships at the Royal Albert Hall and another yearly event – the Star Ballroom Dancing Championships. I was also doing *Postman's Knock* every Christmas morning. Nowadays everything is pre-recorded, but for at least ten years I used to get up early every Christmas and go out to do a live broadcast either with a postman delivering the post (there *was* one in those days on Christmas Day) or at some children's hospital, opening their parcels.

Another annual broadcast in the Royal Albert Hall was the Burma Reunion for the 14th Army, with the emphasis on entertainment from the various stars who had entertained the troops in Burma. Special favourites were Stainless Stephen, Gert and Daisy and inevitably Vera Lynn. So far as the speeches were concerned I generally had to deal with Lord Mountbatten and as with Monty he appreciated the value of a good broadcast and was always most helpful.

It was during this year that I received an unexpected telephone call, which resulted in my taking part in my first and only film. The call came from the film director Herbert Wilcox's secretary, asking whether I could go down at short notice the next day to Shepperton Studios. They were filming *Derby Day* and had suddenly decided that they wanted an interview with the actor Peter Graves on the 'racecourse'.

There would be no script, I was to bring my own morning dress and I was to report at some ghastly hour of the morning. Of course I accepted and on my arrival was greeted by Herbert, who told me my part would last about one minute, that I could work out the dialogue with Peter but that there was one question he wanted asked at the end of the interview.

It all seemed delightfully casual and the cameramen and technicians were most friendly and helpful. Peter was great fun to work with, though he was a terrible giggler. We did one or two takes but I don't think we fluffed too badly.

Now I can understand why film stars so dislike seeing their old films on TV. *Derby Day* was re-shown on BBC-1 in 1972 and I watched horrified as a youthful-looking Johnston suddenly appeared on the screen. It was the first time I had seen the film and I was pleased to see that our interview had not been cut in any way. Herbert is now an old friend of mine and I have seldom felt more proud than when he recently introduced me to someone in Australia. 'This is Brian Johnston. He once played for me in one of my films.'

8 Many a slip . . .

NINETEEN FIFTY-TWO WAS a year of great variety and quite a few 'firsts' for me. In January, Max Robertson fell ill and I went at the last moment as co-driver and co-broadcaster with Richard Dimbleby on the Monte Carlo Rally. We were not competing, as Raymond Baxter used to do in later years, but we travelled in Richard's touring Allard and broadcast from the various report centres along the route.

We were always 'tail-end Charlie' as our broadcasts were so timed that we could describe how everyone was doing at each stage of the Rally. To start with, the weather was fine but the further south we got the worse it became. First it rained, then it froze and the roads became like an ice-rink. Then it started to snow, and we bought some snow chains, which promptly broke. We got miles behind the other competitors and failed to make Monte Carlo for the planned evening broadcast. We sent back a report from a hotel bedroom in Digne, where we were forced to spend the night as the snowstorm made conditions impossible.

Richard had done most of the driving and was dog-tired. We had a steak for supper and as Richard put his fork into his mouth his head fell forwards and there he was fast asleep with the fork in his mouth. We set off early next morning and on arrival in Monte Carlo found that only five of the original 362 starters had completed the route without loss of penalty points. We had a delightful few days on the Côte D'Azur and a leisurely drive back to England.

Richard was a marvellous companion and had a superb sense of humour. The jobs he was called upon to do may have made him appear rather pompous on occasions but he was anything but. I think to all broadcasters he was the greatest – a complete professional, who was never at a loss for the right word. He was a tremendously hard worker and would work for days before a broadcast, collecting what we call associative material about the subject he was to cover. He would then write this on to small cards, which he would keep in front of him as he talked, ready for any emergency. He was thus able to keep talking throughout delays or changes of programme.

Perhaps the best example of this was after Princess Margaret's wedding, when she was an hour late arriving at Tower Bridge on the way to her honeymoon. Richard filled in as if nothing untoward was happening and regaled viewers with details about the Royal Yacht, the Tower, the River Thames – anything in fact which was in sight. He had done his homework and had filled those cards of his with all the information he might need in a crisis. And this – in a broadcasting sense – certainly was one.

It always distressed me that he was never knighted before he died so tragically of cancer. Everyone had known for two years at least that he had not long to live. It always amazed me how he bravely continued to broadcast almost to the end, often in terrible pain. I remember asking my friend Sir Edward Ford, then one of the Queen's secretaries, whether nothing could be done to get Richard honoured before he died. Unfortunately I believe the Palace thought that the move should come from Downing Street, but alas it never did. Richard so far has never been replaced, and there will certainly never be a better broadcaster. Nor a nicer, kinder or more generous man.

As a result of this Monte Carlo adventure with Richard I reported the Rally for radio for the next six years. Another example of how lucky I have been in my broadcasting career. It all happened just because I was available when Max suddenly could not go. It was a very pleasant annual excursion from the cold and fog of an English January to the sunshine and gaiety of Monte Carlo and although it was hard work, we managed to enjoy ourselves as well.

One year I was invited to dinner with Sir Bernard and Lady Docker on board their famous yacht *Shemara* in Cannes Harbour. It was an hilarious evening during which we played tiddlywinks and Lady Docker summoned the Captain to the dining saloon and sacked him on the spot! I must say he did not seem very concerned at the time, and afterwards I discovered it was an almost nightly performance.

A few weeks after my first Rally I shared another broadcast with Richard, this time on the television. It was the funeral of King George VI and we were to do the commentary along the route which the funeral procession took from Westminster to Paddington Station. This was the biggest challenge and opportunity which I had had since joining the BBC six years before and although there was very little time to prepare for it, I was determined to prove that I could do a serious job like this as well as the lighter ones with which viewers and listeners usually associated me.

In this type of broadcast you *have* to get everything right. You cannot correct a small mistake with a laugh or a joke as is possible on lighter occasions. So I thought I would make sure to get a good start. Richard was to be stationed in St James' Street and I was placed at Hyde Park Corner, and it was arranged that he would hand over to me just as the head of the procession came up the slope towards the Corner. I did my homework and discovered that at the head would be five mounted metropolitan policemen. I even found out from the PRO at Scotland Yard that they would be on white horses. So I wrote out an opening sentence – something I would never usually do. But I felt that if only I could get off on the right note all would be well.

On the few nights before the funeral I said to myself before I went to sleep: 'And here comes the procession now. Led by five metropolitan policemen mounted on white horses.' Not brilliant I agree, but at least it would be factual and get me going. From then on I felt I could cope. On the day I was sitting on our stand at Hyde Park Corner listening to Richard in my headphones describing the procession winding its way up St James' Street. Keith Rogers our producer told me to stand by and then I heard Richard cue to me with the words . . . 'The head of the procession should now be reaching Hyde Park Corner, so over now to our commentator there, Brian Johnston.'

At this moment I could just see the caps of the five policemen at the bottom of the slope as Keith Rogers said: 'Go ahead, Brian,' into my headphones. So off I went with my little prepared piece. 'Yes here comes the procession now led by five metropolitan policemen mounted on . . .' and then to my horror I realised that they were not on white horses but black. My mind went completely blank. I had rehearsed and rehearsed 'white horses' so often that I panicked and could not think of any other colour. So what I said was . . . 'mounted on (pause) horseback.' This brought an immediate response from Keith Rogers in my headphones: 'What on earth do you think they are mounted on? Camels?' So my carefully prepared start had gone for a burton and it took me quite a few minutes to recover. Never again did I learn a written piece beforehand.

I had one other nagging thought at the back of my mind as the cortège bearing the coffin approached. I had to keep saying to myself, don't say it, don't say it. It was a phrase often used by commentators doing this type of commentary, but which would have been disastrous on this occasion. It was: 'Here comes the main body of the procession.' Luckily I never said it! But as you can imagine this was not a broadcast I enjoyed doing, though I was naturally honoured to be chosen for such a big national occasion.

It was a key year for television cricket in 1952, because the Holme Moss Transmitter was now open, which meant that for the first time we were able to televise the Old Trafford and Headingley Tests.

The Indians were the visitors and we went to Worcester to televise their first match. As usual it rained and we had to fill in time with interviews under umbrellas. The Indians had an amusing and volatile manager called Gupta, who spoke very quickly but perhaps did not understand English all that perfectly. Anyway I was interviewing him and asking him about the Indian team. 'What about your batsmen?' I asked. 'Oh, we've got seven very good batsmen indeed,' he replied. 'And your bowlers?' 'Oh, six very good bowlers indeed.' I thought we were not getting very far so switched my questions to him personally. 'What about yourself. Are you a selector?' 'No,' he replied. 'I'm a Christian'! I hurriedly changed the subject and asked him what he thought of our weather!

Television could not have wished for a better start to the Test series. The first Test was at Headingley and Len Hutton was captain of England – the first time ever that a professional had been chosen to captain England in this country. It was also the first Test appearance of a young twenty-one-year-old fast bowler from Yorkshire called Freddie Trueman. And to cap everything, in their second innings India were 0 for 4, Trueman taking three and Bedser one. So television's first appearance at Headingley was quite something, though the rest of the four-Test series was disappointing, England winning easily 3–0. The new boy 'Fiery' Fred took twenty-nine wickets in only four Tests, with some really devastating fast bowling which the Indians understandably did not relish. Not a bad start to a Test career.

Later that year, I appeared on a cricket quiz at Eton. This had become a regular annual event following the first one a few years earlier at which Sir Pelham Warner had been on the panel. I am told that he never really recovered from the very first question put to him by a small innocent-looking boy at the back of the hall. 'Please, sir,' he asked, 'was W. G. Grace a cheat?' I gather there was a deadly hush while Sir Pelham turned pale at the iniquity of the question.

In spite of doing so much cricket I still kept up with my contacts in the entertainment world. We continued to broadcast excerpts from the West End shows and during the summer started a new series – *Saturday Night at the London Palladium*. This was at a time when they were featuring big American stars like Jack Benny, Bob Hope, Betty Hutton, Sophie Tucker and Jimmy Durante. We used to broadcast their acts live at the second house to the Light Programme listeners, and it was great fun meeting all these great entertainers.

In addition we began to broadcast the Royal Variety Performance every year. We recorded it on the Monday night and I did a linking commentary for an edited version which went out the following Sunday. The great thing was that it meant that Pauline and I went along to the actual show, and in addition I attended all the rehearsals. With so much of my job now divided between cricket and the theatre I was on top of the world, and had to keep pinching myself to make sure it wasn't all a dream. I was being paid to do what I enjoyed doing most and realised that I was lucky enough to have a job in a million – the only one of its kind.

Nineteen fifty-three was not only Coronation Year but also the year in which England won back the Ashes after nineteen years. Lindsay Hassett led the popular Australian team and it was a splendidly fought series. The first four Tests were drawn, with England just saving the game at Lord's thanks to the defiant fifth wicket partnership of 163 between Willie Watson and Trevor Bailey on the last day.

It was a tense, thrilling struggle as they kept the Australian bowlers at bay for over four and a quarter hours in the heat. I shall always remember the look of intense agony on Bailey's face when he was finally out caught off the first real attacking stroke he had played in his entire innings.

The four draws built up to a wonderful climax at the Oval, and I was lucky enough to be commentating during the final stages, when Denis Compton joined Bill Edrich with England needing 44 runs to win the match and the Ashes. When they were within nine runs of victory Hassett conceded victory by putting himself and Arthur Morris on to bowl. With four runs needed the tension and excitement became unbearable. The crowd, shouting their encouragement, had edged right up to the boundary ropes, ready to rush on to the field. Morris bowled one of his 'chinamen' (an offbreak from a left-arm bowler) outside the leg stump. This is it, I thought, as Compton played his famous sweep. The crowd started to creep over the ropes, but it was a false alarm. Alan Davidson had put out his great paw at backward short leg and stopped it.

The next ball was just the same and this time Compton made no mistake. He swept the ball for four down to the gas holders and bolted for the pavilion. Whether in fact the ball ever reached the boundary I don't think anyone ever knew. It was enveloped by the crowd as they surged on to the field. Edrich and Compton had to fight their way back holding their bats aloft just like submarine periscopes over the heads of the crowd. On television I'm afraid that I was overcome by excitement and emotion. As Compton swept the four for victory all I could do was shout into the microphone: 'It's the Ashes! It's the Ashes!' It was certainly my greatest moment so far, as a TV commentator. It also made Arthur Morris the most televised Test match bowler ever, as for several years this last over was used as a demonstration film sequence in all the TV shops.

For the Coronation I was again one of the TV commentators on the route of the procession.

This time I was in Hyde Park and shared the commentary

there with Bernard Braden. It was a filthy day, and we all got horribly wet. We had had to get up at some unearthly hour in order to make sure of getting to our position, and then of course we had to wait for about six hours before anything happened. By the time the procession had reached us so far as I remember Sir Winston Churchill had 'fallen out' from the line of vehicles. But like everyone else we were enchanted by the friendly buxom figure of Queen Salote of Tonga in her open carriage. In spite of the pouring rain she sat there without even an umbrella waving and blowing kisses to the damp but cheering crowds. A small man was sitting alongside her. When asked who he was, Noël Coward is reputed to have said: 'Her lunch!'

Royal occasions have always been dangerous hazards to commentators and many of the most famous broadcasting gaffes have been made when describing royalty. Audrey Russell once told her listeners that the Queen Mother was wearing dark black – and Max Robertson said of the Queen of Norway, as she arrived at the Guildhall for lunch: 'She is looking charming in an off-the-hat face'!

Then there was the commentator who had to describe the departure of the King and Queen for Canada in 1939. They were to cross the Atlantic on HMS *Vanguard* and there was to be a twenty-minute OB of the scenes at the quayside. The commentator had done his homework and filled in the time with describing the scene, the cheering crowds, the band of the Royal Marines, the decorations, details of the *Vanguard* and the programme of the tour in Canada. That should have been enough, but unfortunately the tugs had difficulty in getting the huge ship away from the quay and it all took far longer than the BBC had bargained for.

Twenty minutes became twenty-five and the commentator was getting desperate for something new to say. For the umpteenth time he mentioned that the King and Queen were waving from the bridge, and then suddenly noticed that the Queen was no longer there. Grateful for something new he said, 'I see now that the Queen has left the bridge and gone below for a moment.' He then got stuck and in desperation a few seconds later added . . . 'and I can see water coming through the side of the ship'!

There was also the Commonwealth commentator who at one of the Independence Day celebrations was talking about the late Duchess of Kent, then representing the Queen. As her carriage passed by he said: 'The Duchess is now going into the President's Palace to take off her clothes ready for the reception.' But of course none of these mistakes will equal that of the newspaper during the Jubilee celebrations in 1935. The reporter had written '. . . Queen Mary then passed over Westminster Bridge.' Unfortunately the printer replaced the *a* in passed with an *i*!

I suppose the most amusing mistake on TV happened when Wynford Vaughan-Thomas was the commentator at the launching of the *Ark Royal* at Birkenhead by the Queen Mother. The producer Ray Lakeland told Wynford beforehand: 'Don't talk while the Queen Mother is breaking the bottle against the bows, and keep quiet as the ship slowly glides down the slipway. We shall be taking the cheering of the crowds and the music of the band. Wait until the *Ark Royal* actually hits the water and then start talking to your heart's content.'

All went according to plan. No. 1 camera showed the Queen Mother making her short speech and breaking the bottle. No. 2 camera showed the ship as it gradually moved, and No. 3 had shots of the cheering crowd. Ray punched all these up in turn so that they came on to the screens of the viewers at home. Then just before the *Ark Royal* reached the water he noticed that No. 1 camera had got a marvellous picture of the Queen Mother smiling in that charming way she has.

Ray was so enchanted that he forgot all he had told Wynford and immediately pressed the button which filled the viewers' screens with the Queen Mother. This unfortunately coincided with the moment the *Ark Royal* entered the water. Wynford was watching this and not his screen, so remembering his instructions started to talk: 'There she is,' he cried, 'the huge vast bulk of her'! He then looked at his monitor and to his horror saw the Queen Mother not the *Ark Royal*. Even this usually volatile Welshman was at a loss for words. But as you might expect when the Queen Mother was told about it afterwards she was delighted.

I appeared on the radio *Twenty Questions* panel for the first time when Kenneth Horne was absent and Richard Dimbleby took over as Question Master. It was fun to do but in my eagerness I wasted quite a few questions and was not too popular with the regular members of the panel – Anona Winn, Jack Train and Joy Adamson. They had evolved a formula for finding out quickly if the object was animal, vegetable or mineral and then what sort of animal or mineral. But I didn't do too badly.

I also became chairman of a regular quiz on radio called *What's it All About?* The panel included Kenneth Horne, Celia Johnson and Dilys Powell. I had to read out cards sent in by listeners relating some extraordinary incident which had happened to them. The panel then had to guess how and why it had happened. It was fairly childish but became quite popular. I also began to cover the Motor Show, a job I always found frustrating with so many wonderful cars well out of reach of my commentator's pocket.

Tommy Trinder used to tell of the very posh salesman in morning dress on the Rolls-Royce stand at the Motor Show. There he was alone on the roped-off stand leaning nonchalantly against a gleaming car costing goodness knows how much. The milling crowd looked enviously at the car and occasionally asked a few questions, knowing full well that a Rolls was really miles beyond their reach. One day a chap leaned over the ropes and asked the salesman the way to the gents. 'I'll show you myself,' said the salesman, and leaving the stand led the enquirer through the crowds to the other side of the hall. When they reached their target, the chap thanked the salesman for being so kind and asked him why he had taken so much trouble. 'Candidly, old boy,' said the salesman, 'yours was the first genuine enquiry I have had all week!'

Pauline and I once again had an increase in our family – this time another boy, Andrew. He started to arrive on the afternoon of Saturday, 27 March just as we were watching the Grand National on TV. I am glad to say we were able to see Royal Tan win the race before rushing Pauline off to the nursing home in Avenue Road.

In the summer Pakistan made their first tour of England and caused a sensation by winning the 4th and final Test at the Oval. They thus squared the series 1–1, and became the only country to win a Test Match on their first visit to England. It was a nasty wet summer and my two outstanding memories are the superb bowling by Fazal Mahmood with his leg-cutters, and an astonishing innings of 278 by Denis Compton in the Trent Bridge Test. It was to be his highest Test innings and only took him four hours fifty minutes. I have only seen one other innings with such an array of orthodox and unorthodox strokes in topclass cricket – Gary Sobers' 254 for the World XI at Melbourne in 1972.

During 1955 I continued to spread my wings in TV when I took part in a quiz series on children's TV called *Ask Your Dad*. I was provided with a 'family' of two and we competed against Ross Salmon and his 'family'. At this time he owned a ranch on Dartmoor and was billed as the TV Cowboy complete with all the gear – hat, ropes, revolver, chaps – the lot. I was also called on to introduce *Sportsview* on several occasions when Peter Dimmock was away.

This was in the early days of the Teleprompter, which is now in regular use by newsreaders and presenters. It's a gadget whereby you can read a revolving script by looking into the lens of the camera. It's all done by a complicated system of mirrors and nowadays is operated by remote control by a special operator. But when I first used it I had to control the speed at which the script revolved by pressing on a switch with my foot – rather like a dentist and his drill. It was a nerve-wracking operation, for if you pressed too hard the script would disappear out of sight on the roller before you had time to read it! You had to apply just the right pressure to keep the next line on a level with your eyes.

Jack Cheetham's South Africans were a magnificent fielding side and only narrowly lost the series 2–3, all five Tests producing a result. I have always thought that the 3rd Test at Old Trafford was one of the best I have ever seen, South Africa winning by three wickets with three minutes to spare after the fortunes of the two sides had swayed backwards and forwards. In this match Paul Winslow scored his first Test hundred reaching it with a six off Tony Lock which nearly smashed one of our TV cameras on our scaffolding. This was a time when England had to rely too much on their captain, Peter May, to make the runs, though in spite of a badly swollen knee Denis Compton supported him gallantly. But their bowling strength was terrific and the selectors could call on Statham, Tyson, Bedser, Trueman, Lock, Laker, Appleyard, Wardle, Loader, Titmus and Bailey. What a choice!

The one sad thing about the series was that it marked the end of Frank Chester's career as an umpire after officiating in forty-eight Tests. He had been in considerable pain for the last two or three summers and towards the end had lost some of his great judgment and authority. But up to then at least he had undoubtedly been the best umpire in the world and Don Bradman always had the highest opinion of him. The overall standard of umpiring has always been better in England than anywhere else, partly because so much cricket is played, but also because our umpires in first-class cricket are mostly old professionals who have played top-class cricket themselves.

This helps them to understand the problems and difficulties of players out in the middle, and accounts for the fact that the relationship between players and umpires is so friendly.

Overseas, even in Australia, very few umpires have ever played first-class cricket themselves. This led to an amusing conversation between Don Bradman and Tom Crawford, the old Kent player, who was watching the Test series on Peter May's tour. Australia had an umpire who wore glasses but who had been highly thought of by Len Hutton's team on the previous tour. However, four years later he was making some quite embarrassing mistakes and Tom was saying that he thought it a pity that none of the umpires in Australia had played first-class cricket, and how much better they would be if they had. Sir Don would have none of it. 'What about X?' he said, referring to our bespectacled friend. 'He played quite a lot of top-grade cricket *until his eyesight went* and he took up umpiring.' He then realised what he had said!

9 How far can you go?

ON THE RADIO, Light Programme asked us to do a short series of a somewhat longer *Let's Go Somewhere* – fifteen minutes instead of the old three to four minute routine. This gave us more scope, so we decided to make the new show a test of the public's reactions to various things – rather like *Candid Camera* which came later on ITV.

This time I had a producer and other people to help me, but as before, each programme with one exception was to be live, not recorded. Our first experiment was at Victoria Station, where we staged various incidents and I reported on the reactions of people to them. I wandered around disguised with a false beard under which was hidden my microphone with a small transmitter in my pocket. We started off with our producer Doug Fleming pretending to be a newspaper seller. He bought up some evening papers and stood there in an old macintosh and peak cap shouting out: 'Paper, paper, get your evening paper.' All this was quite normal except that on his stop press was scrawled the headline: 'Mafeking Relieved'.

I stood watching as people went up to him and bought their papers. Most of them glanced at the placard as they did so. But no one seemed surprised or even remonstrated with Doug for announcing something which had taken place over fifty years ago.

Next, I took a parcel up to the left-luggage office. Inside was a human skull, which I had borrowed from some students. I had purposely split the parcel open in front so that when I presented it to the man behind the counter he could see the empty eye sockets staring out at him. I had expected him to show some surprise or curiosity.

Instead he just had a good look and said: 'How long do you want to leave it sir?'

We had then arranged for the female announcer to say over the public address: 'Will the passengers who took the 6 o'clock train to Brighton from platform 14 please return it as it's needed first thing in the morning!' She repeated this several times and yet I could not spot anyone in the station concourse who seemed to find anything strange or funny in the announcement.

Finally, I went behind a pillar and put on a wolf's mask, which my children had been given for Christmas. I put my hat on top with the wolf's ears sticking up at the sides, turned up my coat collar and walked about among the rush-hour crowds. One or two looked at me and did a double take. But no one challenged me, nor stared for any length of time. Nor did any inspector or porter ask me what I thought I was doing. They all seemed to accept the fact that there was a man with a wolf's face among them. At the end of this broadcast we really did feel that the reputation which the British have for being phlegmatic was fully justified.

Even more so after another broadcast which we did with me disguised as a waiter in a restaurant, with a ginger wig, a phoney French accent and the name of Alphonse. We asked a friendly restaurateur to book us three tables close to each other one evening, and to allow us to plant a microphone hidden in a bowl of flowers on each table. We then got Henry Riddell, Doug Fleming and Cliff Michelmore to ask two people each to dinner at the time of our broadcast, warning them to be punctual. I took my cue in the kitchens and explained to listeners what we were going to do. First we switched on the microphone on Henry's table to see what he and his two guests were talking about. We quickly wished we hadn't as he had asked a Canadian and his wife and the man was busy saying how much he loathed his job and what a terrible man his boss was.

So I hurriedly went out with the soup which Henry had

ordered beforehand. I placed two plates in front of the guests and when a 'commie' handed me the third one, I pretended to drop it and upset it straight into Henry's lap. He had been warned and was wearing an old suit, but as arranged played up magnificently and started to tear the most terrible strips off me at the top of his voice.

I had warned listeners that this would happen and that we wanted to see how the two guests would react. They did so by pretending not to notice what was going on and started a conversation with each other about a film which they would like to see. They just left Henry to it, as if nothing was happening.

I then went to Doug's table, where I served some sole, which he had ordered, to him and his two guests, another husband and wife. I gave the lady and Doug a most beautiful sole each but on the husband's plate there was just the bare backbone of a sole with only the head and tail complete. Doug pretended not to see and asked them both if their fish was to their liking. The wife said yes hers was perfect but the husband instead of being candid said something like: 'Well there's not too much of it, but it looks jolly good all the same, thanks very much.' What manners!

Lastly I went to the final table where Cliff and his wife Jean had asked a wine connoisseur to be their guest. During the afternoon we had drawn the cork of a bottle of the very best claret, poured a little away and then topped up with some Angostura bitters, tomato ketchup and a pinch or two of pepper. We had then given the bottle a good shake and left it to settle down. (I have never dared to tell John Arlott about this!)

Anyway, I presented the bottle to Cliff, saying it was the wine he had ordered and would he like to taste it. He said no but that his friend the expert would do so. This was the big moment. What would he say? I poured out a little of the wine into a glass and the expert sniffed it. 'A most unusual bouquet,' he said, then took a sip. We were watching him closely and he somehow managed to hide his true feelings.

'This is one I haven't met before,' he said without wincing, 'but I am sure it will make a pleasant drink with our dinner.' Like the other two he was not prepared to embarrass his host by any criticism, but goodness knows what he was feeling.

We finished the broadcast by me dropping a pile of plates and getting the sack from the restaurateur in front of everyone. As soon as it was over he and I then rushed round to the other tables to explain what had been happening, while our three hosts made peace with their guests. They all took it very well and we made sure that they then had a super dinner, washed down with some genuine claret.

It was after one of these broadcasts that Berkeley Smith told me it would have been fun to *see* us all performing and could we not do a similar sort of thing on TV? We went into it very carefully but eventually turned down the idea, as we thought it would never be possible to keep it secret and so make it genuine. On radio it was easy with our small hidden mikes transmitting back to a nearby control van. With TV it would have meant hiding the cameras, the cables and the hordes of technicians that normally go with an OB. People would be bound to know about it beforehand and bang would go the authenticity so essential to make such a series viable. Jonathan Routh did it with great success in *Candid Camera*, but how he managed to keep it all secret I have never discovered.

Kenneth Horne helped me when we proved how difficult it is to give real money away in the streets of London. We made the Victoria Palace our base and sallied forth in turn to try to give some ten-shilling notes away to the passers-by.

Kenneth had to have a large black beard to hide his well-known features, and told people that he was carrying out the wish of a dead aunt. It was the anniversary of her death and each year she wanted money to be given away in her memory. 'So will you accept ten shillings?' Kenneth asked. But believe it or not, he failed to get rid of a single note! People just stared or brushed him aside.

I was slightly more successful, getting rid of exactly one to a soldier returning from leave. He grabbed it gratefully. But everyone else seemed embarrassed or pretended not to hear me, though one rather posh elderly lady did mutter, 'disgusting'! I don't blame her really as I was dressed up as a filthy old tramp and in a wheedling, whining voice said that I had just won the pools and wanted people to share my luck with me. I suppose it was rather incongruous for a tramp to be offering brand-new ten-shilling notes but I still find it strange that only one person took one.

For another of these broadcasts I was kitted out in a smart commissionaire's uniform and stood as still as I could for about ten minutes on the staircase at Madame Tussaud's. I was made up with side whiskers and a wax moustache to look as similar as possible to the famous wax-dummy commissionaire halfway up the stairs.

Generations of children have gone up to him and asked the way or the time, only to find that he was not real. I stood at the top of the stairs ramrod stiff, staring straight in front of me, doing my best not to move. People came right up to me, prodded me in the stomach and asked me questions. When I didn't answer one woman even tweaked my moustache! By then I think she was convinced that I was a dummy so I slowly lowered the lid of my right eye and gave her a wink. She let out an hysterical scream which gave the game away.

The one broadcast we had to record was a trip I made in a balloon from Cardington. We did it in March when the weather was really quite unsuitable, and we had to choose the moment when the wind was below the maximum allowed – 20 mph I believe it was. Anyhow we were hastily called early in the morning and told that conditions were just all right, although there was a forecast of snow. I had an engineer with me, Ted Castle, and he, myself and the RAF officer who was to be our pilot, all got into the basket.

Inside there was not much room as our basket contained some sandbags, though not as many as there should have been due to the weight of our recording gear. We were released and soared gently up into the sky, emptying some of the bags over the side as we went, to make us lighter.

We reached about one thousand feet and cruised gently along. It was all very peaceful and so quiet that we could hear people talking on the ground below. It was freezing cold and beginning to snow so I recorded a few impressions of what it was like in the balloon. I then noticed our pilot looking rather anxiously at some high ground ahead of us and he began hurriedly to empty out the remaining sandbags. But I suppose our gear was too heavy as we did not get any higher. We got nearer and nearer to what was a range of hills and the pilot was now seriously worried that we might not clear them. So he pulled the quick-release valve and the balloon began to deflate and we sank down rapidly towards the ground.

Frankly, I was scared stiff, as we were going faster and faster but I managed to record my rather hysterical commentary on our descent. We hit a ploughed field with a tremendous bump and shot about twenty feet up into the air. Our gear was thrown all over the basket and we hung on grimly as we hit the ground a second time. The wind then caught the deflated balloon and we were dragged across the field, finally ending up against a hedge.

I have never been so relieved as when I stepped out of that basket. We had to stand about in the snow until a search party found us. Looking back I am convinced that we should never have taken off in the first place. How dangerous it really was I don't know. I was too scared to learn the truth so never did ask the pilot. Remarkably, we managed to get a programme out of my recordings though my final commentary as we were coming down was largely incoherent, and all the listener heard of the actual landing was a loud crash and then silence as our recording gear disintegrated.

Towards the end of the year I had an accident at the annual Lord's Taverners' Ball at Grosvenor House. Each year there is a sporting event in which the Taverners take on the experts of a particular sport or game. Needless to say by hook but largely by crook the Taverners always manage to win.

The sport this particular year was athletics and I took part in a three-legged race with Macdonald Hobley and Peter Haigh as my partners. I was the middle man with my arms round their necks, and we were going quite well when we slipped on the polished floor. I had no arms to break my fall and landed heavily on my left shoulder. It was agony but luckily Bill Tucker the orthopaedic surgeon was there and gave me some pain-killing pills.

I went to Bill the next day hardly able to move my arm and he diagnosed a dislocated shoulder. This meant going for heat treatment, massage and manipulation for a month or two, which made life a bit difficult. But in OBs we kept to the old theatrical tradition that the show must go on, and I never actually missed a broadcast as a result of it. In fact my contribution to the Christmas Day programme was to be thrown into the sea by the Shiverers Club at Brighton – the only way they could get me to join them in their daily bathe. It was of course freezing cold, but my shouts were more because of the pain from my shoulder as they picked me up and swung me in.

Mention the wet summer of 1956 to any cricketer and he will almost certainly think of Jim Laker, who not only took forty-six wickets in the series against Australia, but performed the incredible feat of taking 19 for 90 in the 4th Test at Old Trafford. Laker thus became the first and only bowler to take ten wickets in one innings of a Test, and I cannot believe that any of these three records will ever be equalled, let alone broken. Peter May's side won the series 2–1 and so kept the Ashes.

The Australians under Ian Johnson just could not cope with Laker's off-spin but they will also tell you that the perfidious Albion prepared pitches to suit Laker and Lock, especially at Old Trafford. As you can imagine, this match provided thrilling television as Jim took all his wickets from the Stretford end where our cameras are always situated. This meant that viewers got a perfect view of the turning ball unimpeded by the batsman and wicket-keeper. I remember going across to the pavilion afterwards to collect Jim to do an interview for TV and he was by far the calmest man on the ground. From his cool, casual air you might have thought he had taken a couple of wickets in a parents' match.

In addition to the cricket I did a mixed assortment of jobs for TV, three of them connected with water. I was surprisingly selected to introduce the Boat Race broadcast and had to talk knowledgeably about the course and the crews. They must have been pushed that year!

I also took part in a number of the *Saturday Night Out* programmes. One of them was from a Turkish bath in Harrogate and the cameras showed me lying on the Begoni cabinet, a kind of massage table which gives the victim a series of electric shocks in the bottom. What for, I never discovered, but it certainly made me jump up and down like a yo-yo.

The cameras also paid a visit to the Serpentine to demonstrate the life-saving abilities of boys' clubs. For some reason I was put in a boat dressed as a city gent in bowler-hat, pin-stripe suit and reading an evening paper. The boys tipped me out of the boat and then proceeded to 'rescue' me and haul me back to the bank. As I reached the water's edge one of them handed me back my bowler-hat and dripping wet I put it on my head and walked off into the crowd as if nothing had happened.

For the radio I went on one of several trips abroad with General Sir Brian Horrocks. He and I became a sort of double act for the unveiling ceremonies of the Cross of Remembrance at the War Graves Commission war cemeteries. Over the years we went to Dunkirk, Nijmegen, Caen, Athens and in this year to Mount Cassino in Italy.

Sir Brian was a wonderfully amusing companion and a great broadcaster. I used to cover the actual service and ceremony, while he did an introduction dealing with the events in that particular theatre of war. It was always a comfort to visit these cemeteries and to see how beautifully they were all kept up and maintained. What was so nice was that in Holland especially the local children used to put flowers regularly on the graves.

Pauline came to Mount Cassino with me on this trip and we spent a glorious week at Positano before going up to Cassino. We had an unusual bath in the hotel at Positano. The end of the bath, where the taps were, was a fish tank, so that as you lay relaxing in the bath, fish were pressing their noses against the glass of their tank, watching you. Highly embarrassing!

On arrival at Cassino we decided to go up the winding road to the monastery silhouetted at the top. Pauline and the General went ahead in one car and at the entrance there was a notice in Italian. I saw them both look at it and Pauline then say something to the General, which seemed to amuse him.

It turned out that the notice said that pregnant women weren't allowed to enter. Pauline had just discovered that week that she was pregnant again, but she had not yet had the courage to tell me, as we had planned to call a halt to the additions to our family. She felt she had to ask the General's advice what she ought to do, and he naturally told her to say nothing about it. He reasoned that if her husband did not even know, the monks were unlikely to find out!

In November I went into King Edward VII's Hospital for Officers for another hernia operation – on the other side. There was a strange coincidence about this. I had gone to see our family doctor, Dr R. Cove-Smith, the old rugger international, who won twenty-eight caps for England. He is a large, burly, genial man now but I would not have liked to have met him in the middle of a scrum. A remarkable thing about him is that for all his size and outward toughness no one could be gentler with children. Anyway he sent me to see a surgeon in Harley Street to fix up an operation.

The surgeon examined me, noted my other hernia scar and asked me when and by whom it had been done. 'By some army surgeon who came from London Hospital and who operated on me in the Military Hospital at Salisbury. I reckon he did a rather good job.' 'Yes, I agree,' said the surgeon. 'I must have been in good form that day and I'll do my best to match it on the other side.' It was the same surgeon!

I don't think he remembered me but recognised his own handiwork and of course knew he had been at Salisbury at that time. Anyway he did another splendid job and I had a fortnight in hospital and then a short convalescence at Eastbourne. This was nice for me as my mother was suffering from rheumatoid arthritis and was in a private nursing home there.

I returned to work in the middle of December in time for all the Christmas activities.

As usual, Raymond Baxter and I broadcast for radio on Boxing Day from the Bertram Mills Circus at Olympia. He used to do the commentary at the ringside and I did interviews with the artists outside the ring, and this year I learnt the value of being able to keep talking. I had finished my interviews and handed back to Raymond to describe the next act, and said to Bernard Mills: 'They're not due to come back to me again, but just in case they do, be a good chap and have an animal available which we can talk about.'

Bernard went off and in my headphones I heard Raymond describing what was going on inside the ring. There was a man on a motorbike circling round and round inside a big cage twenty feet or so above the ring. There was a hole at the bottom of the cage but as Raymond was explaining, so long as the rider kept up his pace his machine would clear the gap each time. But if by chance his speed did slacken or his engine were to stall, he would fall right through on to the sawdust ring below. As Raymond was saying all this the rider was riding the bike with one hand and trying to take off his jacket with the other. As he did so, possibly because his loose jacket caught in his rear wheel, his engine cut out and just as Raymond had said he would, he plunged through the hole on to the ground below.

Raymond had to think quickly. This was Boxing Day with an audience made up of children. It was radio, not TV, so they would not know that an accident had taken place. He made up his mind quickly and said . . . 'and as the act finishes let's go straight back to Brian Johnston behind the scenes for some more interviews.' I heard this cue as I looked through the entrance to the ring and saw the poor rider lying prostrate in the sawdust. I turned round hopefully and there to my relief was Bernard leading a nice-looking white horse towards me.

'Yes, welcome back,' I said. 'We have an interesting animal here to talk about, a horse! What's its name, Bernard?' We then proceeded to talk about this very ordinary animal for three minutes or so, while they cleared up the mess in the ring. We looked at the beast's teeth, felt his fetlocks, patted his rump and talked non-stop about him until Raymond was ready for us with the next act – some performing dogs. The next day hardly anyone knew that anything untoward had happened, though they thought the act had ended rather abruptly, and that the horse was not perhaps worthy of such a long interview. But the point was that the children at home did not have to hear details of the accident. The gift of the gab at least proved useful on this occasion.

10 The show must go on

NINETEEN FIFTY-SEVEN WAS a sad year for me, as my mother died after a long illness. She was seventy-seven and had been a wonderful mother to all of our family. I had been going down to Eastbourne as often as I could to see her and was due to go down again on Sunday, 14 April.

I was at home to lunch on the Saturday as I was to do some interviews in the afternoon at our local garage. It was for a record-request programme and the idea was to ask drivers filling up with petrol for their choice of records. During lunch the telephone rang and it was the matron from the nursing home telling me that my mother had died. It was too late to get someone else to do the broadcast, so I had to go straight off and try to be bright and cheerful as I chatted up the motorists.

I was also due to do a commentary on some Old-Tyme dancing that night but Sydney Thompson kindly did it for me, and I was able to rush down to Eastbourne. It happened at a very busy time as the West Indies touring team arrived on the Sunday evening and I had to get back to interview their captain John Goddard. Worse still I was Chairman of the Cricket Writers' Club that year. This meant that I had to preside at our dinner for the West Indians at the Skinners Hall on the Thursday night before catching the sleeper to Cornwall, where my mother was buried next to my father at the little village church of Stratton, near Bude. This was my first real personal experience of those old theatrical clichés – 'the show must go on' or 'laugh, clown, laugh' – and I found it a pretty trying experience.

But a fortnight later I had something to cheer me up.

Our fourth child, Ian, was born on 2 May. We were once again 'caught short'. This time it was in the middle of the night and at 3 o'clock in the morning I had to rush Pauline off to the nursing home. Her mother was staying with us and came along too. It was a delightful warm morning and as dawn broke I was doing the traditional pacing up and down in my dressing-gown in the middle of Avenue Road. Luckily there was no traffic, but anyway I didn't have long to wait as Ian arrived only fifty minutes after we had left home.

Ian's arrival meant that 1A Cavendish Avenue was now full to overflowing, even though Barry had gone off to boarding-school. Barry was really far too young as he was not quite eight years old, but he had been attending a small kindergarten school in St John's Wood and they said they could do no more for him. He went to Sunningdale School, where the Headmaster was an old school friend of mine – Charles Sheepshanks, formerly Adjutant of the 2nd Battalion Grenadier Guards for some of the time when I was the Technical Adjutant.

Sheepshanks, James Bowes-Lyon who was gunnery officer, and myself had once all been called 'a f...ing lot of nitwits' by one of our Commanding Officers, 'Naps' Brinckman. Naps evidently thought that we had made a mess of a gunnery inspection of the tanks. He was a somewhat explosive character who used to shake his shoulders when he laughed, just like the politician Edward Heath. We gave him the nickname of 'Spanner', because he was always trying to get a grip on things and tighten them up. Anyway I knew Charles Sheepshanks well and did not consider him a nitwit, so I knew that Barry would be in good hands, especially as Charles had a sweet sympathetic wife, who was marvellous with small boys.

But I must admit that when Pauline and I left Barry at the school after a scrumptious tea with the other new boys, we burst into tears as we drove away down the drive.

Foreigners are always amazed and, I fancy, shocked at

the way some of our children are sent away to boarding-school at such an early age. I see their point of view and though I have probably gone soft in my old age, I don't think I would ever again send a son of mine away until he was at least twelve years old. All three of my sons went to Sunningdale, and although Barry and Ian never seemed to mind going back, poor Andrew used to make a terrible fuss. There are many points for and against. A boarding-school undoubtedly toughens a boy and teaches him to live and get on with other boys, and at the same time usually gives him confidence and independence. But a lot of boys and their mothers do undoubtedly go through much misery and on balance I am now slightly against boarding.

There is one thing, however, that supporters of the system quite rightly point out. A boy living at home often sees the worst side of his parents, early in the morning when no one is at their best, and later in the evening when he comes back from school and finds everyone at home tired after a day's work. They are generally telling him to do things – 'get up', 'hurry up or you will miss the bus', 'do your homework', 'don't look at the telly', 'go to bed', etc. The advantage of a boarding-school is that all this dirty work is done by the masters, not the parents!

Our life in St John's Wood over those past ten years had been a very happy one. No. 1A was bright and cheerful, with large rooms with high ceilings and was usually full of our friends or those of our children. It had a small garden, with a lawn, a greenhouse and a hut for the children, and we had the normal array of pets, a lovely Sealyham bitch called Smokey, guinea pigs, hamsters, and tortoises.

St John's Wood itself, though only ten minutes by tube from Piccadilly Circus, has always retained its village atmosphere with plenty of trees and gardens, and in the High Street are some small family shops putting up a bold fight against the supermarkets. St John's Church by the roundabout at the south-east corner of Lord's has always been a nourishing community ruled over for a quarter of a century with benevolence by the Reverend Noël Perry-Gore, who christened all our children.

For holidays each summer we went to Cornwall, the Isle of Wight and later to Dorset for the usual family seaside holiday. I have always loved the sea to look at or bathe in but not to sail on. I enjoy nothing more than playing around on a beach. I also have a passion for those vulgar postcards, especially those by that great artist Donald McGill, which I have collected for years. I had them pinned up on the wall of my office at the BBC and still send them to my friends.

My favourites tend to be rather lavatorial in humour, such as the Bishop in his gaiters dozing in an armchair at his club. The picture shows a waiter squirting some soda water into the Bishop's glass, who wakes up and says: 'Is that you out of bed again Milly?' Or the small boy outside the gents public lavatory shouting to his mother waiting with a pram full of screaming kids – 'It's all right Ma. Don't worry. Dad says he'll be out in a couple of shakes!'

During this period we did a number of radio OBs for a Saturday afternoon programme, which was a mixture of sport, music and other outdoor activities. I found myself gliding, canoeing, sand yachting and riding a tandem bicycle. The gliding was an exhilarating experience, first the towed take-off, then floating serenely through the air, and suddenly finding a thermal and shooting rapidly upwards. The canoeing was fun, trying to avoid capsizing under some rapids by Teddington weir, while the sand yachting gave an exaggerated feeling of speed, racing across the huge expanse of sands at Southport.

The tandem I rode with the announcer Patricia Hughes on a trip to Le Touquet, but we found it very difficult. It's essential for both partners to do the same thing at the same time, especially starting and stopping, and we seldom did!

Peter May captained England to a 3–0 victory in the series against the West Indies, and so became the first captain to win a series for his country, and the championship for his county in the same season. The Test series was really decided by a remarkable record-breaking stand of 411 for the fourth wicket by Peter May and Colin Cowdrey in the 1st Test at Edgbaston. England batting first were 288 runs behind on the first innings and then by Saturday night were 102 for 2.

On the Monday morning, we all packed up and paid our hotel bills, expecting it to be all over that day. But May and Cowdrey were still there at close of play and stayed together till ten to three on Tuesday afternoon. Cowdrey made 154 and May 285 not out before declaring with 140 minutes left, in which time the West Indies lost seven wickets for 72 runs. It was a truly remarkable recovery by England.

England with their great bowling talents won three Tests easily, in spite of the West Indies having the three 'Ws, Sobers, Rohan Kanhai and that dynamic player Collie Smith, so tragically killed in a car accident two years later. Having beaten South Africa, Australia and now the West Indies, England cricket was on top of the world.

For the most part, 1958 was an uneventful year. Where the big three had failed it was too much to expect New Zealand under John Reid to do any better, and although a very nice side, they lost their first series of five five-day Tests 0–4.

Their batting collapsed time after time against the strong England attack and in five of their completed Test innings they were all out for under a hundred. It was the old Laker/Lock partnership which did most of the damage and Lock had a wonderful series, taking thirty-four wickets. It was disappointing cricket for us to try and cover on TV, and due to the easy wins and the weather we lost at least ten days of viewing time.

On radio I sat several times on the panel of *Twenty*

Questions and also spent a week covering the Brussels Exhibition. I was beginning to do more and more interviews for various programmes and one of these was *Spot the Headliner*, which went out on Saturday night on the Light Programme. It was a sort of quiz show based on someone who had 'Hit the Headlines' during their lifetime. I asked questions about the event or incident, when and how it happened and by so doing provided clues for the listener.

I then asked them to guess who the headliner was. We came back about ten minutes later, revealed the identity of the person and I then talked to them about what had happened. Among our headliners were included: M. E. Clifton James, who had been Monty's double during the war – Arthur Bell, a survivor of the R101 airship disaster – Miss Mathieson, who had helped take the Stone of Scone from Westminster Abbey – and so on. It was fun meeting all these interesting people and hearing their stories and the series ran quite a long time.

By the end of 1958 I realised that I had been with the BBC for nearly twelve years. In that time although I had done all the television cricket commentary I felt my cricket education was incomplete. I had never been on a tour abroad with MCC and I decided that it was time that I did. Peter May's side had already left for Australia and I applied for something called 'Grace' leave – nothing to do with the cricketer – to join them for the last four Tests.

The BBC were very kind and gave me eight weeks' absence on full pay, but I would of course have to pay my own expenses. I fixed up some articles with a weekly boys' paper, the Australian Broadcasting Commission said I could join their commentary team and finally the BBC said that once I was there they would of course use me for commentary, reports and interviews. That being so they felt they should pay some of my expenses, which they did! So all was set and I even managed to have Christmas at home with my family.

I flew off to Melbourne in a Britannia on 27 December. It was a forty-eight-hour journey in those days. This trip to Australia was to change the pattern of my broadcasting life for the next twelve years, until I retired as a member of the BBC staff. I reached Melbourne on 30 December and was commentating on my first Test match overseas on the morning of 31 December – not bad going.

I hadn't expected to work quite so soon, and despite having slept the clock round I was still a bit shaky after the journey. I had also, for the first and only time, flown first-class and actually enjoyed some free champagne for breakfast. What is more, Alan McGilvray's plane from Sydney had been delayed so I was thrown in at the deep end and was the second commentator on, twenty minutes after the start.

And what a start! In the third over of England's innings Alan Davidson had dismissed Peter Richardson, Willie Watson and Tom Graveney with his first, fifth and sixth deliveries, and England, having already lost the 1st Test at Brisbane, were 7 for 3 when I took over the commentary.

To make matters worse, no sooner had I begun to introduce myself to Australian listeners than a pigeon from a rafter overhead dropped a message of welcome on to my wrist! Luckily no more wickets fell while I was commentating, but England lost this Test and the 4th and 5th as well to lose the series 0–4. This result was a complete surprise as May's team had been hailed as world champions and the best side ever to leave England.

It was quite an experience being a commentator in Australia for the first time, as I had to learn to say 'sundries' instead of 'extras' and give the number of wickets down before the number of runs scored. In other words our 108 for 7 becomes 7 for 108. This method is all right so long as the score is not 10 or less when it becomes hopelessly muddling. 4 for 7 or 7 for 4 could mean different things to different listeners.

I got back to England towards the end of February after two months of wonderful hospitality and with my appetite whetted for more such tours in the future. It was great fun travelling round with a team and sharing in their triumphs and disappointments – usually the latter on this tour. I also felt it was adding to my cricket education and therefore helping to improve my commentary. Luckily my boss Charles Max-Muller thought the same. He was a white-haired old Etonian, who had taken over from Lobby in 1952. They could not have been more different in character.

While Lobby was somewhat puritan and quiet living, Charlie was a cheerful extrovert, who enjoyed going out and meeting people. He was highly strung and always jingled the coins in his pocket when he got enthusiastic or excited about something. He fought hard for the department and did a marvellous job of public relations with all the heads of various sporting bodies. Luckily for me, he adored travelling and used to go all over the world at the slightest excuse – planning for the Olympic or Common-wealth Games or for some Royal Tour in the far distant future. It was a great race between him and Peter Dimmock as to which clocked up the biggest world mileage in any one year!

Anyway, Charlie realised the value of having someone from his department travelling with a touring team abroad. I had been able to arrange broadcasts and interviews which would never have been possible without personal contacts or a good relationship with the captains and members of both teams. Charlie therefore proceeded to fight to get me appointed as the first BBC cricket correspondent, so that in future I would automatically accompany an MCC team abroad. He won, as he usually did, but it took a long time and it was not until 1963 that I became the first cricket correspondent of the BBC.

Back home in England I seemed to be doing more and more television and had a hat-trick of new commentaries. First I was one of the commentators at the Miss World Contest; great fun reading out all the statistics but very frustrating. Then there was the Lord Mayor's Banquet, full of tradition and pageantry but rather starchy, and finally the Lord Mayor's Show, which I always enjoy. Rather more I imagine than the Lord Mayor himself, whose coach has no springs but sways in a sickening way.

I also began to introduce two programmes, both angled towards children. I suppose they thought that as a father of four I ought to know how to deal with the kiddies! Little did they know!

One was an animal programme called *Dog's Chance*, in which we used to have various obedience tests, discuss a different breed of dog each week and invite celebrities to bring their own dogs along.

The other was *All Your Own*, which I gradually took over from Huw Wheldon, who was going on to higher and better things. This was a programme in which children demonstrated their hobbies and it was my job to chat to them and find out all about them. It meant travelling round to the BBC TV studios in Glasgow, Manchester and Bristol but it was rewarding, and I never ceased to be amazed at the keenness, ingenuity and originality which the children displayed. I suppose I must add to this *Ask Your Dad*, which still continued, so the poor children of that generation had a large overdose of Johnston.

On radio, the *Today* programme in the early morning had now been running for about eighteen months, and Jack de Manio was breaking all previous records in getting the time wrong. I started to do a weekly birthday spot for it called *Many Happy Returns*, in which I picked out the most outstanding birthday of the week and interviewed the person concerned. It ran for about four minutes and I kept it to a regular pattern: how were they going to spend the birthday, what sort of presents, a short bit about themselves and ending with a birthday wish.

My records are fairly hazy, but it seems that I did about eighty of these over the following year or so, speaking to some fairly prominent people – usually on a tape-recorder in their own home as near as possible to their birthday. What does surprise me now on looking at my guest-list, which figures personalities and public figures like Lord Longford, Sir Compton Mackenzie, Gracie Fields, Stirling Moss and Alfred Hitchcock, is that very few people ever refused to take part, which in a way I suppose was rather flattering.

Running currently with this during the next three years was *Meet a Sportsman*, in which I interviewed a famous sportsman or sportswoman and if possible played a recording or commentary on their most outstanding achievements. I did over sixty of these and covered every conceivable sport – even tobogganing. It's really rather frightening as I write this about the year 1959 – and with all the later years still to come – to think just how many questions I have asked people in the course of my career.

One of the best answers I ever had was from that lovable character Uffa Fox, the yachtsman. When I interviewed him he had just married a French lady and it was rumoured that she could not speak a word of English and that Uffa could not speak a word of French. I asked him to confirm this and he admitted it was roughly true. 'How then,' I asked, 'does your marriage work?' 'Oh,' he said, 'it's easy. There are only three things worth doing in life – eating, drinking and making love. And if you speak during any of them, you are wasting your time!'

So far as cricket was concerned, the weather was glorious but the Test series against India a terrible disappointment, England winning all five Tests easily, three of them by an innings. India, under D. K. Gaekwad, were simply outclassed. Trueman took twenty-four wickets in the series and as a comment on the Indian bowling eight England batsmen averaged 50 or over, including Brian Statham of all people, who was top with an average of 70.

Our TV commentary box was enlivened by the arrival the previous year of Denis Compton as the expert between overs. He brought a cheerful but professional analysis of the play with his emphasis always on attacking cricket. Unlike some expert summarisers, he could claim to have practised what he was now preaching.

Over the next ten years or so we were to have a lot of laughter mixed with our cricket and although some of our jokes may have offended the more serious pundits, I genuinely believe that that is what cricket is all about. It is a game to be *enjoyed* by player, spectator, viewer and listener alike.

Before the year was over I had become an 'angel' for the first and last time. At William Douglas-Home's suggestion I invested £100 in his new play, *Aunt Edwina*, and I am sorry to say that I lost the lot. If it were presented today the play would probably be a roaring success, but it was ten years before its time.

Aunt Edwina was all about a Master of Foxhounds, who during a holiday abroad with his wife and two grown-up children, suddenly changes sex and comes home a woman. I thought it extremely funny but the critics slated the play and it never recovered, though William kept it going for six weeks. Possibly Henry Kendall who played the MFH was too 'camp', and the play might well have got by if it had been played straighter. During its short run, as an angel I received a weekly breakdown of the takings and the outgoings, and though none of the latter came my way I found it all very intriguing.

William had previously had two big successes, *The Chiltern Hundreds* and *The Reluctant Debutante*, but at about this time was going through rather a thin patch. It's perhaps fairer to say that it was the kitchen-sink era and his witty country-house drawing-room comedy was out of fashion. But in recent years he has come right back into form with three big hits: *The Secretary Bird, The Jockey Club Stakes* and *Lloyd George Knew my Father.* Alas he has never asked me to be an angel for any of these but he does very kindly give me seats for all his first nights. So perhaps we are quits.

11 A Sporting Chance

IN 1960 THERE WAS another disappointing series, with
England winning the first three Tests and beating South
Africa 3–0. For some reason Jackie McGlew's team
never quite clicked and their batting and fielding were
below their usual standard. A wet summer did not help
them, nor the fact that Cowdrey won the toss five times
for England.

On radio we started a new quiz called *Sporting Chance*
in which the New Towns competed against each other
every week for a cup presented by the BBC. The teams
were asked to identify bits of commentary on matches,
races or fights, answer questions on laws, records and
statistics, and also identify a mystery sporting personality.
I was the chairman and before the broadcast used to test
the teams with some trial questions to get them confident
and relaxed. They were not always serious and included
the following:

Q. Who played at Twickenham one Saturday and at
Wembley the following Saturday – both international
matches? The teams used to try to think of a double
international who had played both rugger and soccer
for England, but of course never succeeded. The
answer was:
A. The Band of Her Majesty's Grenadier Guards.
   Another one was:
Q. Who was the last person to box Jack Johnson?
A. The undertaker.
   The next two really have to be spoken and are given
away if written properly. So I will cheat slightly.
Q. When did fog last stop the Cup Final at Wembley?

A. In 1935. Fogg was the name of the referee.

Q. A football team won a match 3–0 yet never scored a goal. (Their opponents did *not* score through their own goal.) How do you explain this apparent contradiction?

A. Never was the name of the winning team's centre-forward!

The quiz was devised and produced by Michael Tuke-Hastings, who since then has established himself as the roving quiz king of the BBC with *Sporting Chance* and *Treble Chance*, touring the British Isles, Europe and the Middle and Far East regularly over the following twelve years.

Sporting Chance was such a success that we were immediately asked by Paul Fox to do a special version for TV to go out every Saturday afternoon at the beginning of *Grandstand*. To make it more visual we included clips from films of sporting events, photographs for the team to identify and the silhouette of the mystery personality hiding behind a screen.

After one or two shows Paul Fox began to change his mind, as he felt *Sporting Chance* was too static indoors and lacked sufficient action for a programme like *Grandstand*. He finally decided to scrap it and was in the BBC club having a drink when Kenneth Adam, then Head of BBC TV, came up to him and said: 'That's a jolly good quiz show you've got on *Grandstand*. I can't get my two boys away from our set while it's on.'

So we were saved and *Sporting Chance* lasted for some time, with dear old Roy Webber as scorer, adjudicator and question-setter. He was a large, friendly person with a fantastic photographic memory, and after a few casual scorers including John Woodcock, now cricket corres-pondent of *The Times*, Roy became the regular TV scorer and statistician. He also did a lot for radio other than the Tests and he and I spent many happy hours together 'at the cricket' as he used to say. He collapsed and died suddenly in 1962 and our commentary box was never the same again without him, though there was much more room!

Arthur Wrigley – a Lancastrian who bowled a useful leg-break and had a dry sense of humour – was the radio scorer and used to carry a mobile reference library round with him. He always came up with the right answer, as of course did Roy but usually out of his head. These two were the first of the invaluable TV and radio statisticians and were ably assisted by Jack Price and Arnold Whipp. By a sad coincidence all four of them died within a few years of each other. Since then Ross Salmon and Irving Rosen-water on TV and Bill Frindall (the bearded wonder) on radio have continued to provide the high-class and near infallible service of information and statistics which is so indispensable to all of us commentators. Some people may feel that too much emphasis is put on records and the like but from the large number of letters which we receive it is obviously also much appreciated by most viewers and listeners.

One unusual job I found myself doing on TV was inter-views at breakfast time at the Savoy Hotel. It followed the night of the results of the American Presidential Election and was one of the first breakfast-time programmes ever to go out on TV, except of course for our own elections. It was also my one and only foray into the political arena. Just as well perhaps as I am sure I would never be able to hide which side I was on.

I also entered the TV world of sequins and white ties and tails, and for the next eight years or so I was the commentator at the International Ballroom Champion-ships from the Royal Albert Hall. My expert co-commentator was Elsa Wells who had an attractive drawl and was always exquisitely dressed.

Elsa did a fabulous job as she not only organised and put on the whole event but was also one of the judges in the two grand finals which we televised. She used to commentate and judge at the same time which was quite unique as it meant that the viewer knew what at least one of the judges was thinking before the results were announced.

But I suppose the most important occasion on TV that year was Princess Margaret's wedding in May. It was especially crucial for the BBC as for the first time ITV were to challenge the BBC's right to a big occasion and were to match the BBC's coverage with their own cameras and commentators.

We were all very carefully briefed and exhorted to make special efforts to do a good job. I was in a comparatively unimportant position on the Horse Guards Parade, and all I had to cover was the procession crossing the Parade on its way to and from Westminster Abbey.

It was a field day for the TV critics who had two sets in front of them and next day compared the performances of the two channels. Naturally Richard Dimbleby won hands down in the Abbey and later at Tower Bridge. But along the route things were more even and opinion was divided as to who had done best – the BBC or ITV commentators. Of one thing though Peter Black of the *Daily Mail* had no doubt whatsoever: 'By far the silliest remark of the whole day,' he wrote, 'was made by Brian Johnston of the BBC, who when Princess Margaret passed a statue in Whitehall commented: "Princess Margaret is now passing the statue of the 2nd Duke of Cambridge. I am sure he would have waved at her if he could." ' On reading it again I am inclined to agree with him but at the time I was very upset!

This was a great year for all of us at 1A Cavendish Avenue as it heralded the arrival of Mrs Callander, alias 'Cally'. She and her son, Jack, and daughter, Ann, came to live in our downstairs flat, and except for a few weeks she has been with us ever since. She has looked after all the children, cooked, cleaned, mended, washed and answered the telephone. Remarkably, she has remained cheerful throughout and been a real friend of the family. How she has put up with us all I don't know. Just possibly she enjoys being with us as much as we enjoy having her with us. I hope so anyway.

The year 1961 was much better for cricket and Richie Benaud's popular Australian side won the series 2–1 and so kept the Ashes which he had won from Peter May's team in 1959. I flew out in April with a TV camera crew to meet their liner SS *Canberra* at Port Said. I then travelled with them to Malta, doing interviews and taking shots of their life on board, which we flew back to England in advance of their arrival.

For a couple of nights we stayed in Cairo and saw the Pyramids and rode a camel before we went down to Port Said to wait for the ship. It was pouring with rain, so to get some shelter I went into a shoe shop where I spotted a pair of brown-and-white correspondent shoes. They fitted me perfectly so to pull his leg I told the Arab shop-keeper that I would take the left one, and would he wrap it up for me. He got terribly excited and waved his arms about in protest, so I relented and said I would take both. These are the same shoes which I have worn ever since, and they are famous among cricketers all over the world. They are supposed to bring England luck and it is true that England have won more Tests than they have lost since I started to wear the shoes. Now everyone expects me to wear them, even though they look a bit shabby.

Australia were severely handicapped by Benaud's bad shoulder, which prevented him bowling his leg-breaks and googlies properly throughout the tour. But in spite of a lot of pain he bowled Australia to victory in the 4th Test at Old Trafford. Benaud was one of the greatest Test captains and an inspiring leader. He always did his best to see that his sides played attractive and attacking cricket but on the few occasions when they did not, his public relations were so good that it never seemed to be his fault! He broke all tradition by giving a Press conference at the end of each day's play, and never refused to answer a question. It often appeared that he was writing the correspondents' articles for them.

Richie was indirectly responsible for my giving up wicket-keeping some years later. I had been terribly lucky since joining the BBC to play in Sunday charity matches with all the famous Test cricketers of the time. I have let byes or missed countless catches and stumpings when keeping wicket to bowlers like Lindwall, Miller, Trueman, Bedser, Statham, Laker, Worrell, F. R. Brown, Gover, R. W. V. Robins, Compton and Titmus.

One Sunday in the late sixties Richie and I were playing for John Woodcock against the Rugby School Boys' Club at the Dragon School in Oxford. I was crouching behind the timbers reading Richie's googlies, flippers and top spinners. I read them all right but many of them still went for byes. However, when the last man came in Richie bowled him a leg-break. He went down the pitch, missed it and with all my old speed – so I thought – I whipped off the bails and appealed. The umpire put up his finger and there it was: St. Johnston b. Benaud. I felt very proud and pleased with myself as I walked off.

Then the school bursar came up to me and said: 'Very well stumped.' I looked suitably modest and thanked him. 'Yes,' he went on, 'I should also like to congratulate you on the sporting way you tried to give him time to get back!' I was speechless and much shaken. If that's what people thought of my lightning stumping it was time I hung up my gloves. So I did.

It was during this year that Rex Alston on reaching the age of sixty retired from the BBC staff and became a freelance commentator. I missed him a lot as he was a kind and charming person, but in fact his departure did make me the number one cricket man on radio so far as the staff were concerned. It also opened up the way for me to be the BBC representative on future MCC tours.

Rex continued to commentate for the next decade,

specialising as he always had on cricket, tennis, rugger and athletics. He had a very clear precise delivery with a touch of the schoolmaster about it, and looked, and still does, wiry, fit and amazingly young for his age. I have always thought that he was at his best when doing athletics, which is not surprising as when up at Cambridge he had been second string to Harold Abrahams in the 100 yards.

Throughout his broadcasting career Rex was plagued, possibly more than most of us, by a small word which is the bugbear of all commentators. He is recorded as saying: 'It's a colourful scene here during the tea interval. The ground is full of small boys all playing with their balls.'

Or again at Wimbledon when there was a pause while the ball boys were getting the new balls and Louise Brough was waiting impatiently to serve. 'There's a slight hold-up here,' said Rex. 'Miss Brough hasn't got any balls.'

After he left the BBC, Rex did a voice-over commercial on ITV, advertising a well-known brand of soft lavatory paper. Someone commented: 'If he *is* going to do commercials he is quite right to start at the bottom!'

In 1962 I was very busy. On radio I was asked to do another new series called *Married to Fame*. In this I talked to the wives of well-known people to find out what sort of life they led, and how they helped their husbands in their careers.

Among the wives I visited and recorded were those of Sir Compton Mackenzie, Herbert Morrison, Ted Dexter, Douglas Bader, Jimmy Greaves, Lord Robens, Graham Hill, Jack Warner, Scobie Breasley, Humphrey Lyttleton, H. E. Bates, Harry Secombe and Sir Francis Chichester.

The ladies were an interesting and varied selection, who proved to me how important it is for a man to have a wife who can provide sympathy, encouragement and a happy and peaceful home life. Admittedly I picked successful marriages but some of us have indeed been lucky. The series was brought to an end with a 'cod' interview with Dick Emery using one of his sexy female voices, which somewhat spoilt the saintly image of my previous wives!

Sporting Chance was replaced by *Treble Chance*, a quiz with more varied ingredients: general knowledge, current affairs, show-business, and guess the year or the voice. I was Chairman and a BBC panel toured the seaside towns each week to take on the local team. The town which got the most points against the BBC eventually won the cup.

There were three people on the panel – Nan Winton (the first lady ever to read the news on BBC TV), who was an expert on music, films and the theatre; Charles Gardner, the old BBC air correspondent, who covered all the sporting, technical and scientific side and Wynford Vaughan-Thomas, who covered almost everything else. Wynford is a man with a vast knowledge of history, geography, literature, serious music, food, wine, travel and world events.

Our panel was strong, but even so, the occasional town used to beat us, and gained bonus points for so doing. This quiz has been tremendously popular and it has always amazed me not only that so many people are keen to air their knowledge but that they have so much knowledge to air. Wherever it goes large audiences turn up to watch the show and support their teams, which is highly encouraging in this TV age.

Talking of television, I had a fleeting appearance as one of those people for whom I always feel so sorry – the compere in *Come Dancing*. He must sit at a table surrounded by a bevy of beauties (?) and act as a sort of local cheerleader.

The venue was a vast ballroom in Purley and my team represented south-east London. I did my best but I am afraid we lost and in spite of a polite note of thanks from the producer I think the BBC rightly thought that in future the beauties deserved a younger and more 'with it' cheerleader. I wasn't sorry.

But I was pleased to join Peter West, Polly Elwes and David Dimbleby in an information-type programme on TV called *What's New?* It was produced by Brian Robins and as its name suggests was a forerunner of *Tomorrow's World*. We weren't quite as technical and scientific as Raymond Baxter is today, but did try to explain new inventions and ideas. *What's New* became a regular feature for the next year or two and was great fun to do, though we were all terrible gigglers and always trying to make each other dry up.

Brian was the ideal producer to work for, and always took great care of the human needs of his team. He was small, wiry and full of infectious energy and enthusiasm and the word 'no' did not exist in his vocabulary. He was also a man of instantaneous decisions, and once when I reported to Lime Grove in my best suit to do a studio interview, I was suddenly whisked off to catch a plane to Switzerland. I just had time to collect my passport and next day found myself on the top of a ski-slope, inter-viewing some skiers – still in my pin-stripe suit. They must have thought I was mad. All I know is that I was jolly cold.

Life was full of surprises like that. I had had a lovely family holiday in a cottage at Swanage, which Pauline had bought with some money left to her by her mother. It was on the top of a hill two miles above the town in a small quarry village called Acton. It had the most perfect view of the sea and of the Isle of Wight, too, on a clear day. To my mind Swanage was, and still is, the most unspoilt and delightful place for a seaside holiday.

The bathing is safe, it is usually near the top of the sunshine league, and there are sandy beaches for the children, good sailing for the sailors and perfect walks for miles round the cliff paths. In recent years we have spent most of our holidays there, and now have a holiday home on the cliff-tops.

On my return from a family holiday in Swanage my

telephone rang and it was TV Light Entertainments from the White City. Was I free that evening and if so could I come down to the TV Theatre at Shepherd's Bush and introduce *This Is Your Life*? My heart sank. Me do an Eamonn Andrews for half an hour? My first thought was that I would break down and blub when some aged sister whom the victim had not seen for thirty years hobbled in, just flown by the BBC from Sydney.

But I need not have worried. They just wanted me to open up the programme and explain that Eamonn was busy trying to trap the victim and would appear, they hoped, at any moment. It was in the days when the programme was done live and it often really was touch and go whether the victim would turn up, and having done so, agree to appear. In case he or she failed to do so, there was always one pre-recorded show in the can, but so far as I know the only person who turned up and then refused was the footballer Danny Blanchflower.

Somewhat reassured I went down to Shepherd's Bush and after the dramatic opening music walked out on to the stage, much to the surprise, and I'm sure the disappointment, of the audience. But I soon explained what was happening, and luckily Eamonn and his victim appeared more or less immediately. It was the actor Rupert Davies, of the TV series, *Maigret*, whom Eamonn had trapped in another studio.

Pakistan under Javed Burki were the cricket tourists and after the excitements of 1961 it proved to be another disappointing series. England won 4–0 and would have won all five but for the weather at Trent Bridge. Peter Parfitt, Tom Graveney, Ted Dexter and Colin Cowdrey were the main run-getters for England and Fred Trueman with twenty-two wickets the best bowler. But all these runs and wickets were cheap as Pakistan were completely outclassed and none of their bowlers took more than six wickets in the series.

The Pakistanis were a friendly side and strictly managed by a military consortium of Brigadier R. G. Hyder, the manager, and his assistant, Major S. A. Rahmann. The Brigadier was a genial and charming soldier who did not profess to know anything about cricket. He was determined that his team should behave well, be popular and be good losers and he succeeded in all three.

At times the Brigadier's methods were more suitable to a military campaign than a cricket tour. In the 3rd Test at Headingley Pakistan were beset by injuries and player after player left the field, which became full of substitutes. This was too much for the Brigadier who decided to put a stop to it when he saw another of his bowlers hobbling from the field. It turned out afterwards that this bowler had a very serious groin injury and did not in fact bowl again on the tour. But as he stumbled up the steps to the dressing-rooms he was met by an irate Brigadier who waved him away: 'Go back on to the field at once and fight for Pakistan,' he cried, and back limped the unfortunate bowler.

In this same match Pakistan had collapsed in the first innings and were 123–9. The Brigadier walked into the dressing-room and saw the opening bat, who had actually made 50, lying asleep on the massage table. The Brigadier shook him awake: 'Get up, and get your pads on at once.' 'But I have already been in,' protested the batsman. 'No matter,' said the Brigadier, 'get your pads on again. We are fighting for Pakistan!'

On the other hand the Major was quite a useful cricketer and played for me one Sunday in an annual match which I used to run against the village of Widford in Hertfordshire. It was a perfect setting surrounded by trees and gardens with a little thatched pavilion. The local side was captained by John Pawle, the old Cambridge blue, and Racquets player, and I usually got some well-known players to join me and my broadcasting friends.

In 1962 when Major Rahmann was playing we were

twelve-a-side and created what must be a record. When the village batted I made the usual bowling changes to start with and found that the first four wickets had fallen to four different bowlers. So from then on whenever a bowler took a wicket I took him off and put on someone else. Believe it or not, at the end of the innings eleven bowlers had each taken one wicket apiece. It must be unique and we did not cheat in any way. No catches were deliberately dropped, nor did any bowler stop trying once he had taken a wicket.

We were all highly delighted with the record and celebrated in the village pub – all except Major Rahmann, who was exceedingly puzzled as to why he had been taken off immediately after taking a wicket. They did not play cricket that way in Pakistan! Incidentally, Roy Webber used to be our regular umpire and on one occasion called off play for bad light, before he discovered he still had on his dark glasses!

During the summer I started to do a column for the *Cricketer* magazine, in which I used to relate my experiences round the grounds, and tell the occasional story. I reported on a match between Lord's Taverners and Old England, which was played at Lord's one Saturday before a large crowd.

Denis Compton could not be with Peter West and me in the TV box as he was playing for Old England, so we thought we would try an experiment. We gave him a small pocket transmitter and a microphone the size of a button pinned to his shirt. We also fitted up Richie Benaud, who was playing for the Taverners, in the same way.

When Denis was batting and Richie bowling we had a combined commentary. Richie would tell us what type of ball he was going to bowl: googly, leg-break or top spinner. But Denis could not hear this and as the ball was delivered he told us what he thought it was and how he was going to deal with it. The viewer sitting at home could then judge who was right. It was a fascinating experiment, and it is a pity that it has not been repeated more often as with two such good players who could also broadcast it made a marvellous way of coaching young boys.

During the same match Norman Wisdom was playing for the Taverners and when he was batting kept the crowd in roars of laughter with his clowning and antics at the crease. He finally did a succession of his mock falls in the middle of the pitch and collided with and knocked down his partner. The crowd's laughter shook Lord's.

In the pavilion there was an elderly MCC member in a Panama hat with I Zingari ribbon who hadn't really cottoned on to what match he was watching. However, Norman made him chuckle and he nudged his neighbour: 'I don't know who this player is but he'd earn his fortune as a comedian.'

12 Cricket correspondent, BBC

NINETEEN SIXTY-TWO WAS A happy year with a touch of nostalgia for me, as Barry left his private school at Sunningdale and went to Eton College. In spite of dour reports from his headmaster, Mr Sheepshanks, he had passed the Common Entrance quite easily and in fact 'took' two forms higher than I had done when I entered Eton in 1925.

Nowadays it is the fashion for some Old Boys to run Eton down and to reveal all the scandals and terrible goings-on that have taken place there. Perhaps I was just one of the lucky ones, but during my five years at Eton I enjoyed some of the happiest times of my life.

The great strength of Eton lay in the quality and character of its masters. I may be falling into the old trap but they certainly seemed greater characters then than the masters are today. By far the wittiest was Tuppy Headlam, who taught me history. It was during one of his classes that I was to learn the importance of timing in making a successful joke. I discovered that, however bad the material, if it is put over well, with the right emphasis at the right time, it can produce laughter.

We were doing history and Tuppy was talking about the wives of an historical figure called Henry – I forget which one.

'His first wife died,' said Tuppy, 'and now let's talk about his second one, Henrietta.'

'Did he really?' I said quickly from the back of the class. Bad joke, but big laugh, which Tuppy enjoyed as much as anyone.

It was amusing to go back as a parent and notice the changes after thirty years. The fees were at least double what they had been and the boys, though still in their tails and white ties, no longer had to wear top-hats – they were too expensive. There was no longer such an emphasis on games and in the summer, for instance, the boys were now allowed to play tennis, golf or do athletics, rather than being forced to play either cricket or to row. This I think is a good idea as it means that those playing cricket, though fewer, are keen and want to play. Towards the end of his time at Eton I fear that the only thing Barry played was his guitar and he spent most of his leisure hours composing and writing songs.

One other thing I noticed about Eton was that the masters no longer live in the comparative luxury to which they had been accustomed in my day. In the twenties all housemasters and masters in digs had butlers and cooks. Now Barry's housemaster spent hours chasing round Windsor looking for Spanish maids, while the poor young masters had to cook their own breakfasts after early school. *Tempus fugit* seemed to me the appropriate cliché.

I ended the year by flying off to Australia to join Ted Dexter and his MCC team. It was rather sad in one way as it was the first time I had ever missed Christmas at home with Pauline and the children. But the BBC, urged on by Charles Max-Muller, this time were keen that I should go and represent them, though they had not yet officially appointed me their cricket correspondent.

This was the tour on which the Duke of Norfolk was the surprise manager. There had been much speculation as to who it was going to be and late in July the Press and the BBC were all asked to assemble in the Press Box at Lord's, to hear the announcement, and meet the mystery manager. It had been an amazingly well-kept secret and not even the keenest ferrets in the Press had the faintest idea who it was going to be.

When the Duke of Norfolk's name was announced it was a cricket sensation. The box rapidly emptied, as correspondents rushed to their phones to warn their sports editors. They were even more surprised when they returned and heard a statement from the Duke telling how and why he had got the job. He had evidently woken up in the middle of the night and thought that he would rather like to go to Australia. So he woke up the Duchess and asked her if she thought it would be a good idea if he told Lord's that he was available, if required, for the job. She said yes, so he did and he got it.

But this unorthodox choice proved a great success and the Duke was extremely popular and a wonderful ambassador for MCC wherever he went. He owed a tremendous lot to his assistant Alec Bedser, who worked like a beaver and carried out most of the day-to-day chores of the tour with admirable efficiency.

During the tour the Duke used to visit as many race-meetings as possible and even had an interest in a horse, and the following story was told about him. He went to a small country meeting to see the horse run and strolled into the paddock to see it saddled. It was in a far corner and as he approached, the Duke noticed the trainer put his hand in his pocket and slip the horse something to eat. Remembering his position at home as a member of the Jockey Club and the Queen's Representative at Ascot, coupled with all the dope scares of recent years, the Duke went up to the trainer and said: 'What's that you've just given the horse to eat?'

'Oh, your Grace,' said the trainer looking a bit guilty, 'not to worry. It was just a lump of sugar. Here, have one yourself. I am going to.'

So saying, the trainer gave the Duke a lump and popped one into his own mouth. The Duke somewhat relieved thought he better follow suit and eat his too. He walked off to talk to someone and the jockey joined the trainer who began to give him his riding instructions, 'Take the horse steadily for the first five furlongs, just keep him on the bit and tuck him in behind the leaders. But when you have only two furlongs to go, let him go and give him all

131

you've got. If anyone passes you after that, it will either be myself or the Duke of Norfolk.'

I joined the team at Adelaide just before Christmas and we stayed at a beach hotel about ten miles along the coast. I was greeted by *When Shepherds Watched Their Flocks by Night* over the intercom of my plane from Sydney and it was strange to be celebrating Christmas with temperatures in the eighties and nineties. On Christmas Day itself the Press and BBC played MCC in a riotous game of beach football and then gave all the players a champagne party before lunch.

With the Rev. David Sheppard in the team we were kept on our religious toes and not only attended early service but went to hear him preach in the cathedral. He did this in every city and people used to come in from miles away in the outback to hear him and he always had a full house.

On this occasion I went with Colin Cowdrey and John Woodcock of *The Times* and we decided to have a sweep on the length of his sermon. I had taken my stopwatch with me and there was great excitement as he approached the various targets. He had a habit of pausing so that it seemed as if he had finished and once I was about to pay out to John Woodcock when David suddenly went off on another tack and did another four minutes. His final time was twenty-eight minutes, which may seem long, but he spoke superbly and appreciated that people had come especially to hear him. Cowdrey assessed his form better than us and won the sweep.

David had a good tour with the bat and made a fine hundred in the 2nd Test at Melbourne, which we won. Unfortunately his absence from regular first-class cricket had made his fielding a bit rusty and he dropped a lot of catches. As so often happens in cases like this, the ball seemed to follow him wherever he fielded and down it would go. This surprised Fred Trueman who commented:

'After all, when the Rev. puts his two hands together he must stand a better chance than any of us.'

The series was drawn, each side winning one Test. This meant that Australia kept the Ashes and it was the first time that a five-Test series in Australia had ever been left undecided. The teams were evenly matched but in the last two Tests both seemed scared of losing and the final Test at Sydney played on a very slow pitch was the dullest I have ever watched.

Ted Dexter has always had a splendid sense of humour and one night I thought he would never stop laughing. When I was a child in Herefordshire we had a groom called Dean. He had enormous ears which he could tuck in. He taught me how to do it and I can still tuck my ears in today. I was dining with Ted Dexter, Ron Roberts and John Woodcock in a restaurant in Launceston so I thought I would challenge my companions to do the same. Ted and Ron both failed, but John promptly tucked both in as if he had been doing it for years. We all began to laugh and the noise attracted the attention of all the other diners. Soon everyone in the room, including the waiters, were trying to tuck their ears in, and John and I went from table to table to give them aid and advice. We found ourselves trying to twist complete strangers' ears into the right shape in order to tuck them in. The whole place was in an uproar and everyone, including Ted, became quite hysterical. I must add that we found no one's ears pliable enough to 'take the tuck'.

After Christmas, Pauline flew out to join me travelling with the Duke's three daughters. As Sue Dexter and Grace Sheppard were also accompanying their husbands we didn't lack female support and company, which all helped to enliven the social scene. When there is no cricket many of the team and Press nowadays play a lot of golf but I have always gone off to the nearest beach to swim and sunbathe. I must confess though that I have never mastered surfing and gave Jack Fingleton some good laughs once when he took me to Bondi beach. I know all the technical terms to shout: 'one out the back', which means a big wave is coming or 'there's too much water in that one', which still means nothing to me. But however small the wave I am usually well and truly 'dumped'.

At the end of the tour I had to fly back to England but Pauline went on to New Zealand where she had an amusing experience.

On her last day, Ted Dexter gave her lunch and she then said that she would like to have a short sleep before flying off that night. Ted suggested that she should use one of the beds in the Duke's suite, the sitting-room of which was used as a team meeting-place. Ted explained that the Duke was away for the day and that she would not be disturbed. So she took off her dress and lay down on one of the beds and was soon fast asleep. She awoke some time later to hear a gruff voice saying: 'Who's that sleeping on my bed?' It was the Duke who had returned unexpectedly. But unlike the three Bears he did not chase Pauline away. After hearing her embarrassed explanation he did the British thing and gave her a cup of tea.

On my return to England at the end of February 1963 I found an additional assignment lined up for me in April. Jack de Manio was going to take three weeks' leave and they asked me to take his place and introduce the *Today* programme while he was away.

This was quite a challenge, as it's never easy taking over someone's regular spot and there was also the contrast in our styles. Jack has the most casual and natural approach of any broadcaster I have heard, and speaks with a slow, rather upper-class drawl. I would not dare to analyse my delivery, but I do know that I talk fast – too fast probably – and that compared to him my presentation must have sounded like machine-gun fire.

In those days there was only one presenter and I used to get a call from the BBC and set my alarm at 5.50 am.

The BBC sent a car for me and I was in the studio by 6.30 am. The overnight staff and producer had prepared most of the items and a secretary was usually typing out a rough script when I arrived.

I quickly scanned through all the daily papers to bring myself up to date with any news item with which we might be dealing. I also looked for any 'funnies' to use as fill-ins between items or in an emergency. There was sometimes an interview to be recorded before the programme with someone in their home or abroad or perhaps one or two people were actually in the studio to be interviewed live in the programme.

This meant chatting them up beforehand to find out what the interview was all about. Once the script was typed with the timings allowed for each spot, I went through it and made adjustments to suit the way I would normally say it. It was therefore quite a hectic forty-five minutes before the programme went on the air at 7.15 am.

An hour later we had a second edition with one or two of the items changed and in between we were given a rather poor breakfast of coffee, fruit juice and soggy toast and marmalade. The toast was always soggy because the BBC claimed that if they provided a toast rack it was always pinched. We were usually short of a bottle-opener, too, for the same reason.

One thing I was determined to get right was the time. The main danger was getting the hour wrong so for each edition I always wrote a large 7 or 8 on a pad in front of me, and though even then I sometimes got it wrong, I never touched Jack's form. It was all a good experience but at the end of three weeks I felt pretty tired, as I was doing my normal work as well. It also made any social life extremely difficult, as I tried to have a 10 o'clock curfew, and it was especially tough on Pauline, who had to put up with an alarm and the telephone at 5.50 am every morning. I just don't know how Jack stood it all those years.

Except for odd shows for TV like the Ballroom Championships and the Miss World Contest, *Treble Chance* and the Royal Variety Performance for radio, I shall always remember 1963 for its cricket. During the year I was at last appointed the first-ever BBC Cricket Correspondent and from then on my broadcasting life gradually centred more and more on cricket and less on other types of programmes.

The summer of 1963 saw the start of the Knock-out Competition, now known as the Gillette Cup, and when Sussex beat Worcestershire in an exciting final, Lord's for the first time experienced the real cup-tie atmosphere which has existed every year since then.

The West Indies under Frank Worrell beat England 3–1 in an exciting series, which produced some brilliant batting, some fine fast bowling and attracted huge crowds. For England, Dexter, Close, Ken Barrington and Phil Sharpe made the runs and Trueman with thirty-four wickets had his best-ever series.

Led by the genius of Kanhai, all the top West Indies batsmen came off and Sobers proved himself a great all-rounder. Wes Hall and Charlie Griffith made a devastating and frightening pair of opening bowlers, though they both bowled too many bumpers and there was considerable doubt about the legality of some of Griffith's deliveries.

The match of the series was undoubtedly the 2nd Test at Lord's – almost certainly both the best and the most dramatic that I have seen. For four days the fortunes of the two teams fluctuated, and then on the fifth day came that famous last over at the start of which any of four results could have occurred.

As Wes Hall started his long run, eight runs were needed by England to win with two wickets in hand, one of them being Cowdrey with his left wrist in plaster. David Allen and Derek Shackleton were together and they each scored a single. Then off the fourth ball Shackleton was run out and out of the pavilion emerged Cowdrey to cheers and counter-cheers from the excited crowd. Six runs were needed and two balls left and Allen resisted the temptation to try for a six for victory and played the two balls out. So Cowdrey did not have to bat, but had he done so he had intended to stand as a left-hander but using only his right hand.

Once again I had my usual luck and was the TV commentator for the finish. Earlier as the excitement grew, the TV programme planners decided that we should not return to Alexandra Palace for the usual 5.50 pm news. But in the middle of the second-last over someone apparently changed their mind, as I was told to wrap up quickly and hand over to Alexandra Palace for the news, which so far as I can remember started with a rather boring item about President Kennedy.

Luckily for cricket viewers Kenneth Adam, Head of BBC TV and himself a cricket fanatic, was viewing and got straight on to the news people and ordered them to return to Lord's at once. So we had the unique event of the national news fading out for cricket. They just got back in time for the start of the last over. So all was well in the end and it was certainly the most dramatic of all our television broadcasts of cricket.

In 1964 *Treble Chance* gave me the opportunity of seeing more of the world, and we set off on a six-week trip to Aden, Bahrain, Nairobi, the island of Gan in the Indian Ocean, Singapore and Hong Kong.

Led by our producer Michael Tuke-Hastings, our team consisted of the panel: Wynford Vaughan-Thomas, Nan Winton and Charles Gardner; a secretary; an engineer and myself as chairman. We travelled everywhere by RAF Transport Command and played teams from the three services wherever we went. We had a fantastic time and were royally entertained.

This was my first experience of the mysteries and customs of the East and of course the smells and the heat.

I couldn't believe it when we went on to one beach and were told that the — of — had a close-circuit television set on which he watched the beach, and invited 'up to tea' anyone he particularly fancied. None of us were asked!

In Nairobi we visited the big game reserve just outside the city early one morning and enjoyed an unique experience – or so we were told. We saw a pride of lions and witnessed the lion and the lioness 'performing' twice within a quarter of an hour. Just to put the record straight I must add that it was definitely the lioness who wanted and instigated the repeat performance.

The island of Gan is an RAF staging post in the Maldives in the Indian Ocean – it has a large airstrip, some huts, some powder-white beaches and coral strands, and clear blue water containing multicoloured fish of all shapes and sizes. It was an idyllic place to stay for three or four days and we spent hours with our snorkels watching the fish.

The RAF do a two-year stint and when we visited them, there was only one lady on the island – a senior WRAF welfare officer. So you can imagine the sort of reception which Nan Winton and our secretary received!

There were several small islands dotted around from which the natives used to row across to work on the airstrip. We visited one of these called Hitadu – as near to a Robinson Crusoe setting as you could find. No domestic pets nor wheeled vehicles were allowed, except bicycles, and we pedalled our way along steamy jungle paths to visit the Chief of the island in his hut. He bade us welcome and gave us a delicious cup of tea.

We attracted the attention of the children, who followed us around with large staring eyes. We demonstrated cricket to them with a piece of wood and a stone and they soon began to copy us and join in. When we got back to England we sent the Chief some cricket gear for the boys, but whether they ever played or not I never heard. It was all so beautiful and peaceful with the tropical trees and plants and no one seemed to have a care in the world. Yet sadly we were told that the maximum age most of them reached was about forty-five.

Singapore and Hong Kong were every way as good as I had expected though Singapore was perhaps too sticky. The view from the heights looking down on Hong Kong Harbour at night is one of the most breathtaking sights I have ever seen. The city itself is overcrowded and teeming with people, but there is a wonderful atmosphere of bustle and activity and, as so often in the East, a painful contrast between the living standards and conditions of the very rich and the very poor.

As one arrived on the steamer from across the harbour there were queues of rickshaws lined up like taxis. But I could never bring myself to ride in one. I felt it was the final degradation for the poor rickshaw 'boys' – many of them tired, thin, old men, doing the job of an animal.

My one complaint was the Chinese food, which I just could not stomach. While the others picked away at a communal dish and ate birds' nest soup and the like, I used to settle for a fried egg and bacon. I visited the famous Hong Kong Cricket Club with its ground right in the middle of the city, surrounded by skyscrapers and giant office blocks. The site is worth millions and there was always tremendous pressure to get them to move. They rent it from the civic authorities and now at last they are being ejected and given another ground outside the city. It was here that Keith Miller hit a six through a window of the Red Bank of China and nearly lost us Hong Kong – fifty years *before* we had to hand it back to the Chinese.

We returned at the beginning of March in time for me to fly up to Scotland for the wedding of my god-child, Meriel Douglas-Home. Her father, Sir Alec, was then Prime Minister, so the telly, radio and Press made a lot of fuss about it. I was able to help the happy couple escape from their clutches as I travelled down in the same plane and smuggled them out of London Airport in the back of my Ford Zephyr. We thus avoided hordes of newshawks waiting in cars to follow them to their honeymoon destination.

My first big job after I had welcomed Bobby Simpson's Australians at London Airport was to commentate on a firework display from Southend on the opening night of BBC-2. It was due to take place on Sunday, 19 April 1964 but due to an electricians' strike there was a black-out, so the opening was postponed for twenty-four hours.

A commentary on fireworks is almost an impossibility. What is there to say? I remember in 1951 at one big firework display on the embankment, Stewart Macpherson had a list of adjectives written down in front of him – brilliant, fantastic, magnificent, dazzling, sparkling – and he crossed out each one as he used it. Anyway, I asked the man in charge to give me a list of all his fireworks, the order in which he was going to let them off, and their correct names. We also asked him to pause between each lot so that they could register on TV and I should have time to describe what they were.

Alas all my well-laid plans went for a burton. When he got the signal, the man panicked and rushed from rocket to display, from display to banger, from banger to Catherine wheels – in any order and at a terrific pace. All my notes were useless, and not only did I not know what to say but would not have had time to say it anyway. But muddle or not at least the opening of BBC-2 went with a bang!

It was, in general, a fine summer but, typically, rain spoilt three of the Tests, otherwise England might at least have drawn the series. As it was Australia won the 3rd Test at Headingley and then made certain of not losing the series by winning the toss at Old Trafford. They batted into the third day and made 656 for 8 before declaring, Bobby Simpson making his first-ever Test hundred – a small matter of 311! England replied with 611 with Barrington and Dexter, England's chief run-getters of the series making 256 and 174. So with rain at the Oval, Australia won 1–0 and still kept the Ashes.

The series against Australia had been made brighter for us by one of our leg-pulls on Jim Swanton during the 1st Test at Trent Bridge. For some reason at the start of the season Jim decided to have a chauffeur to drive him around. The only other cricket writer I ever remember having one was C. B. Fry when he wrote for the *Evening Standard* in 1934 and coined the lovely phrase about Bradman: 'The Don was at his donniest today.'

Jim as usual was doing television with us and Trent Bridge was packed on the first morning. At about 12 noon Denis Compton went down to see the man on the public address and asked him to read out a message. We had composed this up in the TV box when Jim wasn't looking, and during a silence between the overs the loudspeakers gave out: 'If Mr E. W. Swanton has arrived on the ground yet will he please go to the back of the pavilion, where his chauffeur has left the engine of his car running!'

I have rarely heard such a roar of laughter on a cricket ground and I'm afraid Jim soon knew where to put the blame! Wherever cricketers meet, Jim's name is bound to crop up sooner or later. He looks big and thinks big and is fearless in giving his opinion, no matter how unpopular he knows it is. People who don't know him sometimes think that he is pompous. So I suppose do his many friends – and he has legions – which is why we enjoy pulling his leg.

Jim also has a habit of staying with Governor Generals or dining with Prime Ministers when on MCC tours, and this produced the now famous but rather unkind remark by someone about him: 'Jim is such a snob that he won't travel in the same car as his chauffeur!'

He is one of the really great cricket writers and has had the necessary strength of character to ensure that he is given adequate space to reflect his opinions. He started broadcasting on cricket way back in 1938 and goodness knows how many Tests he has covered on TV or radio. Jim's summaries are still infinitely superior to those by anyone else in the business though they are now restricted to radio only.

There were some classic moments when he did the summaries on TV. He had the guts – and he needed them – to stop in the middle of one, snap his fingers and tell some small boys to stop moving about behind the camera. When they did so, he continued quite unabashed. But he *was* slightly taken aback once at Trent Bridge when he finished his summary and removed his field glasses from around his neck and placed them on the table in front of him, as he always did. 'Well it's been a day we shall never forget. A fine day's cricket. Let me just give you the final score once again.'

So saying, he looked up at the giant electric scoreboard and to his horror saw that it had been switched off! As happens on occasions like that his mind went blank and he could not remember what the score was! But a snap of the fingers and a hurriedly written note was slipped in front of him on the table and all was well.

13 Johnston's choice

DEXTER HAD NOW LOST three series as captain – against India, West Indies and Australia. With the general election in October, he turned his attention to politics and stood as a Conservative for Cardiff SE.

This meant that Mike Smith was given the captaincy for MCC's winter tour of South Africa. The BBC had decided that we should give it full coverage, so towards the end of October 1964 Pauline and I sailed for Cape Town in the *City of Exeter* – a pleasant ship of the Ellerman Line.

An aunt kindly moved into 1A to help Cally run the house and look after the children. But I must admit that I did not enjoy the voyage as much as I had hoped. The sea does something to people: within a few minutes of meeting a complete stranger you are hearing intimate details of his or her private life, often accompanied by a show of photographs. Ugh! Pauline is far better than I am at this sort of thing and thoroughly enjoyed herself. But I got plenty of sunshine, scrabble and swimming so I don't really know why I am complaining!

This tour was one of the happiest on which I have ever been. It was without incidents, the country was beautiful, the people friendly and the hospitality superb. But most important of all was the MCC's team spirit. As on all his three tours as captain, Mike Smith proved himself to be the ideal leader of a touring side. As a batsman he was utterly unselfish and on the field he never asked anyone to do anything which he would not do himself. As a result he was usually to be found in the most dangerous close-catching positions.

Mike never flapped or got excited and had the ability to deflate gently anyone who tended to get temperamental or swollen-headed. His teams would do anything for him and he was rightly known as 'the players' captain'.

By winning the 1st Test at Durban on a spinner's wicket, England won the series 1–0 and although the next four Tests were drawn they were usually good to watch. But the pitches were too placid and the batting of both sides stronger than their bowling. For MCC that great tourist Ken Barrington averaged 101 in the Tests and all the other batsmen averaged over 42. For South Africa the batting and fielding of Colin Bland and the batting of Eddie Barlow and Graeme Pollock were outstanding.

From a personal point of view, there was the added enjoyment of seeing my sister Anne for the first time for nearly thirty years. She came down to Durban to meet me on our first visit for the Natal match and when we returned for the Test, Pauline and I went up to visit her in the little fishing village of St Lucia Estuary, about 150 miles up the coast from Durban. Anne had been there since 1937 and became a mother-figure to the RAF during the war, for they spent their leaves up there.

If you like the quiet life, that part of the globe is a paradise. It has a lovely climate, monkeys swinging from tree to tree in the garden or hippos wandering around at night. It only has sandy roads and is now a popular weekend fishing resort and a good centre for two game reserves. Anne loves the simple life, has her grandchildren around her and goes to bed at about 8 pm and gets up at 4 am. Definitely not the life for me!

My popularity with the team sunk somewhat when we were at Port Elizabeth the first time round. We were playing football on the beach and I was racing through the centre with the ball at my feet when I was tackled by Bob Barber. Our feet met and he came off worse with a suspected broken toe. He missed a match and at one time it looked as if he would not be able to play in the 1st Test. But luckily for me he recovered in time.

I renewed my friendship with Charles Fortune

(nicknamed 'Outrageous') and he and I were the regular commentators throughout the series. With his slow, articulate delivery and good command of English, Charles is a fine broadcaster and has a big following in South Africa, where for years he commentated on cricket, rugger, tennis and soccer.

There are, however, critics of Charles' cricket commentary who maintain that he neglects the score and the play and talks instead about the seagulls, scenery or what have you. They quote the story of him commentating at Adelaide one day when Ray Lindwall was bowling. At the beginning of the over he gave Lindwall's analysis as 0 for 32 and then proceeded to describe the beauties of the ground, the backdrop of the blue hills and Mount Lofty, the spire of St Peter's Cathedral, the gum trees, the seagulls settling by the sightscreen and the gay frocks and hats of the ladies. After about three minutes of this he is reported to have said: '. . . and that brings us to the end of Lindwall's over, his analysis is now 3 for 32 . . .'

A likely tale! But Charles loves to hear it told. He has made his name with that particular style of commentary and why should he change it? He was kindness itself to me and we had a most friendly atmosphere in the box. I was a bit shaken though on one hot and sticky day in Johannesburg. I handed over to Charles who had just slipped into the seat alongside me, and after so doing noticed that he was sitting there in his underpants, his trousers hanging on a peg.

Pauline had left us before Christmas to spend it at home with the children, but before leaving she bought a small present for each member of the team, which I duly presented to them on Christmas Day.

At the end of the tour I flew to Cyprus via Athens to join the *Treble Chance* team for another tour of the forces. This time it was a short one in the Middle East, taking in Cyprus, El Adam, Tobruk, Malta and home via Gibraltar. It was a tour of contrasts, with snow in Athens, sunshine in Cyprus and a dust storm in Tobruk. It was a case of 'Join the BBC and see the world'.

On returning home I was selected to introduce *House-wives Choice*, quite an accolade in those days. The producer picked out twenty or so requests for each day from the many thousands of postcards received, and the presenter then wrote his own links based on what was written on the postcards. As you can imagine, it gave me ample scope for corny gags and I think my worst one was about a request by a Mr and Mrs Morley for the Seekers to sing *I'll Never Find Another You*. I couldn't resist adding: 'Sounds the sort of song that a blind ram might sing.' I remember writing the scripts one weekend at our cottage at Swanage, where during the course of a walk on the cliffs Pauline revealed that Johnston No. 5 was due in November.

For this year's Boat Race, radio decided to have a second commentator in addition to John Snagge on the launch. The previous year, the launch had failed to keep up with the race and listeners had had to listen to the TV commentator. In case this should happen again, I was stationed on Chiswick Bridge just beyond the finish – so that at least listeners would know who had won, in the event of the launch breaking down altogether.

After Barnes Bridge, John Snagge also loses sight of the two boats for about a minute as they go round a big right-hand bend. At this point he hands over to me for about a minute, though I am always extremely careful to hand back to him in time to describe the finish.

What a marvellous career John has had with that deep, distinctive voice. Until he became famous as a newsreader with his *This Is London*, he was in OBs and not only started *Let's Go Somewhere* but even commentated on a cricket match!

John has always had his leg pulled about his famous remark during that thrilling boat race in 1952. The boats were racing canvas to canvas and John shouted: 'It's a desperately close race – I can't quite tell from here who is ahead – it's either Oxford or Cambridge!'

The first year of the experimental double tour was 1965. Following the tremendous success of the West Indies in 1963 it was generally agreed that they ought to have another tour as soon as possible, so a series of shared tours were arranged.

New Zealand and South Africa were the guinea-pigs and New Zealand were unlucky to come first and to experience cold wet weather for most of their tour. They were a young, inexperienced side and the wet wickets and damp atmosphere proved too much for them – they lost all the Tests.

South Africa were luckier with the weather, and by winning the 2nd Test at Trent Bridge won the series 1–0. They owed a lot to the two Pollock brothers – Peter and Graeme – and to the thrilling fielding of Colin Bland. His policing of the offside and his swift accurate throwing alone were worth the price of admission. For the first time I heard people saying that they must go to a match especially to watch a fielder. His two run-outs of Barrington and Jim Parks at Lord's when he hit the stumps each time from an 'impossible' angle were fantastic.

At Canterbury, Colin Bland gave a special demonstration for us on TV of picking up and throwing at a single stump. Watched by hundreds of small boys, he hit it more often than not. This was putting fielding where it belongs – at the top of priorities for all classes of cricketers. To attain this perfection, Bland used to practice for hours on end, throwing at a single stump with a hockey net at the back to stop the ball. I can't help feeling that his example on this tour did much to encourage some of the many fine fielders whom we have in county cricket today.

At about this time BBC-2 entered the cricket arena and broadcast on Sunday afternoons the limited-over matches between the International Cavaliers and the counties.

These were usually run for a charity and the county beneficiary and attracted large and enthusiastic crowds. They came to see the great Test cricketers from all the countries playing together in one team and these Sundays became a family occasion. The matches not only brought money into the game but also a fresh approach, with the gay dynamic cricket which was played. I shared the commentaries with John Arlott, Peter West and Richie Benaud with Sir Learie Constantine as the regular summariser – and how he used to enjoy it. This type of cricket was just up his street and he would have played it superbly. I once heard him give his philosophy on cricket . . . 'I never wanted to make a hundred. Who wants to make a hundred anyway? When I first went in, my immediate objective was to hit the ball to each of the four corners of the field. After that I tried not to be repetitive! . . .'

Sunday, 28 November was to be a very important day in our lives. In the early evening Pauline went into the nursing home to have her baby and I sat waiting in the hall downstairs. It seemed an awful long time, but at last a nurse came down the stairs to tell me that I had a daughter and that Pauline was fine. But she looked embarrassed and didn't look me straight in the face, and went off before I could ask any more questions.

Dr Cove-Smith then came down and said that our little daughter was in an incubator and that he wasn't quite happy about her and would consult a specialist the next day. I went up to see Pauline who was still in the delivery room and had not yet really seen the baby, but seemed blissfully happy at having a daughter. I didn't say anything about it to her but already I suspected that something was wrong.

After leaving her, I was allowed to peep at the tiny baby lying naked in the incubator and then went home to tell Cally the news that we had a daughter. She was thrilled as she loved children and had we not had another might even have left us in search of one to look after! At this stage I told her nothing but I realised that everything was not quite right.

I spent as much of the next day as I could with Pauline, but it was a busy one for me and she was left much on her own, without yet seeing the baby. I felt desperately sorry for her as she had so looked forward to another child. Meanwhile Cove and a paediatric specialist from St Mary's Hospital had examined the baby again and as a result Cove came in during the evening to say that the specialist would like to see Pauline and myself alone together the next day, with the baby.

You can imagine how we felt and neither of us slept much. I told Cally what was going on and she was wonderful and said she didn't mind what the baby was like, she would look after her. The next morning, the specialist came to Pauline's room. He was a charming man, gentle and kind but did not beat about the bush. The baby, he said, had Down's Syndrome but in a milder form called Mosaic. He and Cove had made sure that she was physically perfect, but she would undoubtedly be backward and not quite like other children. He said that she would be pretty, loving and a source of great happiness. (He was right on all three counts.)

The specialist also pointed out that some parents in our position might have to put the baby into a hospital due to their circumstances at home, but that a happy home life was the best medicine a child like this could have. Of course we didn't hesitate. Talking it over after he had left, we both realised how lucky we had been with our lives and that most of its worst features had passed us by. Now we felt it was our turn, and that this whole thing would be a challenge to us which we would accept. We promised there and then that we would do everything in our power to make Joanna – as we named her – as near as possible the same as any other child.

One thing was certain. With Cally, three brothers and a sister she was not going to lack love and care. Because she was such a rare type Guy's Hospital took a special interest in her and for the next five years she went regularly to them and Great Ormond Street for blood and development tests and an EEG on her brain. The reports got progressively better but the doctors never led us to believe that she would ever be completely normal.

Although Joanna was a happy and loving child she was naturally not always easy to bring up and train, and Pauline and Cally had to exercise a great deal of patience. They also noted down every detail of her progress in walking, talking and so on, and compared this with the rest of the family at her age. The three boys and Clare were wonderful with her from the moment we told them the facts, a few weeks after she was born. They helped look after her, bathing her and playing with her. Except for her big saucer eyes she didn't look so different to them. I am sure that this happy home life has helped her enormously and she has certainly added to the happiness and enjoyment of our own lives.

Meanwhile my life and career in the BBC had to continue, and on Boxing Day I once more flew off to Australia to cover the MCC tour for the BBC. I arrived just before the 2nd Test at Melbourne, and as usual went straight to bed and slept round the clock in the comfortable Windsor Hotel – one of my favourites anywhere in the world.

I have always found that after twelve hours sleep I am as good as new and quite unaffected by a long flight, whereas some people take several days to recover. One quite good tip is to keep your watch on English time instead of advancing it as you go further east. You can then eat something at normal English mealtimes, even if it means refusing the regular airline meals, and making do with snacks. By so doing, your usual eating habits remain unaltered and your stomach will be duly grateful.

This was another enjoyable tour under Mike Smith's

captaincy and Billy Griffith's friendly and helpful management. England won the 3rd Test in Sydney, and Australia the 4th in Adelaide, and so the Ashes remained in Australia. England's victory at Sydney was due to some fine fast bowling by David Brown and the spin of Freddie Titmus and David Allen but more especially to a magnificent innings by Bob 'Ali' Barber. Going in first he made 185 off only 255 balls and thrilled the Sydney crowd with his stroke play. It remains one of the most exciting Test innings which I have ever seen.

By now, I had come to look on Australia as a second home, with cricket, sunshine and friendly hospitality. I particularly like the contrast in its cities. Melbourne is sedate and dignified, with its large city offices, vast department stores, wide tree-lined streets with trams still running, and the fashionable and social suburbs. The Melbourne Club is a wonderful institution and I have been lucky to be elected an honorary member on all my visits. Its peaceful olde worlde atmosphere rivals that of the Athenaeum in London – without the bishops.

This reminds me of the two bishops who were having tea together at the Athenaeum during one of the Synods, which are periodically held at Church House. They were discussing the agenda for the next day, which included a debate on pre-marital sex. Both were married and they were trying to decide what line they would take. 'For instance,' said one of them, 'I never slept with my wife before I married her. Did you?' The second bishop paused for a few seconds as he nibbled a crumpet. 'I can't remember,' he finally said. 'What was her maiden name?'

Anyway, to get back to Melbourne. The cricket ground is an enormous arena about 190 yards across, surrounded by towering stands. It looks a desolate sight when only a few thousand spectators are present, but when full it is unique so far as cricket goes. It has held 90,800 *on one day* of the 5th Test against West Indies in 1961 and I personally have seen over 80,000 there. The noise and excitement has to be seen to be believed, with the players looking like small white puppets at the bottom of a large bowl.

Sydney is one of the most exciting cities in the world. In the centre near its famous bridge is the crowded business and shopping centre. At King's Cross – a combination of Montmartre and Soho – there is every kind of entertainment, restaurant and hotel. Then only fifteen minutes away are the magnificent beaches. The standard of living is high and the quality of food and drink in the restaurants is extremely good. It's a friendly place and if I were a millionaire I would buy a flat overlooking Rose Bay and fly out there in the winter. The cricket ground ranks high with all cricketers and many consider it the best in the world on which to play.

Adelaide is the most beautiful city with its broad streets, gardens and lakes and its quiet cathedral-like atmosphere. The tempo of life is slower, there is some lovely countryside and its oblong cricket ground is top of the pops for beauty.

Brisbane, where the 1st Test is usually played is more down to earth and has no attraction for me. But Perth on the Swan River is delightful and undoubtedly the city of the future, though it is so far to the west that one gets the impression of being on another continent.

From this latest MCC tour, I flew back via San Francisco and New York, spending two of my six days in America aboard the train, the *California Flyer*. Fitted with an excellent observation car, the *Flyer* wended its way across America, round mountain gorges, through deep valleys or over miles and miles of flat dull plains. It was a good way to see America – but I had never realised before that the country had so much space and so few people. Sometimes we would travel for miles without seeing a living soul!

I could have stayed longer in hilly San Francisco with its trams, Chinatown and Golden Bridge. But two days in a freezing New York was enough, for me. I saw two musicals – *Funny Girl* and *On a Clear Day* – went up the Empire

State Building and watched skaters on an open-air ice rink in the heart of the city. I don't suppose I would dare to do so now with all this mugging, but then I wandered for miles looking at famous landmarks like Broadway, Times Square, Central Park, Fifth Avenue, Wall Street and Greenwich Village.

Yet the pace of everything in America was too fast. Everyone seemed to be in a mad rush. It was nice to get back home to the family for a rest at the end of February.

14 The compleat commentator

I WAS SOON OFF again with *Treble Chance* to Germany, this time including West Berlin. It was unpleasant standing by the wall, thinking of what went on behind it, and equally eerie peeping out from our sealed train as we travelled through the Eastern Zone on our way to the Rhine Army. It was a relief to go on to Gibraltar where Pauline joined me to try to get a sun tan while we played quiz games with the forces.

In the summer of 1966 the West Indies beat England 3–1, the tour being a personal triumph for their captain, Gary Sobers, who averaged 103 in the Tests with 3 hundreds, and also took twenty wickets. His performances at this time certainly justified the claims made that he was the greatest all-rounder cricket had ever seen – though it is something impossible to prove. It was not just his batting but the fact that he was three bowlers in one and a brilliant fielder close to the wicket – and incidentally a charming and most modest person.

England were a disappointing side under three captains: M. J. K. Smith, Colin Cowdrey and Brian Close. But I have some happy memories of the series.

After an absence of three years, there was the return to Test cricket of the graceful Tom Graveney on his thirty-ninth birthday. It was a fairy-tale return, as in his first innings at Lord's he just missed his hundred by four runs, but then made up for it by making one in the 3rd Test and another in the 5th. I have always been a Graveney fan and consider that he was grossly under-played for England. But selectors, and some of his fellow players, too, always maintained that he had no stomach for a fight when the chips were down. Be that as it may, to me he always *looked* a class above most of his contemporaries.

Just before he retired Tom was sweeping the leaves away from the door of his house in Winchcombe. Two boys passed him on their bikes and he heard the following conversation: 'I say, I think Tom Graveney lives somewhere here'.

'Yes, he does, in that house where the old man is sweeping the leaves.'

Next came the emergence of Colin Milburn as a Test player. He was run out for 0 in his first innings at Old Trafford but followed with 94 in the second and 126 not out at Lord's. He was a magnificent hitter of a cricket ball and with his Billy Bunter figure was the type of crowd-puller that cricket so badly needs. But he too failed to be one of the selectors' favourites over the next three years.

It was during this summer that the BBC decided that I should divide my commentary time between TV and radio. They felt that as the BBC Cricket Correspondent it was only natural that I should do both, especially as I was now doing so much broadcasting overseas during the winter months. So long as I stayed on TV for home consumption only, my voice would not be familiar to the audiences of the various cricketing countries, and with the West Indies tour coming up it was important that the Caribbean should learn what to expect!

The two techniques are, of course, totally different and I am often asked which I have found the more difficult. The answer, perhaps surprisingly to many people, is television. On radio, with a gift of the gab and a knowledge of cricket, you are halfway there. Personality and broadcasting technique learned by experience, make up most of the other half. It is important to remember that you are the eyes and ears of the listener at home in his armchair, in his car, on the beach or listening surreptitiously to a small transistor in the drawer of his office desk.

Lobby always told us to imagine that we were describing

what was going on to one particular person, and so try to make the commentary as intimate and conversational as possible. You have in effect to paint the scene with words and that is why John Arlott has been such a great commentator. He is a poet at heart with an immense knowledge of cricketers and their history, and his vivid word pictures of a cricket match have won large radio audiences for cricket. To many people his gravel voice and Hampshire burr *are* cricket, and to me certainly they conjure up the smell of bat oil and newly mown grass.

Cricket owes John Arlott a great deal and his witty, picturesque phrases are something unique to him. Who could better his 'Mann's inhumanity to Mann', when Tufty Mann bowled George Mann in South Africa in 1948. So given a knowledge of cricket, a good vocabulary, the ability to talk and a personality to put it across, radio cricket commentary is certainly an art but not an impossible one.

Perfect television commentary is on the other hand virtually impossible. There are certain golden rules such as: 'Never speak unless you can add to the picture'; 'Do not try to describe what the viewer can see on his screen'; 'Let the camera tell the story.' But that is really putting it all far too simply.

Cricket has a mixed audience made up of possibly 25 per cent experts who know and understand what cricket is all about. The remainder are what are called fringe or marginal viewers, ready to be entertained and even educated but not essentially keen on cricket. All the experts want to hear from a commentator is who has won the toss, the state of the weather and the pitch and of course the score. They know the players by sight, they know the fielding positions and the laws and regulations of the game.

In contrast, the marginal viewer will almost certainly not know the names of all the players. He or she will not have detailed knowledge of the very difficult laws, such as what constitutes a no-ball, or place-names such as gully or 3rd man. The commentator is on a hiding to nothing, and if he compromises, which perhaps seems the obvious thing to do, he may end up by pleasing nobody at all!

By the way, people often ask me whether I ever feel nervous before or during a broadcast. I know the right answer should be 'yes', because it's always said that a performer can never be at his or her best without butterflies in the stomach. But to be truthful, except at the start of my broadcasting life, I never worried, and have no nervous tension or pains in the tum. Perhaps it would have been better if I had!

Once the cricket season was over, the Johnston ménage prepared to make its first and so far, only move. Our lease of 1A Cavendish Avenue was due to end in 1968 and our road was losing a lot of its peaceful charm since the arrival of Paul McCartney in a house opposite to us. At all hours of the day and night there were crowds of Beatle fans outside his gate. There were occasional screams and cheers as he rushed out of the electronically locked gates in his black-windowed Mini, but usually the house looked unoccupied with drawn blinds and no sign of anyone.

The explanation of this I got from Paul's butler, whom I used to meet when taking their large black dog for a walk. He said that because of the crowds the pattern of life at the house was topsy-turvy with breakfast at 11 pm, and night becoming day for the Beatle and his friends. Anyhow with the arrival of Joanna, and the other four growing up and needing rooms of their own, we felt that it was time to move. But not far! Once again my brief to Pauline was St John's Wood and almost immediately she found just what we wanted, about a quarter of a mile away in Hamilton Terrace, a broad tree-lined road between Lord's and Maida Vale.

Our new house was large and bright with plenty of room for all of us, and Cally and her two grown-up children, Jack and Anne. Furthermore, it has a wonderful garden, unusual for London, with a large lawn, a big copper-beech, pear trees and plenty of flower beds. We moved in during November and for the first time were able to enjoy central heating, something we had never had at 1A. We were naturally sorry to leave after eighteen years, but we soon liked our new house even better and I was still only ten minutes' walk from Lord's.

Unusually for me I spent the winter at home as the only tour abroad was by MCC's under-25 team to Pakistan. This gave me the opportunity to go round the country in my spare time and give lectures or make speeches at Dinner Clubs or Ladies' Luncheon Clubs. These were fun to do and quite lucrative, though I have never taken money for speaking at any cricket function – a small way of paying back all I owe to cricket.

The Luncheon Clubs are great institutions and especially strong up in the North. I have often been the only male present among two hundred women, most of them wearing exotic hats of all shapes and sizes. I normally talk for about fifty minutes about my life and experiences at the BBC, and then answer questions afterwards.

I have never been taught the art of public speaking. I just stand up and with a few notes in my hand rattle off a succession of anecdotes and stories, linking them with my life at the BBC. From experience I have learned the importance of getting a good start and for years have used the following:

'I was extremely flattered to receive Mrs X's kind invitation to speak here today, especially as she added: "You are such an expert at this sort of thing I am sure it will be no trouble to you." I told my wife: "There's someone here who thinks that I am an expert. Isn't that marvellous?" But you know what wives are: "Better look it up and make sure," she said. So we got out an Oxford Dictionary and of course she was right. There it was. *Ex* means you've had it and *Spurt* is a drip under pressure – which is exactly what I feel standing up in front of all you ladies.'

It usually gets a laugh.

Besides standing in again for Jack De Manio in *Today* for a few weeks, I was also called in to chair a TV quiz called *Top Firm* when the late Kenneth Horne suddenly fell ill. On reflection, I have been one of the biggest 'stand-ins' in the business. For Richard Dimbleby on *Twenty Questions*, for Leslie Mitchell in *How Do You View*, for Huw Wheldon in *All Your Own*, for Jack De Manio in *Today*, for Peter Dimmock in *Sportsview* and for Franklin Engelmann in *Down Your Way*.

I suppose that in some ways it is a compliment to be a stand-in, though in fairness I must point out that there was an added incentive for the BBC to use me. Against my name in the final accounts for the programme were the letters 'SNF' in brackets. They stood for 'staff no fee', so that in place of the fee that some of the others got I cost the BBC nothing!

There was another double cricket tour with India and Pakistan as the two visitors. It was a terrible May, the worst for nearly two hundred years and India lost all three of their Tests, and Pakistan two of theirs, drawing the first one at Lord's. Neither of these countries, normally so difficult to beat on their home pitches, had yet learnt to master English conditions. Their chief weakness was a lack of fast bowlers and their batsmen's inability to play the moving ball.

Barrington and Geoff Boycott were England's chief run-getters though Boycott was dropped after scoring 246 not out in the 1st Test against India at Headingley. He batted all the first day for only 106 not out and to show their disapproval of his methods the selectors dropped him from the next Test, just as they had Barrington for similar reasons in 1965.

After spending a happy family Christmas at No. 98 Hamilton Terrace I flew off on 31 December to Barbados where

I joined the MCC party in the middle of their New Year celebrations, and quickly sampled my first rum punch.

This was Colin Cowdrey's first MCC tour as captain, though he had been vice-captain five times before. He started off at a disadvantage as the selectors had somewhat irresponsibly let it be known that they would have preferred Brian Close and that Colin was only their second choice. However, with his fellow Kent Hopper, Les Ames, as his manager, Colin did a great job, and England won the series 1–0, so gaining the Wisden Trophy for the first time. Even more important than the result was the fact that Colin's side was a very happy one, with the most wonderful team spirit. They hardly put a foot wrong the whole tour, in spite of several incidents not of their making.

Colin is by nature a modest, gentle character, a practising Christian who sets himself a very high standard, and expects the same from others. As a result he has often been severely buffeted by this evil world of ours. But by his own example and understanding he has always inspired great loyalty from his players, both on this tour and during his fifteen years as captain of Kent. His Achilles heel has been a lack of confidence in his own ability – remarkable in a man who has played in 113 Tests – and a certain difficulty in making up his mind, due largely to his efforts to see and listen to everyone else's point of view. But on this tour he grew from strength to strength both on and off the field, and England were unlucky not to win the 1st and 2nd Tests as well as the 4th.

The batting of Wes Hall of all people saved West Indies in the 1st and England were undoubtedly robbed of the 3rd at Kingston by the now-famous bottle-throwing riot. This occurred when the West Indies followed on and was sparked off when Butcher was caught by Parks down the leg-side, with West Indies still 29 runs behind and only five wickets standing. Bottles poured on to the field, mostly from an open stand to the right of our broadcasting box.

The combination of heat and rum had obviously affected the crowd, who shouted and jeered at the police as they tried to restore order.

At considerable danger to himself, Cowdrey went and pleaded with them to no effect, so the police decided to use tear gas to empty the stand. Unfortunately, they forgot all about the direction of the wind. It blew the gas away from the stand, past the Press and broadcasting boxes, and right across the ground to the Pavilion, where VIPs and their ladies, players and officials were caught in its flow. There was a mad dash by both sexes to take shelter in the ladies' loo at the back, but everyone was weeping and holding handkerchiefs to their eyes as if they had just heard Al Jolson sing *Sonny Boy*.

We tried hard to continue broadcasting but were spluttering and choking so much that we had to hand back to the studio, while in the Press box next door the clattering of the typewriters gradually ceased altogether. Pauline, who had joined me in Jamaica, took some splendid photographs of the cloud of gas drifting over the ground, with Colin reluctantly leading his players off the field.

Play was resumed about eighty minutes later in front of a half-empty ground. But England were naturally affected by what had happened and lost the tight hold they had had on the game, and in fact nearly lost it when extra time was played the next day. If ever there was justification for the expression 'we was robbed' this was it.

The victory by seven wickets in the 4th Test was a splendid performance by England, who won with only three minutes to spare. Even more exciting was the draw in the 5th Test when on the sixth day England just held out with the last man, Jeff Jones, playing a maiden off the last over bowled by Lance Gibbs. He was surrounded by the entire West Indies side and I doubt if his bat touched the ball once! The whole success of the series depended on him staying there, and I have always nominated this as one of the most thrilling Tests which I have ever watched.

Off the field we had a fabulous time on the glorious beaches and especially enjoyed the scenery of the smaller islands like St Lucia and Antigua. But though it was paradise on the surface underneath it all one felt a current of nationalist and political feelings. Barbados was, and still is, the least spoilt and is the most friendly to visitors. It was here that we had the near-tragedy of Freddie Titmus' toes.

We were all bathing at Sandy Lane Beach, and some of the boys were playing around with a small motor boat, which had a propeller underneath the middle of the boat instead of at the stern, as in most boats. Freddie went to give it a push and in the buoyant salt water his legs were sucked under the boat and his four toes on his left foot were cut off, luckily just above where the nerves go into the foot. He was rushed to hospital, where an efficient team of doctors were waiting to operate on him. The remarkable thing is that he felt no pain at all at the time and has never done so since. What's more, he played for Middlesex in the summer and nearly did the double, taking 111 wickets and making 924 runs, which only goes to show how small a part our toes play in our movements. It's the big toe which is the vital balancing factor and had he lost that, Freddie might never have played again.

A happier occasion was the night when some of us were dining in a restaurant full of American tourists. Our waiter – as they all do out there – soon got talking about cricket and told Colin Cowdrey that he was a useful fast bowler and would like to bowl at MCC in the nets. We decided to try him out and cleared a few tables from near the dance floor. We then put down an ice bucket as the stumps and Colin with a large serving spoon took up his position at the wicket.

Then, to the amazement of the Americans, this tall, athletic-looking waiter took a long run, wending his way through the tables and delivered a fast yorker with a round bread roll. It hit the base of the ice bucket without Colin getting a touch and he there and then invited the waiter to bowl at the nets next day, which he duly did. Where else in the world could such a thing happen?

I have spared you most of my puns which I fear have been the bane of my friends' lives for countless years, but I can't resist telling one I made in Port of Spain. One of my press colleagues had made friends with a pretty American girl who was staying out there and he used to see quite a lot of her! One evening we were going to have a drink and a swim at the Hilton and as we arrived my friend and the girl emerged from the hotel. He couldn't avoid us, so rather sheepishly introduced her to us as Annette: 'Oh,' I couldn't stop myself saying, 'that's what you've been doing. I thought you were going to practise cricket every time you said you were about to have a net (Annette!)', I am glad to say that she laughed but I'm not so sure about him!

One interesting side to the tour was that BBC TV sent out a producer, two cameramen and a sound recordist to film the Test matches. Denis Compton and I did the commentaries and the films were flown back to London each night. It meant a lot of hard work for me, as no sooner had I finished my ball-by-ball commentary session on radio, than I had to climb a ladder to join our TV team and do a stint for them. It had never been done before at cricket but it seemed to work well, and we actually received a congratulatory note from the TV chiefs on returning to England – a rare enough event to be recorded!

15 Simply not cricket!

I GOT BACK TO England in early April after what had been a lovely tour, and I am glad that I went when I did, as from what I hear the Caribbean is not now such a happy and carefree place as it was.

That summer Bill Lawry captained the Australians and the series was drawn with Australia winning the 1st Test at Old Trafford and England under Colin Cowdrey the 5th at the Oval, though it's probable that bad weather robbed England of victory at Lord's as well. Except for a swash-buckling 83 by Colin Milburn at Lord's, my main memory of the series is of the dramatic finish to the 5th Test and the repercussions which followed Basil D'Oliveira's 158 in the same match.

To take the result first. At lunch on the last day, Australia, set 352 to win, were 86 for 5 with three and a half hours left. It looked odds on for an English victory until during lunch there was a cloudburst and the Oval became a lake.

Although the sun came out, further play looked impossible to everyone except Ted Warne, the groundsman, and Colin Cowdrey. Ted recruited volunteer labour from the crowd, who with a collection of blankets, mops and squeegees helped the ground staff to dry out the ground. It drained rapidly until only miniature lakes were left. Soon even these disappeared, and miraculously the umpires decided that play could start at 4.45 pm, giving seventy-five minutes of possible play.

Thanks to Derek Underwood who took 7 for 50 on a pitch made to measure for him, England won with six minutes to spare. I still think that the photograph of all eleven Englishmen appealing for the final lbw against

Inverarity is one of the most remarkable cricket pictures I have ever seen – every man in the team within a few yards of the bat.

But much as England owed to Underwood and the volunteer band of drier-ups, they owed as much to Basil D'Oliveira, who, although missed when 31, and three more times after his hundred, went on to make a magnificent 158, and so started one of the most unfortunate chapters in the history of modern cricket.

Basil had had an unsatisfactory tour of the West Indies, where he not only missed a lot of catches but was out of form with both bat and ball. After his performance on that tour, I think it is fair to say that of those who went to the West Indies, either to report, broadcast or just watch, very few would ever have picked him for any future MCC tour.

But then fate played a hand. Roger Prideaux had been selected for the 5th Test against Australia at the Oval, but came down with tonsilitis. So Doug Insole, the Chairman of Selectors, consulted the captain, Colin Cowdrey, whose opinion was that Dolly's bowling might be useful and he'd like him to play. So he did, and if Jarman had caught him when 31 nothing more would have come of it. But after his 158, made when England were up against it, everyone agreed that the selectors could not leave him out of the MCC team to South Africa.

They met at Lord's on the Wednesday and Thursday after the Oval Test and there was a conference called for 6 pm to announce the team. It was my job to give the team first to the world as I had a microphone just outside the committee room and the 6 pm news were prepared to take me live as soon as the team was chosen. With the smell of drama in the air, the meeting was packed, as it was realised that if Dolly were chosen, the tour could be in jeopardy as no guarantee had been given (or asked for) that he would be acceptable to the South African Government. They had announced in April that teams of mixed race would be able to tour South Africa if they were teams from countries with which South Africa had traditional sporting ties, and 'if no political capital was made out of the situation'. This last sentence was vital and seemed to put a question mark against Dolly. As a native of South Africa his presence might be political dynamite to the South African Government.

There was a deathly hush as Billy Griffith read out the names of the team selected in alphabetical order. By halfway down it was obvious that Dolly had *not* been chosen and there was a buzz of excitement round the room. I could not wait to hear the explanations and I rushed out to announce the team over the air, within seconds of it being given. I read it out in my usual way when giving teams, batsmen first, then bowlers, wicket-keepers and all-rounders. As Dolly would have been in the last category listeners did not know whether he was in or not until I had finished.

From that moment on, all hell was let loose. The ordinary man in the street could not understand how he could have been left out after his 158. The Press as a whole took a cynical view of Doug Insole's statement that the selectors had looked on Dolly as a batsman and not as an all-rounder for overseas purposes. The selectors were accused of racism, bowing to political pressure and sheer incompetence. A group of indignant MCC members called for a special meeting to censure their committee and the *News of the World* finally put the cat among the pigeons when they engaged Dolly to report the tour for them.

Things were not helped when, ironically, Tom Cartwright, the *all-rounder* who had been selected, declared himself unfit and cried off the tour. The selectors then promptly chose in his place D'Oliveira, whom they had previously said they did not rate as an all-rounder for overseas. This was the last straw so far as the South African Government was concerned. Mr Vorster, the Prime Minister, announced that he could not receive a team forced on

South Africa by 'political influences', and MCC accordingly cancelled the tour.

It was all terribly sad for cricket and everyone felt great sympathy for Dolly, the unwilling cause of all the trouble, who behaved impeccably and with dignity throughout. I still think the selectors were right in their original selection, but some of their statements made their final choice of Dolly appear to be contradictory and to justify the accusation that they had yielded to pressure.

And so robbed of a winter in South African sunshine, the rest of the year slipped quietly by with the usual number of quizzes and interviews, and a month introducing *Today*. But MCC managed to arrange a short tour of Pakistan and Ceylon and I persuaded the BBC to let me cover the three Tests in Pakistan, arriving in time for the first one at Lahore in the middle of February.

Except for the occasional stop-off at an airport, I had never been to either India or Pakistan and it was quite an experience. The pungent smells of the East, the heat and dust, the beggars, the noisy markets and the apparent lack of care for either human beings or animals, were all quite new to me. So were the disorderly crowds at the matches. It was a time of political unrest and the left-wing students seemed to be in control almost everywhere, in spite of the efforts of the police in Lahore and Karachi.

During one of the noisiest demonstrations in the 1st Test, seats were being hurled about in all directions and it was a wonder that no one was seriously hurt. Aftab Gul, the local student leader, was batting for Pakistan at the time and when he was out, instead of returning to the pavilion, he went straight across to the students and appealed to them to be quiet, and this had some effect.

MCC were due to play the 2nd Test at Dacca in East Pakistan but the trip was on and off because of serious street fighting there, which had resulted in many deaths. Colin Cowdrey and Les Ames, who managed the tour with great patience and tact, had conferences with the British

High Commissioner who finally persuaded them to go, on the assurance that they would have full police protection at the match and that the army would meet them and escort them from the airport. If MCC had refused to go and play a Test in Dacca the local students threatened more riots and burnings, and the lives of the Europeans would obviously have been in danger. So a cricket tour had become wholly political and MCC were being used as a lever to achieve the students' ends.

We flew off to Dacca full of foreboding but encouraged by the promise of police and army support. Imagine everyone's surprise when the local representative of the British High Commission welcomed Colin and Les with the news that there was no army about, though he hinted they were in reserve if needed, and that there would be no police whatsoever at the Test match. The students had insisted on organising the whole thing and Colin had several conferences with their leaders in his hotel bedroom before agreeing to go on with the match. Remarkable to relate, the crowds were the best-behaved of the whole tour, though admittedly they were behind wire-netting so could not invade the field of play. But whenever there was a disturbance in a stand the students' committee sorted it out straightaway, and we never saw a single policeman during the whole match.

But the police were back in force at Karachi where political tension was just as high and there was strong feeling against the Pakistan selectors for failing to make the local hero, Hanif, captain in place of Saeed. On the first two days there were the usual interruptions of play and scuffles with the police. The third day had been declared a general strike in Karachi and the students made it known that they thought that there should be no cricket either on that day. There was clearly going to be trouble.

Colin, after making 14, had flown home on the death of his father and Tom Graveney was captaining England, who went on batting into the third day. I was doing TV com-

mentary for the local Pakistan station when Alan Knott
reached 96. David Brown was his partner and together
they had put on 75 runs for the eighth wicket. All seemed
set for Knotty's first Test hundred when a section of the
crowd suddenly erupted and jumped over the fence,
reinforced by a crowd of students who had somehow
gained entry to the ground. They raced across the ground
towards the pitch shouting and screaming as they went. It
was bedlam. Both Knotty and David had seen them coming
and though hampered by pads and bats set off for the
pavilion, followed by the fielders and umpires.

They must have been near to breaking the Olympic 100-
metre record as they dived into the safety of the dressing-
rooms. I tried to commentate on the TV but someone
pulled the plug out and the picture and sound disappeared.
The rioters did what damage they could to the pitch and
then swept towards the VIP stand, where there were
comfortable armchairs and thick carpets under a giant
awning. The VIPs were no fools and had already sensed
danger some time before and were sheltering in the pavilion. Just as well.

Their stand was completely wrecked, chairs broken,
carpets ripped up, tables overturned. It was a horrifying
sight to watch a mob at work and I admit to feeling scared
even though I was up in the TV tower. But there was no
guarantee that they would not wreck that too. However,
they decided to set fire to some of the other stands and
the English Press and myself managed to dash for the
safety of the English dressing-room.

Police reinforcements arrived and we were smuggled
into cars and whisked back to our hotel. I think there were
at least twelve of us in our car, piled on each others laps
– and the driver's! I had to go out again to the local radio
station to send my report back to England but this was not
easy as there were no taxis and the streets were not too
safe. Anyway I managed somehow, after first doing a quick
recording with Les Ames, who was busy arranging an

immediate flight home, the match obviously having been abandoned.

We hurriedly packed and flew back that night, arriving at London Airport on Sunday morning, highly relieved but not highly amused. The team had all behaved extremely well under all the stresses of the tour but politics had come first and cricket had suffered.

In the final Test, England had scored 502–7 when play was stopped. Top scorer was Colin Milburn with a brilliant 139. He had been summoned from Australia to join the team during the second Test and his arrival had boosted the morale of the team. They went to meet him at Dacca airport and as he came down the steps of the aircraft they garlanded him with flowers.

He then solemnly shook hands with the lined-up team to the amazement of the airport staff, who were even more amazed when Olly and the team burst into a chorus of his theme song, *The Green, Green Grass of Home*.

Here was a cricketer who by his exciting batting and his cheerful Billy Bunter personality exuded an aura of fun whether on or off the cricket field. The crowds loved him. So did his fellow players. He and I used to sing *Underneath the Arches* and *Me and My Shadow*, using the question and answer technique.

B.J. Where were you last night, Ollie?
C.M. Underneath the Arches.
B.J. Did you have a bed?
C.M. On cobblestones I lay.
B.J. Where did you say?
C.M. Underneath the Arches.
B.J. What do you do there?
C.M. I dream my dreams away . . . *and so on*.

Luckily, his singing drowned most of my wrong notes on the piano. You can imagine therefore how I felt when our newsroom rang me at Lord's on Saturday, 24 May and asked me to do a piece about Colin Milburn in the 1 pm news. He had had a car accident and had lost his left eye.

I was really shattered. What a loss to cricket. Just when he had shown that he must be a regular choice for England. Only a week before, Colin had made what was possibly his most brilliant hundred – 158 in seventy-seven overs with five sixes and sixteen fours. I did my best to do him justice but for the first time on radio I nearly broke down. I took him a bottle of champagne the following week when I went to visit him in hospital at Northampton. There he was, as big and smiling as ever, and we even slipped into 'The Arches' for a few bars. But cricket had been his life, not just playing but the whole social side of it, and in the winter he had become just as big a favourite in Western Australia. He was to find the next few years hard going, in spite of a bumper benefit of over £20,000.

This was one of the double tour years with West Indies in the first half, and they lost two Tests and drew one. Colin Cowdrey had damaged his Achilles tendon in a Sunday match at the end of May so Ray Illingworth, after only a month as captain of Leicestershire found himself captain of England for all six Tests – the start of a long sequence.

As England also won two Tests against New Zealand, Illy got off to a good start. But the Tests were undistinguished and there were few outstanding performances. The most important feature of the season was the start of the John Player League in which each county plays the other once, on Sundays, in a single innings match of forty overs each. It was an immediate success and drew large family crowds who had learnt the fun and excitement of instant cricket from the International Cavaliers.

The Cavaliers were badly treated by the counties, who dropped them as soon as a sponsor came up with some money, seemingly forgetful of how the Cavaliers had helped their beneficiaries, besides providing their members and crowds with some capital entertainment.

With no MCC tour scheduled, I was delighted to receive a novel invitation from Charles Fortune in South Africa. He invited me to be the 'neutral' commentator in the four-Test series between South Africa and Australia due to start in January. So far as I know this was the first time that any cricketing country had asked an outsider to join their commentary team except when his own country was taking part in the series.

The BBC very kindly allowed me to accept, and after spending Christmas in bed with 'flu I looked forward to two months of sunshine and sharing the commentaries with my old colleagues, Charles Fortune and Alan McGilvray.

We were to see the annihilation of the Australians, tired after a strenuous tour of India. They were completely outplayed by the superb South African team who, captained by Ali Bacher, won all four Tests by large margins.

For pure perfection, I doubt if I have ever seen a partnership to rival that of Barry Richards and Graeme Pollock in the 2nd Test at Durban. They added 103 in one hour for the third wicket, matching each other's strokes boundary by boundary. It was technically perfect cricket, Richards scoring 140 and Pollock 274. I shall never forget it.

There was obviously much talk of the coming tour of England in the summer. Would it take place? Would the anti-apartheid campaigner, Peter Hain, and his friends carry out their threats to stop the games? Was barbed-wire really being put up on the cricket grounds of England? The South African cricketers themselves were keen to make the tour, no matter what difficulties lay ahead. They were undoubtedly the best team in the world and they wanted to prove it against their old opponent, England.

I am one of those people who do not think that politics should interfere with sport. I happen to believe that in spite of the inevitable minor incidents, it is still a good thing for people of all races, religions and colours, be they capitalists or communists to play and compete against each other. If we only competed against those whom we liked or of whose politics we approved, there would soon be no people left to play.

Which brings me to South Africa. I love the country and have many friends there, but I definitely do not support apartheid and the way it inflicts unnecessary indignities and restrictions on the coloureds and black people. But this does not stop me visiting the country – any more than I would refuse to go to Russia, Greece or Argentina if I wanted to.

I am convinced that things are slowly getting better in South Africa and will continue to do so if the people there are left alone to sort out their great problem. Our Lord made a good statement about this once. 'First cast out the beam out of thine own eye . . .' As Lord Montgomery once said in a speech when quoting a saying of our Lord '. . . and I quite agree with Him'.

16 From ashes to Ashes

As soon as I got home in the middle of March I had a personal problem to deal with. I heard whispers that while I had been away, TV had decided not to use me as a cricket commentator any more.

As I had heard nothing official, I went to seek confirmation from my boss Robert Hudson, the head of radio OBs. He confirmed it unofficially but said that he would rather I waited to be told officially by TV. But to my relief he did add how delighted he was, from radio's point of view, as this would mean he could now have me for all the Tests. His remarks were cheering, as I must admit that I was a bit shocked at the suddenness of it all, though relieved that it had happened.

For the last few years, TV had been changing. The powers that be said they wanted an increasingly professional and disciplined approach – which so far as cricket was concerned meant sticking rigorously to the play to the exclusion of all else. Jokes, stories, anecdotes or light-hearted asides were frowned on and the camera was no longer encouraged to find off-beat pictures of a blonde in a bikini on the grass or small boys playing cricket round the boundary edge.

The emphasis was to be on an analysis of technique and tactics with an efficient appraisal of what was happening on the twenty-two yards of pitch. So be it. But it was not my cup of tea. A cricket match includes so many other things besides what goes on in the middle. It is a game full of character and fun and there is always laughter not far away. But not if you have a producer shouting down your ear . . . 'Steady – no jokes – stick to the cricket!'

As a result of this policy, TV has now become a highly

efficient purveyor of cricket with superb camerawork and great expertise from the old Test players who now do the commentary. But it has lost its soul and humour and is angled towards the cricketer viewer, and not the majority who don't play and don't know too much about the game, either.

As I write this just after a Test match, four newspapers have praised the efficient and highly technical service given by TV. But each one has added that it lacks the humour and friendliness of the radio, ball by ball. It is because of this that more and more people watch the TV picture and listen to our radio commentary.

The same thing was happening in Australia when I was last there. So although my pride was hurt – no one likes to be dropped, whatever the reason – I was secretly pleased to be leaving TV after twenty-four years. *But it would have been nice to have been told!* It is unbelievable but true that I am still waiting to hear from the Head of Sport in TV OBs. He presumably made the decision, but I have never heard from anyone in TV that I was being dropped nor the reasons for it.

After about a month, when told I had heard nothing, Peter Dimmock, General Manager of TV OBs, wrote me a short note in his own hand saying he personally would miss me but that it was radio's gain! But no explanation, no thanks nor appreciation from the Head of Sport, which was not too much to expect after twenty-four years, in which I had re-started the cricket after the war and helped to create and develop the commentary technique. In addition I had done countless cricket interviews and pro-grammes and had been their consultant on all cricketing matters for a quarter of a century.

I am afraid I sound bitter, and in this very small context I am. I think it is time that TV grew up and learned to deal with people properly. I know it's the technical playground of whizz-kids, but they still ought to have good manners and behave as normal human beings in their relations with the people they employ.

I am saying all this, partly to get it off my chest but also because some freelances, whom I know, have been treated far worse than me. I at least had the welcome refuge of radio. This is my only complaint against the BBC in my long career with them. They have always been kindness itself. But I just hope that this may catch the eye of one of the top TV men, who may then ensure that in future, TV matches radio in the quality of its manners and behaviour.

The spring was largely taken up with speculation about the coming South African tour. There were meetings, conferences and demonstrations, and Peter Hain and co. threatened to disrupt the matches if the tour did take place.

The Cricket Council came under strong pressure from the Home Secretary, James Callaghan, and was 'requested' to withdraw the invitation to South Africa. That was as good as a directive, and on 22 May the tour was cancelled. It saved cricket commentators from possible verbal embarrassment. In the South African side was A. M. Short of Natal. I personally was dreading having to announce that Boycott had been caught Short in front of the pavilion!

In place of the South African tour a five-Test series was quickly arranged against a strong 'Rest of the World' side containing, ironically, five top South African players: the two Pollocks, Barlow, Richards and Procter. The Cricket Council designated these Tests as unofficial and the England players were to be awarded home caps. On this basis the series was sponsored in order to give an extra incentive to win and to avoid suspicion that they were in any way exhibition matches.

On the guarantee that the Tests were to be unofficial – and so count in Test match records as unofficial – BBC TV and radio both gave their usual full coverage. But ever since the International Cricket Council has queried the right of the Cricket Council to have staged even unofficial Tests without their approval. Statisticians too have had heated arguments among themselves as to whether the figures should be included in records of Test careers. Personally I am strongly in favour of recognising the Tests but think that an awful lot of unnecessary fuss has been made about the whole thing.

England, not unexpectedly, lost the series 1–4 against this very powerful Rest of the World side captained by Gary Sobers. In addition to the South Africans it included Lloyd, Kanhai, Murray from West Indies, Mustaq and Intikhab from Pakistan, Engineer from India and McKenzie from Australia. If a game against a side like that is not a Test match, what is?

Ray Illingworth captained England and, remarkably, was top scorer with 476 runs averaging 52.88. This form ensured his selection as captain of MCC for the winter tour of Australia and New Zealand, but not without a certain amount of unpleasantness and controversy.

The trouble was that many people in authority felt that Colin Cowdrey would make a better *tour* captain than Illy. After all, he had already been vice-captain on three previous Australian tours. Illy's selection was a bitter disappointment to the sensitive Colin and it was some time before he could be persuaded to accept the vice-captaincy for the fourth time. You could hardly blame him, but it was not a good way to start the tour.

For the first time there were to be six Tests in Australia so as to include Perth for the first time, and for the first time, too, I was to cover all the Tests for BBC. Previously I had always missed the 1st Test at Brisbane.

But before making my preparations to leave for Australia Pauline and I spent a delightful holiday in Jersey at the end of September, when most of the crowds had gone. It was a splendid place to relax after all the excitements of the last few months. Maurice Allom, the Chairman of the

Cricket Council, and his wife Pam were also there, and Don Wilson of Yorkshire and his wife Jill.

One night Pauline and I went to a night club and we were recognised. The compere, an eccentric extrovert called Ronald Ronalde (not the whistling one) announced that he would sing a song in our honour which he had recently sung in front of the Queen at the Royal Variety Performance. The holidaymakers lapped it up. Here is the song, sung to a catchy old music-hall tune:

> Show me your winkle tonight
> When the lights are low.
> Show me your winkle tonight
> And set my heart a-glow.
> Oh, what a surprise
> When it dangles in front of my eyes.
> My heart is thumping with fright
> Show me your winkle tonight
> That's right!

A few nights later we all returned to the club and Maurice, Don and myself were invited to stand up and sing it to the night-club audience. Not a bad advertisement for cricket I thought at the time. President of MCC and Chairman of the Cricket Council, a Yorkshire and England cricketer, and a BBC commentator, singing a trio in a night club. I don't know about the singing but at least it proved the harmony which exists among cricketers.

This was to be the last tour which I covered for BBC and except for one or two incidents, I enjoyed it as much as I had all the others. Pauline joined me after Christmas and we saw more of Australia than we ever had before, when we motored the 1,100 miles from Adelaide to Sydney with John Woodcock as our companion.

The first part of the journey was miles and miles of nothing with the temperatures in the nineties. But then we came to the peaceful Murray Valley and the beautiful

Snowy Mountains. Many of the small towns we passed through were reminiscent of the one-street cowboy towns of the films and it was an education to see how the other half of Australia lived, away from the big cities.

On our way down to Sydney we stopped to pay homage at the house in Bowral where Don Bradman was brought up as a child. We saw his tiny bedroom and the small backyard where he started his cricket.

Ray Illingworth was not the usual type of MCC captain. He saw it as his sole job to win back the Ashes and if he had to devote more time to cricket than to the social side of the tour then that was too bad. He had always appreciated the tough way Australians play their cricket and he was prepared to match them. They respected him for it.

Illy was more Yorkshire than Yorkshire itself. Honest, blunt, fair, with not too much time for the niceties of life. But he had the backing of his team, who were intensely loyal to him, and he got the best out of them on the field. Illy was a good tactician and reader of a game and an accurate assessor of his opponents' weaknesses.

He achieved his object of regaining the Ashes by winning the two Tests at Sydney and the series 2–0, though the final Test at Sydney was at one time a close thing and a magnificent team effort.

Geoff Boycott was the outstanding batsman of the tour, scoring 657 runs in five Tests, averaging 93.85. But he had his left wrist broken by McKenzie in a one-day game and he could not play at Sydney.

Similarly, John Snow was the outstanding bowler taking thirty-one wickets in the series. But he broke a finger when fielding in the vital second innings at Sydney and could only bowl two overs. Even without their two best players, England won in the end by 62 runs, and his team chaired Illy off the field.

Once again – as in 1953 when England last regained the Ashes – I was lucky to be on the air for the *coup de grâce* and Radio 2 stayed open all night to hear our ball-by-ball commentaries. Once again, too, I was able to share the triumph of a team with whom I had been touring for four months, living with them through the good times and the bad.

After the stress and excitements of Australia we spent a very happy and relaxed eighteen days in New Zealand. I am ashamed to say it was my first visit, as the BBC had never thought it worth the expense to send me. In fact, even this time I went at my own risk, being paid by the New Zealand Broadcasting Corporation for all my commentaries.

This was an unusual procedure, as in the past McGilvray, Fortune, Lawrence and myself have always been paid for by our respective bosses and so have broadcast without fee when visiting other countries. We were lucky with the weather, and the team thoroughly enjoyed the chance to unwind slowly before returning home.

New Zealand is a gorgeous country with magnificent scenery and I hope one day to return there for a long holiday. During our stay we decided to try and emulate the England World Cup XI and record a victory song. I scribbled out some words and aided by John Henderson of Reuters we produced four verses designed to fit the tune of the *Winkle Song*, which at least we all knew.

We rehearsed in hotel bedrooms and even on the plane home via Los Angeles, and finally gave the song full treatment as we crossed the English coast, much to the surprise of some American passengers, who kept on looking for the Ashes we said we were bringing home.

Although we got back on 12 March we did not record the song until 19 April when the team were all going to be in London for an MCC dinner in their honour. This delay was to prove fatal to the success of the song. At any rate that's our excuse! In spite of quite a lot of publicity and airings on Radio 2, our record never caught the public's fancy and try as we might we failed to get on *Top of the Pops* on TV.

But though we failed to make a fortune we had a great deal of fun doing it. We had to wait for the spring of 1973 before we heard that our royalties had reached the princely sum of £53.86! We decided to have a draw for four prizes rather than distribute it among all of us. I asked Illy to do the draw at the Test trial at Hove in 1973 and guess whose name came out of the hat first. It was Illy himself who won the first prize of £25, with John Henderson, John Edrich and Bob Willis being the other lucky ones. Here are the words of the song and perhaps they are the best explanation of why it never became a hit!

We've brought the Ashes back home
We've got them here in the urn
The Aussies had had them twelve years
So it was about our turn.
But oh! What a tough fight
It's been in the dazzling sunlight
In spite of the boos of the mob on the Hill
We've won by two matches to nil.

When we arrived people said
The Aussies would leave us for dead
But we knew we would prove them wrong
And that's why we're singing this song
Oh! The feeling is great
For losing is something we hate
So Sydney we thank you for both of our wins
But not for those bottles and tins.

Our openers gave us a good start
And the others then all played their part
We usually made a good score
Seven times three hundred or more
The Aussies however were apt
To collapse at the drop of a hat
If they were bowled any ball that was short
It was ten to one on they'd be caught.

In the field it was often too hot
So sometimes we felt very low
Whether rain was forecast or not
We always knew we'd have Snow
So now to go home we are free
And we're sure the Aussies agree
Though the series has been a long uphill climb
We've all had a real bumper time.

But there is one happy note with which to end the saga of our victory song. The Prime Minister, Edward Heath, gave a reception to the team, the accompanying Press, and the broadcaster at No. 10, and we presented him with a disc of our song. This was rather a cheeky and presumptuous thing to do in view of his love of good music and skill as an organist. But he was kind enough to send a letter to me and my opinion of him as a judge of good music rose even higher than it had been before.

He said of the record: 'I enjoyed listening to it – and congratulate you on your musical and literary skills'! It is my exclamation mark, not his, but I think you can now better understand how he became the top politician in the country.

17 A bang, not a whimper

IN THE SPRING OF 1971 I managed to spend a week on a boat on the Thames with my sons Andrew and Ian, and we travelled up as far as Oxford and down just below Windsor. I appointed myself non-playing captain and let the boys do everything.

All went well except once when we forgot to pull up the anchor and dragged it for several miles before we discovered why the boat was going so slowly! Travelling like this is a holiday which I thoroughly recommend. There is a splendid camaradarie on the river, and it was encouraging to see as many novices as ourselves doing equally clottish things. We spent a pleasant day at Oxford seeing the colleges and I must admit it did my ego good when we went into the pavilion on the New College Cricket Ground and found my picture as captain of the 1934 side still hanging on the wall, with my Sealyham, Blob, sitting at my feet.

The double tour by Pakistan and India gave final proof that they were both now in the top league and that England were not going to have it their own way on future tours of this country as they had had in the past. Pakistan lost their series 0–1 but rain undoubtedly robbed them of victory in the 1st Test at Edgbaston, and England only just won at Headingley by 25 runs.

India were more successful, and at the Oval in the 3rd Test beat England for the first time in this country amidst scenes of tremendous enthusiasm. Back in India there was wild rejoicing and the team became such national heroes that their Prime Minister, Indira Gandhi, had their plane diverted so that she could personally congratulate them on their success.

If not so good for England, it was wonderful for cricket, especially as India's success was largely due to superb spin bowling by Venkat, Chandrasekhar and Bedi. What a relief from the dreary old seam, and the England batsmen short of practice against class spin, just could not cope. There was one unusual feature of the England batting. John Jameson the hard-hitting opener played in the last two Tests and was run out in three of his four innings. None were his fault and Boycott was not playing in either match. How unlucky can you be!

My co-commentators on the six Tests were John Arlott, Alan Gibson and Neil Durden-Smith, with caustic, expert and witty comments from Trevor Bailey. We also had summaries from Pakistan and India but in truth did not always find them easy to understand. But we had plenty of fun in the box and offered the listeners a variety of styles in our commentaries. I am afraid that some of the names offered tempting opportunities to make puns. When the wicket-keeper let byes off Bedi's bowling they became 'Bedi byes', or when comparing two of their batsmen it was 'Sardesai' which was the better.

After a pleasant holiday with Pauline in Cornwall I returned to the BBC for my last year as a member of the staff. Retirement age is sixty and I was to reach that frightening target on 24 June 1972. As this would be in the middle of the cricket season it was decided that I should stay on until the end of the season and retire on 30 September. I was due for a lot of compensatory leave so I arranged to take it at the beginning of the following year which would enable me to go to Australia to follow the series there against a World XI, which as with us, had taken the place of a cancelled South African tour.

I filled in the autumn by temporarily taking over the chairmanship of *Sports Forum* from Peter West. This was a sporting brains trust, which was recorded at some sports club on Thursday nights and transmitted in *Sport on Two* the following Saturday afternoon. The panel consisted of a columnist like Jim Manning or Peter Wilson and two top sports stars. It was a useful forum for presenting opinions, criticisms and informal discussion on any sporting topic.

I have known Peter West since he joined me on TV cricket in the late forties, and he has been the most versatile of all the TV commentators. His wide range of sports has included cricket, lawn tennis, rugby, football, athletics and hockey, plus of course his winter invasion of the dancing world as the genial compere of *Come Dancing*. I suppose it could be said that he tried to do too much, but I am sure that his reply to that would be that he is still on friendly terms with his bank manager!

I enjoyed my years with him on the TV cricket commentary team immensely. With Peter and Denis Compton about there was always plenty of laughter and I honestly cannot remember a cross word ever passing between the three of us.

We had our usual family Christmas with all of us having stockings and everyone (Barry 22, Clare 20, Andrew 17, Ian 14 and Joanna 6) opening them on Pauline's and my bed at 8 o'clock in the morning. I must admit I am a sucker for Christmas and we have been lucky to have our children to share it with us over so many years. Three days later I flew off to Australia.

Once again I had been invited to be a neutral commentator – this time by ABC television – and I covered the matches with Alan McGilvray and Lindsay Hassett. We were lucky enough to see one of the most fantastic innings ever played in international cricket – Gary Sobers' 254 at Melbourne.

I have never seen more thrilling stroke play, much of it unorthodox, with feet a long way from the ball. By the end, even the fielders were applauding the scorching drives, hooks and cuts. ABC TV made a film of it with a commentary by Don Bradman, who said it was the best innings which he had ever seen in Australia. I think he still considers Stan McCabe's 232 at Trent Bridge in 1938 as the best which he saw anywhere.

After the last match at Adelaide I flew to South Africa for a fortnight's holiday. Pauline and Andrew met me at Durban and after a week by the sea at the lovely Oyster Box Hotel we went up to St Lucia to see my sister Anne once again. We left Andrew with her to spend a year in South Africa to see a bit of life and get used to looking after himself.

I got back to England in the middle of February 1972 and on Thursday, 2 March heard the very sad news that Franklin Engelmann had died suddenly of a heart attack in the night, only a few hours after recording *Down Your Way* on the Wednesday. It was decided that this would still be used at the usual time on the Sunday, but there was no immediate decision as to who would take over the programme at such short notice, although it would have to be recorded in six days' time.

Franklin Engelmann – known as 'Jingle' – had been presenting *Down Your Way* since 1953 and after 733 programmes everyone associated the programme with him. It was going to be an impossible task to follow him and needless to say after a couple of days I was asked to do it! Once again I was to be a stand-in but only for a week or two, I was told, while a permanent substitute was found.

In the end I did ten programmes before my cricket commitments forced me to give up, and four different interviewers were selected, to fill in during the summer. I had evidently not done too badly as I was asked to take over the programme again in October, when of course I would be a freelance after retiring from the BBC staff.

I must confess that the very first programme which I did at Hyde in Cheshire the week after Jingle died was not easy and I felt very diffident and humble following in his footsteps. He had had such a large faithful following that I thought they would regard me as an intruder and resent me taking over. But I need not have worried. I received nothing but the most friendly and encouraging letters, and it is one of the most satisfying and rewarding programmes which I have ever done.

In April we enjoyed a happy family occasion when we went along to the Savoy Hotel to hear Barry's group 'Design', who were appearing as the main act in the cabaret. Barry had left Eton at the age of seventeen and a half after taking his A Levels. It would be untrue to say either that he had left his mark on the school or that Eton had left its mark on him. He was always a bit of a rebel and found it difficult to conform to discipline and regulations, so, unlike me, had never enjoyed his school days.

But he has always acknowledged that Eton gave him the valuable gift of confidence, and also the opportunity to learn to play the guitar and compose songs. I thought at the time that it was an expensive way of attaining the latter two objectives, but as things have turned out it may well have been worth it. Anyway, again unlike me, he knew exactly what he wanted to do – to sing and to compose.

I remembered my own experience when through lack of guts I failed to train as an actor but went into the family business in which I was not really interested. I was determined that so far as possible all the children could start by doing what they wanted. If they then failed they could never complain that they had not been given the chance. So Pauline and I tried to help and encourage Barry in every way we could.

Within a few weeks of leaving Eton he went to work at the Decca Recording Studios in West Hampstead. He stayed there for nine months and learnt all the tricks of the recording business. He then spent the next two years working in various record shops, living with us at home and using all his spare time composing songs, often late into the night.

In 1969 with three other boys and two girls he formed the harmony singing group, Design. They gradually got recording dates on many different programmes on Radio 2. Then came television with appearances on a variety of comedy shows.

The comedians seemed to like their style and songs, and among those for whom they have appeared are Morecambe and Wise, Benny Hill, The Two Ronnies, Tommy Cooper, Rolf Harris and Spike Milligan. They have also been in the musical programmes of Cilla Black, Val Doonican and Nana Mouskouri.

The group all live together in a flat and have produced several LPs and singles. Their LPs, especially, have been highly praised by the critics but neither they nor the singles have yet reached the charts. One problem is that their type of music is a trifle square for Radio 1 producers and disc jockeys and unless a record gets a good airing it does not stand a chance.

Anyhow all goes well with Design and they were so successful at the Savoy that they were asked back later at a bigger fee. They certainly make a pleasant sound and are slick and professional with their arrangements and harmonies. They go round the clubs, especially in the North, have done a summer show at Skegness with Tommy Cooper and keep popping up on the TV and radio.

The Australians were welcome visitors for my last summer on the BBC staff, and it was one of the best series since the war, very closely fought with each side winning two Tests. This meant that England kept the Ashes which Illingworth's side had won in Australia.

The Australians gave me an opportunity to play my nickname game. 'Laguna' was obvious for Lillee but I was quite pleased with 'Chusetts' and 'Melon' for Massie and Colley respectively. They were a most friendly side, admirably managed by Ray Steele and Fred Bennett and extremely well-captained by Ian Chappell, both on and off the field.

Ian's younger brother, Greg, established himself as one

of the leading batsmen in the world. I well remember his hundred against England in his first Test at Perth. It was on a Sunday and I felt compelled to say that the English bowlers looked as if they had had too much 'Chappell' on Sunday.

The other great success of the tour was Dennis Lillee, who took thirty-one wickets in the series. With his long, dark mane and even longer run he is a genuine fast bowler and a magnificent sight as he runs up – so long as you are not the batsman! It looks as if he will be plagued with a bad back unless he cuts down his run. At the moment he takes far too much out of himself.

The most surprising thing about the series was that no England batsman managed to score a hundred in the five Tests, but John Snow, as usual, produced his best against Australia and took twenty-four wickets.

For the first time there were three one-day Internationals sponsored by the Prudential. For these Brian Close was dramatically recalled to captain England in place of Ray Illingworth, who had an injured ankle which he had turned over in the Oval Test. England won the mini-series 2–1 and in spite of dull weather the matches were good fun and attracted satisfactory crowds, though the Australians, at the end of a long and tiring tour were not too enthusiastic about them.

The Prudential made a fifty-five-minute film of the three matches for which I wrote the script and did the commentary. I was amused that the only reaction to it was because of something nothing to do with cricket. At Lord's the sun came out suddenly for a short time and its reflection shone into the batsman's eyes off a board advertising Prudential. The umpires ordered it to be turned face downwards on the grass so I said: 'That must be the only time the Sun has got the better of the Prudential,' which caused some chuckles in the insurance world.

After the three Internationals there was only a fortnight left before I retired as a member of the BBC staff. I had been due to leave on 30 September but I was owed some leave. So I had to rush around arranging things like pensions and clearing up all the clutter in my office. I also had to sign a contract for *Down Your Way*, which I was to re-start in October and for which, now as a freelance, I would be paid. I had agreed with Robert Hudson that all goodbyes and leaving parties should wait until October or November as most people in OBs took their leave in September when the summer activities died down.

Meanwhile I had two cricket commitments before I left. First the annual Gillette Cup Final at Lord's, which has become the biggest day in the cricket season. The rival supporters really care who wins, and St John's Wood rings with their cheers and applause. This year it was between Lancashire and Warwickshire, and Lancashire completed a hat-trick of victories for the third time running under Jackie Bond's captaincy.

Clive Lloyd made a magnificent 126, one of the most exciting innings which I have ever seen, and once again my good luck held. One of the sports programmes came over to me for a score flash at exactly the moment when Clive reached his hundred. From Lord's I went to Edgbaston to see Warwickshire clinch the County Championship by beating Derbyshire. So I finished on a high note so far as cricket was concerned, and went off to Swanage for my holiday – self-employed for the first time in my life.

It was not long before I got my first job, and strangely enough it was for Thames TV – the opposition. They were planning a series of thirteen weekly programmes called *A Place in the Country*, in which they were to visit a National Trust property every week.

Each programme was to be introduced by a different presenter and they had asked me to do the one from the beautiful village and abbey of Lacock in Wiltshire. Although I was still with the BBC till the end of the month, with their usual kindness they allowed me to go to Lacock for a day's filming on 16 September. The main filming was to be done in November but they wanted to catch the local fair, a village cricket match and the harvest festival. It was strange to be working for the opposite side but they were most friendly and one hundred per cent efficient.

So I thoroughly enjoyed my first day's work as a free-lance, especially as Larry the Ram escaped from his pen, where he was on view for people to guess his weight. We were filming the cricket at the time and Larry obligingly ran right across the pitch followed by half the village trying to catch him. Ram stopped play but it made a good shot for our film.

I returned to my interrupted holiday in Swanage, where Pauline had recently bought the two top floors of a house on the cliffs, looking out on a magnificent view of the bay and Old Harry's Rocks between Swanage and Studland. Pauline had made it very comfortable and from now on this was to be our second home. The idea was that I should write this book there in peace, away from the telephone, and looking out to sea for inspiration. I have in fact written much of it there but have always found the sun and the sea more of a temptation than an inspiration, and have often found myself sneaking off to the beach.

My immediate future was mapped out for the autumn based on *Down Your Way* every Tuesday and Wednesday and this book for the remainder of my spare time. I had one important thing to do and that was to register at the local Labour Exchange. The BBC had advised me to do this on the first day after I had officially left their employment. So I took their advice and I am still not sure if what happened really did!

I went along and a nice man recognised me and directed me to a counter reserved for the professions. There I asked another nice chap what I had to do, explaining that the BBC had told me to come. He asked if I was working that day. I said that I had no actual job to do, but would be doing some writing for this book and the next day would be off to record *Down Your Way*. He advised me to go to another counter to register as out of work as, so I understood it, I would be entitled to some pay. I couldn't believe what he had said, and asked whether the unemployment figures would go up by one if I signed and he said yes they would.

I was staggered that in my sort of profession I could draw the dole for a day on which I had no actual job. I asked if the rule would apply to a famous singing star who gave, shall we say, a concert at the Royal Albert Hall on the Wednesday for which he might be paid a thousand pounds or more. Supposing he rested on the other four working days would he be entitled to draw the dole for those days? The answer was, yes he would. I still cannot believe it – perhaps I was dreaming or he was pulling my leg.

And yet I can remember once seeing that an actor was on the dole, though I knew he had just been in quite a long run. Anyway I thanked the nice man and declined to register and at least felt that I had reduced the unemployment figures by one. It still worries me, but perhaps explains why the figures are still so high even though most people say they have a shortage of staff or labour.

When working at our home in London I tucked myself away at the top of the house in my daughter Clare's bedroom, which I turned into an office. She had gone to Australia for a year's look-around as we wanted her to see this wonderful country which offers so many opportunities to young people. After a month or so of temporary secretarial work she landed herself a super job as the sales representative of the island of New Caledonia in Australia and New Zealand, with her base in Sydney.

New Caledonia is a French island in the Pacific, off the coast of Queensland, and Clare got the job because of her fluent French. Pauline had wisely sent her to La Rochelle as soon as she left school. There she stayed with a French family and was the only English girl to attend the local lycée.

The family consisted of the police inspector, his wife, three sons and daughter. The latter four were all more or less Clare's age or a bit older and taught her all she wanted to know. After six months she returned speaking the language like a Frenchwoman and she also taught herself Spanish, Italian and a smattering of German. This ability to speak languages coupled with all the necessary secretarial skills got her some good jobs here before she left for Australia. Already she has been to New Zealand, Fiji, New Hebrides and Singapore, and when in Sydney she has been wonderfully looked after by all our friends. So that's Number Two happily settled and I am beginning to wonder whether we shall ever get her back!

There were three parties to 'celebrate' my leaving. First Pauline and I gave a supper party at Lord's for all my old OB colleagues and their wives. Owing to 'universal demand' John Ellison and I did our old cross-talk act with a few extra gags which had not been considered 'suitable' when we originally broadcast it in *In Town Tonight*.

B.J. I call my dog Carpenter.
J.E. Why?
B.J. Because he's always doing odd jobs about the house. You should see him make a bolt for the door.
J.E. I haven't seen him about lately.
B.J. No. I had to shoot him.
J.E. Was he mad?
B.J. Well, he wasn't too pleased. I must go now to see my wife.
J.E. What do you call *her*?
B.J. Radio 4.
J.E. Why on earth Radio 4?
B.J. Because she has nothing on after midnight.

Luckily, our guests had been well wined, and John and I

knew enough about the business to take it all at a great pace, so it went down quite well.

Next followed a cocktail party given by the Managing Director of Radio, Ian Trethowan, in the Governors' dining-room. When I had gratefully accepted the invitation I had begged that there should be none of those farewell speeches which are usually so embarrassing to all present. But Ian did give me a beautiful briefcase and a clock from all my colleagues and I made a 'brief' speech of thanks.

Finally, OB Department gave me a dinner at Lord's with all the old heads of OBs present – Michael Standing, Lobby, Charles Max-Muller with Robert Hudson in the chair. Robert had taken over from Charlie as Head of OBs and in character was very much in the Lobby mould. He was an excellent and sympathetic boss, because he himself is a first-rate commentator – not just for ceremonials but for cricket and rugger. He therefore understands the difficulties and problems which commentators have to face, and he has always been a most helpful critic and friend. He was always of enormous help to me in arranging various cricket trips abroad.

It was an hilarious evening though I'm afraid Robert did make a very kind speech, and I could not resist making one far too long in reply.

18 A silver lining

URING THE WINTER, MCC were touring India and Pakistan but as I was no longer their Cricket Correspondent, there was no question of my going there for the BBC. However, I had got so used to my winter sunshine that I was determined to get some somewhere. I toyed with the idea of the West Indies, but I finally settled for five weeks in South Africa where Derrick Robins was taking a team to play the Provinces and two representative sides and I arranged with *Down Your Way* to be absent for four programmes.

Once again I was dead lucky. I happened to mention casually to Derrick that I would be following his team around and he immediately offered me the job of Press Liaison Officer – all expenses paid and to travel as one of the team. It was a marvellous offer and I naturally accepted at once, and SABC kindly asked me to broadcast all the matches for them.

Before I left, we had our first Christmas at Swanage with Barry, Ian and Joanna, but minus Clare in Australia and Andrew still in South Africa. It was a pleasant novelty for all of us to spend Christmas Day overlooking the sea.

Just before we went down to Swanage I had been asked to do an unusual type of broadcast for me – the short religious programme *Thought for the Day*. I was interviewed and asked to say exactly what Christmas means to me. This gave me an opportunity to put across one point which has always worried me. At Christmas time people are kind and friendly. Everyone has a cheerful greeting for each other, people are generous and take pleasure in giving. Overnight they become good neighbours. What a pity therefore that this spirit of goodwill does not exist for the rest of the year. What a better place the world would be if only it did. That was one thing I said, trite and unoriginal perhaps, but no less true for all that.

The other thing I was able to explain was my simple philosophy of life. I am afraid that I have never been a very good Christian. I believe in God and in some sort of after-life, though I don't pretend to understand how it will work.

As a child and at school, I went to church regularly, probably far too often. Instead of an occasion it just became part of a hum-drum curriculum. As a grown-up I have always gone to communion at Easter and Christmas and have attended one or two other services during the year. Pauline and I have always taken the children to Sunday School or children's services, but they, like me, have had a surfeit of chapel while at school.

We both feel guilty at not making them go to church on Sunday but as we don't go ourselves we have felt it wrong to expect them to do so. I really regret not showing them a better example as we have always had such a flourishing Christian community at St John's Church, and I enjoy the services when I do attend.

But somehow, Sunday morning is the time to do all the things one has not done during the week. That's no excuse. Just a very poor reason. I do in private try to say thank you to God for everything, and to pray for people less fortunate than myself in the way of health and living conditions.

In addition, I have also given myself a standard to try to follow, based on that character in Charles Kingsley's *The Water Babies* – Mrs Doasyouwouldbedoneby. I try to apply this philosophy in all my dealings with people, and say to myself: 'How would *I* like it if he spoke to *me* like that?' or 'If someone did that to *me* how would *I* feel?' Of course I frequently fail, or speak or act too swiftly to give myself time to ask myself the questions. But it is a useful guideline for a workable Christian way of life and it has undoubtedly helped me. Here endeth the sermon and I do hope it doesn't sound too terribly smug.

The Robins tour was a great success and the most enjoyable of all those I have accompanied. There were none of the stresses and strains of Test matches. The team had been carefully selected for character as well as form and there were no prima-donnas. The weather and hospitality were superb. The cricket was of high quality and the matches attracted enthusiastic crowds.

I had no daily reports nor countless interviews to worry about as I had always had on other tours. I was accepted as a member of the team, ate, lived and travelled with them, and used their dressing-room and attended all the team meetings.

These included the famous Saturday Night Club which is a feature of all MCC tours. This is a compulsory meeting for the whole side after play every Saturday. They meet in one of the hotel rooms under a different chairman each week, who ordains what dress – or lack of it – shall be worn. There are various rituals which I must not reveal, and a certain amount of drink (hard or soft) is consumed, orders for which are taken in advance by two 'barmen' appointed weekly. The whole thing only lasts about half an hour and after attending and enjoying all of them on this tour, I feel that they are a very worthwhile and informal get-together and good for a team's morale. In these days of motels, with meals and TV in the rooms, players on a tour often only meet at functions or on the field of play. This Saturday night ritual does at least bring them all together.

Derrick Robins is an amazing character, a cheerful extrovert with tremendous energy and drive. He is a splendid companion and he and I found two mutual likes – old-time music-hall comedians and the local South African white wine – a dangerous combination! We indulged in a cross-talk act on all possible occasions and he even taught me some new jokes. The one I particularly enjoyed was from one of the routines of that wonderful comic Jimmy James, of the stuttering legs.

Jimmy always had two stooges and he announced to the audience that one of them would shortly do a parachute jump from 20,000 feet. He went on to say that the stooge would not open the parachute until within ten feet of the ground. 'What happens if the parachute doesn't open then?' asked the stooge nervously. 'You can jump ten feet can't you?' was Jimmy's unsympathetic reply.

I shall always be grateful to Derrick for this tour as it also gave me a chance of seeing my sister Anne again, and of meeting Andrew for the first time since we had left him there a year earlier. He was very tall, fair and suntanned and had had a marvellous time. He has always been keen on shooting and fishing and he had enjoyed plenty of both, including a fishing trip to Mozambique.

Andrew had worked on a farm, helped to build an airstrip, and went on a wilderness trail through one of the game reserves. He also accompanied the game wardens when they darted the rhinos. They chased them through the undergrowth in a Land Rover and then fired a dart into the rhinos to immobilise them. They could then be lifted into a truck and shipped off abroad to a zoo or to another game reserve which was short of rhino.

For the last part of his stay, Andrew had hitch-hiked down to Durban and got himself a job with South African Railways driving a fork truck in Durban harbour. This was long and arduous work and meant leaving the small hotel where he lived with a number of other young people at 6.30 am, sometimes not getting back till 9 pm.

But he loved it all, especially the climate and was loath to return to England. But we thought he had had his year and that it was time he came home to decide what to do in life. As I write he is working in Foyles bookshop in Charing Cross Road. He enjoys this but obviously still hankers after South Africa.

I returned to England at the beginning of February and

immediately got down to my weekly but pleasant chore of *Down Your Way*, which in my absence had been introduced by that splendid character from *Tonight*, Fyfe Robertson.

The most important date ahead in my diary was Sunday, 22 April, which was Pauline's and my Silver Wedding Day. This gives me an opportunity to say thank you to her for such wonderfully happy twenty-five years. She has always been of great help and given me every encouragement, though never afraid to criticise if necessary. She has also been remarkably patient and tolerant of my unusual job, with its irregular hours, few free weekends and always working on Bank Holidays when most people are not.

I have lost count of the number of times we have had to refuse or cancel invitations to parties because of some programme which I have had to do. The 22nd of April was a good example as I was booked to commentate on the Battersea Park Easter Parade for TV, so we could not even have a celebration lunch. Actually I nearly missed this broadcast because on the Saturday I had twenty-four hour 'flu but luckily was all right on the Sunday. Had I missed doing the commentary it would have broken my twenty-seven-year-old record of never missing a broadcast through ill health.

There have of course been compensations for Pauline, such as trips abroad and attending shows or ceremonies which we were broadcasting. I suppose it's also true that she has met more interesting and famous people than she would otherwise have done. But she has inevitably had to play second fiddle, except in her home town of Sheffield, where I am known as Pauline Tozer's husband!

But it must have been frustrating at times as she is artistic, musical and an expert photographer and if she had not been tied to me might have become a well-known person in her own right. As it is, of course, she has had to bring up our family of five and I know they all endorse my verdict that she has been a jolly good mother.

I think our marriage proves that you don't have to be compatible in all things and that a little give and take on both sides works wonders. Our chief incompatibility has been on the question of time. She likes to go to bed late, and sleep late, and I am an early bird and can never sleep beyond 8 am. She is also very unpunctual while I, with my Grenadier training, am usually five minutes early. Most of the 'little local difficulties' have been because she has kept me waiting before going out somewhere. But I gather from other husbands that this is nothing unusual! Anyhow if that's the only thing that's wrong, the next twenty-five years shouldn't be too bad either!

The Lord's Test in June prevented me going down to Bradfield School to see my youngest son, Ian, perform in their famous Greek play. There was no danger of his forgetting his lines – not that he knows any Greek – as all he had to do was to stand naked except for a loin cloth and act as a guard. So I doubt if he will follow me into the entertainment world nor alas as a cricket commentator, as he is the third of my sons to dislike the game, and in fact does not even play it at school, preferring sailing and swimming.

It was Ian who met me when I got home from a *Down Your Way* in Lincolnshire in July. He gave me the shock news that Joanna – now aged 7 – had diabetes. She had recently been drinking far more than usual and Pauline suspected that something was wrong and took her to our Doctor 'Cove'. He quickly discovered that she had far too much sugar in her blood, and she was immediately admitted to the Hospital for Sick Children in Great Ormond Street. There they did tests to find out how much insulin she needed and what sort of diet, because for the rest of her life she was going to have to have an injection every day – unless some cure comes up in the meantime.

It was terrible luck on poor Joanna, coming on top of everything else. She had been getting on so well. Until she was five, Pauline organised a small play-school in our house with three or four other children. Joanna then went to a special school run by the Westminster Society for Mentally Handicapped Children. Here she received individual attention and unlimited kindness and thoroughly enjoyed herself.

After eighteen months she went to the Roman Catholic Convent of St Christina just off Avenue Road, where she quickly became an ordinary member of the school. The nuns and teachers were kind and understanding and all the other children seemed to love Joanna and accept her as one of them. She has made many friends there who come and play with her in our house or vice versa. We had always wanted her to mix with normal children as soon as possible and, touch wood, it has so far worked wonderfully well.

Joanna is still as happy and friendly as ever, and a perfect hostess whenever we have a party. She has grown quite tall, which is unusual, and can read and write as well as the rest of our family could at her age. She is still behind normal children in her conversation and her reasoning and seems unable to store up memory of past events. Now that she has diabetes her life will inevitably be more restricted and disciplined with the daily injections and strict diet. But I have no doubt, whatever, that Pauline and Cally will cope as they always have done.

The summer of 1973 had been a very busy one for me as I had to combine *Down Your Way* with cricket commentary on all the six Tests, plus a certain number of County, Benson and Hedges, John Player and Gillette matches.

As for cricket, so far as finance and weather were concerned, it was a bonanza. The glorious sunshine brought out the crowds but it was a sad year for England at Test level. Although New Zealand lost the first series of the double tour 0–2 they gave England plenty of shocks in the first two Tests. For England, Boycott, Fletcher and Amiss all batted well and Geoff Arnold was the star bowler.

But there were ominous signs of lack of class and technique in the England batting line-up.

These were even more evident in the series against West Indies, who won it 2–0 because they batted superbly and England batted badly. England's crushing defeat by an innings in the 3rd Test at Lord's forced the selectors to replace Illingworth as captain after a spell of thirty-one Tests, and Mike Denness was appointed captain of the MCC Team to tour West Indies in 1974.

But of course the shock of the series was the bomb alert on the Saturday of the Lord's Test. A capacity crowd were basking in the sun and enjoying some splendid cricket when suddenly in the middle of an over, the voice of MCC Secretary, Billy Griffith, came over the public address asking everyone to leave the ground immediately due to a bomb threat. It really was a tremendous shock and at first people just could not believe it, though everyone remained perfectly calm. After frequent requests from the police most of the crowd went out into the streets of St John's Wood while the police searched for the alleged bomb. Even so some 5,000 concentrated round the square in the middle of the ground and refused to leave.

Once again I was lucky or unlucky depending on the way you look at it. I was commentating at the time and continued to do so for the next forty-five minutes trying to keep people at home and outside the ground advised as to what was going on. It was an uncanny situation that this should be happening at Lord's of all places. But with the usual 'it can't happen to us' feeling, we all stayed put in our new commentary box on the top balcony of an almost-deserted pavilion. We somehow felt that if the bomb *did* go off we wouldn't have so far to go! Luckily it all proved to be a false alarm and after a loss of eighty-eight minutes, play was resumed. I had been present at riots on grounds abroad but this was the first time ever that 'bomb stopped play'. A rather inauspicious start to my new career as a freelance commentator.

Well, there it is. As I sit in my deck-chair in the garden I just can't believe it. I have finished this book. I never really thought I would. But it has been fun to do, and if you have reached this far, I hope that you have enjoyed it too.

I would just like to say a final thank you to my wife and family and all my personal friends and relations for helping to make my life such a happy one, and for laughing occasionally at some of my jokes.

To all my friends in the BBC, and in the world of sport and entertainment I want to say how grateful I am for the way in which they have befriended and accepted a relative amateur like myself.

And finally to the general public, my warm thanks for many faithful years of viewing and listening and for the kind and generous treatment which I have always received from them.

Now I must stop. Perhaps we shall meet one day – possibly Down *Your* Way.

St John's Wood
September 1973

PART II:
IT'S A FUNNY GAME

19 As I was saying . . .

IT WAS THAT GREAT *Daily Mirror* columnist, Cassandra, who, on re-starting his column at the end of the war, began: 'As I was saying when I was so rudely interrupted . . .' I have no such excuse for starting another book. Except perhaps for two things. A number of people after reading *It's Been a Lot of Fun* assumed that I had retired. No such luck for the listeners! I *did* retire as a member of the BBC staff in September 1972 but have continued to work as a freelance ever since.

The other thing became obvious to me on 25 January 1975 – that in spite of my career as a broadcaster for thirty years I was still not as well known as I had thought. This was brought home to me when flying back from Australia. Our aircraft had stopped at Bahrain to refuel at about two o'clock in the morning. I was pacing up and down the transit lounge to get a bit of exercise when an Englishman in an elegant overcoat approached me. Why he was wearing an overcoat in Bahrain where the temperature was in the nineties I don't know. Anyway, he came up and said, 'Excuse me, I think I recognise you.'

So I put on what I thought was a friendly smile at that hour of the morning and began to reach for my pen. 'Who do you think I am, then?' I asked him. 'Tell me,' he said, 'did you ever drive a bus in Watford?' I gasped out a firm 'No,' and he went on, 'Well, you are the dead spit of a chap who did.' With that he turned and walked off without another word. I am convinced he was not joking nor had done it for a bet.

This lack of fame was further emphasised a few months later at Euston Station – of all places. I had come down on the sleeper from Manchester and at 7 am was walking up the cold dark platform, not looking my best I must admit after a night on the train. I heard footsteps behind me, and soon a man drew level with me. He gave me a good hard look then said, 'Do I know you?'

'I don't know,' I replied, 'who *do* you think I am?' 'Aren't you Alan Dixon?' he asked. Well, poor Alan, who was a BBC sports commentator in the North Region, had died about six years before. So I said, 'Alan Dixon? But he's dead.' 'Yes,' replied the man. 'I know he is!' To this day I still cannot work out what he meant!

Anyhow, with *Down Your Way* as a weekly basis, life in my 'retirement' in the autumn of 1973 was as busy as ever. I went up to Manchester to record two programmes of the television panel game, *Call My Bluff*, something I had always wanted to do. I was in Paddy Campbell's team and although I did not do too badly, I could not match the skill and ease with which Paddy and Frank Muir played. We recorded the two programmes during the evening in front of the same audience. We changed our ties, shirts and coats before the second one but kept on the same trousers.

I expect that, like me, you imagined that the panel made up their own meanings of the words. This was, I believe, tried originally, but now the *True* or *False* explanations are cleverly composed in advance and typed on to little cards. An hour or so before the show you are 'summoned' to the captain's dressing-room where, after consultation, he allots you your cards, either *True* or *False*. You then learn these and have them in front of you during the programme. You can vary them to suit your own particular style. Much of the art of winning the game depends on the selection by the captain of the right person to give the *True* version of a particular word. A deadpan face and the ability to lie convincingly are essential ingredients for the contestants. It's certainly as much fun to do as it is to watch, but alas I have not been asked back (yet!).

In November 1973 the Lord Mayor's Show came round again for TV and this has become a hardy annual ever since. The timing has always been dicey, the ideal being for the Lord Mayor's coach to pass our commentary position opposite St Paul's about a minute before the end of our broadcast. But this is the longest *unrehearsed* procession in the world and I regret that on two occasions we have missed the Lord Mayor before we had to hand back to the studio. But in 1976 we achieved perfection with the Lord Mayor reaching us on the dot, and what is more, for the first time ever, he surprised viewers by speaking a message to them from the window of his coach as it passed our cameras. The secret was that our engineers had been along early to Mansion House before the Lord Mayor got dressed in all his finery and robes, and had wired him up with a small microphone and pocket transmitter.

I had often been to the Festival of Remembrance at the Royal Albert Hall but 1973 was the first year I had commentated on it for radio. Previously I had resisted doing it as I feel that this service and the Two-minute Silence are very personal matters for people who, like myself, lost many friends during the war. But it went all right – unlike the Two-minute Silence service broadcast once by a West Indian radio station. The programme was being recorded in the main square of the town and at about five minutes to the hour the engineer in the control room sat listening to the hymns and the bands playing. He then unfortunately dozed off, but awoke a few minutes later and to his horror heard nothing coming over the air. Thinking that there had been a breakdown he automatically went into his emergency drill and put on a record of martial music. Result – the Two-minute Silence was shattered. So was the poor engineer when he realised what he had done.

At about this time I was a member of the panel on the radio quiz series, *Sporting Chance*, on which I used to be the chairman. It is always fun to do and keeps one informed about sports other than cricket. One of my friends who heard the programme was inspired to send me a rude postcard, which showed a quiz master putting a question to a panellist.

Quiz master What did Eve say to Adam the first time she saw him?
Panellist (After a long pause) Ah – that's a hard one.
Quiz Master Quite right – two marks!

In mid-November 1973 there was Princess Anne's wedding to Captain Mark Phillips and as usual the BBC went to town and pulled out all its ceremonial stops. I had previously been a commentator for TV for King George VI's funeral, the Coronation and Princess Margaret's wedding. But this time I was selected for radio and had a superb position on the corner of the Mall and Horse Guards Parade. I had to describe the procession on its way to and from the Abbey, and also did some interviews with the crowd. I was lucky enough to be one of the few to go to Buckingham Palace the evening before to see the wonderful collection of wedding cakes which had been sent to the Princess. There were dozens of them, many with horsey motifs, and it was nice to learn that they were all being sent off to hospitals. We were also shown the seating plan for the wedding breakfast – round tables for about ten people each – and a preview of the menu and wines. I can assure you they were mouth-watering and I thought of them as I munched a ham sandwich in my car, as I rushed off to Shropshire to do a *Down Your Way*.

Our daughter Clare flew back from Australia and all seven of us had a very happy family Christmas at our cliff house in Swanage. I love Christmas, but must admit that a well-known vicar got the retort he deserved when he said in his sermon: 'Christmas is a time of great and enduring joy for all of God's two-legged creatures.' One of his parishioners was heard to say in a loud voice, 'Try telling that to a turkey'!

The year 1974 started off with a quick trip to West Germany to record some quizzes with the forces, one of which took place in an RAF hospital. I was told that the Queen Mother had been there six months before and as usual had gone round all the wards talking to the patients. She came to a man who was writhing with pain in his bed. 'What's wrong with you?' she asked sympathetically. 'Oh, Mam,' replied the man, 'I'm in great pain. I've got an awful boil on my bum.' 'Oh dear, very painful,' said the Queen Mum, not batting an eyelid. 'I do hope it gets better soon.'

She passed down the ward and when she had left the sister came back and gave the man a terrific rocket. 'How dare you mention a word like that to Royalty – or to any visitor for that matter. Make something up. Say you've sprained your ankle. But never use *that* word again.' The man said he was very sorry and quite understood and promised never to do it again.

Three months or so later, Princess Margaret came out to Germany to visit one of the Highland Regiments of which she is Colonel. She came to the same hospital and like her mother talked to all the men in the wards. Eventually she came to the man with the boil (he was still there), and asked him what was wrong. Remembering the sister's instructions he replied: 'I'm in great pain, Mam. I have a badly sprained ankle.' 'Oh,' said the Princess with some surprise, 'so the boil on your bum is better, is it?'

I hope the story was true. But I doubt it!

Most of January and February 1974 was taken up with launching my autobiography, *It's Been a Lot of Fun*, and all the publicity connected with it. Radio did us proud and I appeared on most of the programmes such as *Today, Open House, Be My Guest, Jack de Manio Precisely, Desert Island Discs* and quite a bit of local radio round the country. Television was not so generous, only *Pebble Mill* in Birmingham giving me a spot. I had long wanted to receive the accolade of appearing on *Desert Island Discs*, the longest running programme on the BBC. Roy Plomley had not only thought up the idea during the war but presented it ever since, and was a most friendly and sympathetic interviewer. My selection of eight records was a fair reflection of my tastes and was as follows:

1 *Eton Boating Song* sung by Eton College Musical Society
2 *All the Things You Are* sung by Hutch
3 *We'll Gather Lilacs* sung by Vanessa Lee and Bruce Trent
4 *Double Damask* A sketch by Cicely Courtneidge
5 *Strolling* sung by Bud Flanagan
6 Elgar's *Enigma Variations* played by Philharmonia Orchestra conducted by Sir Malcolm Sargent
7 *Tie a Yellow Ribbon Round the Ole Oak Tree* sung by Dawn
8 *End of the Party* sung by Design and composed by Barry Alexander (my eldest son, so called because there was already another member of Equity named Barry Johnston)

The book I chose to take with me was John Fisher's *Funny Way to be a Hero*. It is an analysis of British Music Hall with biographies and routines of all the great comics and comedy acts.

My book was published in the middle of February 1974 and I'm happy to say received a very kind press. Unfortunately we had to battle with the three-day week and the General Election, so we lost some of the impetus of the early publicity, but in the end my book did quite well. Not in the David Niven class, of course, but not too bad. I suppose I should have put in some of my early sexual experiences, though I'm afraid they would not have been as amusing as his undoubtedly were!

Our publication date was also not too cleverly timed, as the following week Pauline and I flew off to Barbados for a long-planned holiday – thanks to *Down Your Way* allowing me to pre-record three programmes. The main idea was to see the 3rd Test between England and West Indies at Bridgetown. It was strange to sit in the stand and just watch the cricket *without commentating*. I must confess that at the end of the day I was far more exhausted than if I had been working.

England, already one down in the series, managed to draw the match after being put into bat by the West Indies captain, Rohan Kanhai. They got off to a terrible start but were saved by Tony Greig with 148 and Alan Knott with 87, and England finally made 395.

West Indies replied with 596 for 8 declared, of which Lance Rowe made 302, the highest innings by a West Indian batsman against England. It was the third score of over 300 which I had seen in a Test and I must admit I'm not too keen to see another. The other two were 311 by Bobby Simpson at Old Trafford in 1964, and 307 by Bob Cowper at Melbourne in 1966. Rowe's was the most entertaining of the three, but however good the batsman, it's rather like a brilliant after-dinner speaker going on too long.

England, thanks to a not out hundred by Keith Fletcher, drew the game, which was remarkable for the fact that altogether ninety-nine no balls were called – seventy-nine not being scored off by the batsmen. This is a record but not one to be proud of, although of course with the present front foot law it is not as easy as it seems. However, I am always surprised that even the greatest bowlers give so many runs away, simply because they fail to put their front foot in the right place during their delivery stride.

This Test was the turning point of the tour for England. They batted well in a rain-spoilt match in Guyana and then went on to win a thrilling game in the Final Test at Port of Spain, winning by 26 runs with one hour to spare, and so squaring the series. It had been a triumph for Dennis Amiss who, in the Tests, scored 663 runs with an average of 82.87 and 3 hundreds. Tony Greig also emerged as a formidable all-rounder with 430 runs and 24 wickets, mostly taken by his off-spin, which was helped by the bounce in the wickets.

Back in England after three glorious weeks of sunshine, I appeared in Derek Nimmo's chat show, *Just a Nimmo*, which was great fun. The theme of the programme was sporting commentary and the others on the show were Cliff Morgan and Jimmy Hill. I had often seen Derek do his 'toe-twiddling' act, which he performed goodness knows how many times during the long run of *Charlie Girl*. He had evidently heard that I can tuck my ears in, and quite out of the blue, without previous warning, he asked me to do it during the show. So for the first time after nearly thirty years on TV, I tucked my ears in for millions to see. It caused some hilarity and had an amusing sequel a few weeks later.

We were doing a *Down Your Way* in Kirby Lonsdale and had got lost in the dark on our way to interview someone just outside the town. I spotted a lane leading up to a farm, so we drove up and I knocked on the door.

After some delay, a woman came to the door and peered out into the gloom. Her face lit up when she saw me and her first words were, 'Can you really tuck them in?' Only after proving that I could, did she say, 'Good Evening, Mr Johnston,' and showed us the right way to our prospective victim.

He happened to be a prosperous farmer and as we sat in front of a crackling log fire, I learnt a very good tip from his wife. They had some beautiful carnations in a vase, and when I admired them, she said they were over a fortnight old. I asked her how she kept them so fresh, and she explained that instead of putting them in water, she always used fizzy lemonade. I have tried it ever since and I can assure you it works – they really do stay fresh for far longer.

Incidentally, while recalling the farmer's wife who asked me to tuck in my ears, I couldn't help thinking of the stupid story of a man who also called at a house late one night. He was telling a friend about it and said, 'I knocked and a woman opened the door in her nightdress,' and the friend remarked: 'What a funny place to have a door!'

After commentating on the 1974 Boat Race from Chiswick Bridge for radio, and the Battersea Easter Parade for TV, I introduced a charity concert at Welwyn for my friend Martin Gilliat. It was a serious musical occasion and I was taught an object lesson of when not to try to be funny. The lady accompanying the singers at the piano was a Miss Nunn, and although her name was in the programme I thought I ought to give a verbal credit, so I said: 'And now, ladies and gentlemen, I am sure you would like to show your appreciation of the lady at the piano. Before the show started I was talking to her and asked her what her name was. And answer came there Nunn!' And deservedly, except for a loud guffaw from Martin in the front row, laughter also came there none!

It was a wet summer for the double tour of India and Pakistan. England under Mike Denness beat India easily 3-0 and so avenged their defeat at the Oval in 1971. The England batting averages were remarkable and must be a record for any top-six batsmen for any country in a Test series. Here they are:

David Lloyd	260.00
Keith Fletcher	189.00
John Edrich	101.00
Mike Denness	96.33
Dennis Amiss	92.50

and Tony Greig a comparative failure with only 79.50.

Pakistan were a tougher nut to crack and all three Tests in 1974 were drawn. Rain interfered with the first two matches at Leeds and Lord's. The 3rd Test at the Oval was a very different affair. The sun shone and both sides made gigantic totals on a slow, easy pitch – Pakistan 600 for 7 declared; and 94–4, England 545. For Pakistan, Zaheer Abbas, spectacles gleaming in the sunlight, played superbly for his 240, his first Test hundred since his 274 on his Test debut against England at Edgbaston in 1971. For England, Amiss scored his eighth Test hundred and as usual did not give up after reaching three figures, going on to make 183. Both he and Fletcher had a splendid summer, but with the Australian tour coming up the England batting still lacked a consistently successful opening pair. They were far too liable to early collapses, with someone like Alan Knott or Chris Old having to come to the rescue later on.

We had our usual number of amusing incidents in the commentary box. In the 1st Test against India at Old Trafford there was no play on the Saturday until 1 pm. I was due to begin the commentary at 11.30 am when play should have started. But it was a cold miserable day with rain and dark clouds, and the Indian spectators were sitting miserably huddled together in one of the stands. I heard my cue from Radio 3 in my headphones, '. . . and so to find out the prospects of play, over to Brian Johnston at Old Trafford.'

'It's raining here,' I said, 'and there certainly won't be any play for some time yet.' I then meant to say, 'There's a dirty black *cloud* here.' Unfortunately, what I *did* say was, 'There's a dirty black *crowd* here!' Collapse of everyone in the box, including the former Maharajah of Baroda – or Prince as we called him – who was one of our summarisers throughout the series.

20 A life full of moment

D URING MY SEPTEMBER 1974 holiday in Swanage I caught a bug – and still have it. Golf. As a boy I had played the occasional nine holes with my old Mum, but never seriously. Most of my shots sailed over extra cover with the usual cricketer's slice. After that, with a family of five and generally working for the BBC every Saturday and some Sundays, I never seemed to have any spare time. Whenever I did, in the summer I played cricket, and in the winters on tours with MCC I was quite happy to go to the beaches.

I am a very bad golf player, and still have no handicap except for my slice and my swing. But my friends have been incredibly kind and patient, and allow me to play with them: we normally play a greensome in which all four of us drive off and then each partnership chooses which of their drives they wish to play. This is not always the longest drive, as if mine has gone a reasonable distance and is fairly straight, it is good tactics for my partner to play the second shot. In this way a bad player like myself can have some slight influence on the result of a game. But with a four-ball I trail miserably behind, and it virtually becomes my partner versus our opponents.

I have worked out my own philosophy of golf. During a round – if lucky – I may play as many as six reasonably good shots. Afterwards it is these that I cherish and remember, and forget all about the many bad ones. My friends on the other hand are all pretty good average golfers. So they play many good shots and only a few bad ones. But judging from their conversation it is these latter that they remember and worry about, so that I often end up happier than they do.

Now that I play, I appreciate golf on TV all the more and try to discover its secrets by watching the masters. I am encouraged to see that even they play a few slices or hooks, but am immediately depressed by the ease with which they invariably get out of trouble. Mind you, they do have one advantage over me. When *they* slice, the ball often hits the long line of spectators, and bounces back on to the fairway. But nobody comes to watch *me*, so that my slice disappears into impenetrable undergrowth.

Inevitably, I suppose, I have begun to collect golf stories which make a change from cricket. It's interesting that quite a few of them have to do with death, starting with that oldest of chestnuts:

Two golfers were putting on a green by a road, when a funeral procession went slowly by. One of the players took off his cap and stood reverently to attention. His opponent remarked on this unusual display of respect for the dead person. 'Well,' said the player, 'it's the least I can do. I was married to her for forty years.'

Then there was the very bad golfer with a terrible slice, which always went into the rough. When he died, his will requested that his ashes be scattered on the fifteenth fairway. So after his funeral his friends took the urn up to the course and as requested emptied it out on to the fifteenth fairway. But unfortunately a strong wind was blowing and blew the ashes straight into the rough!

There was also the elderly golfer, who was worried whether he would get any golf when he died and went to heaven. So he found a crystal gazer and asked him about the prospects for golf in the after-life. The crystal gazer looked into his crystal ball for a few moments and then announced that he had two bits of news, one good, one bad. The golfer asked for the good news first. The crystal gazer told him he could see a beautifully laid out course with perfect fairways and smooth lush greens. The golfer was delighted but said he supposed he had better hear the bad news, too. 'Here it is,' said the crystal gazer. 'I am sorry to tell you that I can see you driving off the first tee at 9.30 am next Thursday!'

On a slightly more corny note there was the golfer who always carried a spare pair of socks in his bag – just in case he ever got a hole in one.

And then there was the long driver of the ball who regularly hit it two hundred and fifty yards or more. But gradually over a period of a few months he found that he was beginning to hit the ball shorter and shorter distances. From two hundred and fifty yards he went down to two hundred and twenty-five, then to two hundred, and a hundred and fifty until in the end he couldn't hit it more than a hundred yards. So he decided to go to his doctor to find out if there was anything wrong with his health. The doctor examined him thoroughly and then told him he had two things to tell him, one good, one bad. 'Let's have the bad first,' said the golfer. 'Okay,' said the doctor, 'stand by for a shock. You are gradually changing into a woman.' The golfer turned pale and croaked out, 'Come on, quick, give me the good news.' 'Right-ho,' said the doctor, 'from now on you'll be able to drive from the ladies' tees!'

Jimmy Tarbuck tells a lovely story of the golfer who was always accompanied by his dog when playing a round. Every time the golfer made a good shot or sank a long putt, the dog would stand up on his hind legs and applaud his master with his front paws. A friend asked him what the dog did when the golfer landed in a bunker or missed an easy putt. 'Oh,' said the golfer, 'he turns somersaults.' 'How many?' asked the friend. 'It depends on how hard I kick him up the arse,' was the reply.

In between learning golf my September holiday was twice interrupted. First I went to Manchester to record *Reunion* for BBC TV. This was a series where three people who had been at school together met to discuss their schooldays and the paths which their lives had taken since then. My old school chums were William Douglas-Home and Jo Grimond. We had been at Eton and Oxford together and before the war had occupied the same house at 35, South Eaton Place. It was kept by a lovely couple called Mr and Mrs Crisp. Since then, William had become one of our most popular and prolific playwrights, with an unerring touch for dialogue and light comedy. At the time of our recording he had had sixteen plays in the West End, averaging three hundred and fifty performances each – not bad! Jo had been leader of the Liberal party from 1956–1967 and was the father figure of that party. My favourite remark by a Liberal was attributed to that great character Lady Asquith. When asked what she thought of the two-chamber system she is said to have replied: 'I personally couldn't do without it. You see, my husband is a liberal peer.'

Anyway, under the tactful and friendly chairmanship of Brian Redhead, William, Jo and I were given our heads and encouraged to talk non-stop for about forty minutes – not something which any of us found very difficult to do! But somehow we each managed to get a fair share of the conversation. We came to no very profound conclusions except that Eton was the best trades union in the world and that all three of us had been very lucky in the jobs we had chosen to do.

Towards the end of September 1974 I flew off to South Africa for a week as I had been asked to share the commentary with my old friend, Charles Fortune, on the Datsun International Double Wicket Competition. I wonder what Lord Harris would have had to say about a Japanese car firm sponsoring cricket matches! Anyway, it is a splendid form of cricket consisting of two-a-side, with a maximum of eight overs an innings – and each team playing the others once in a one-innings' match.

It must have been an eye-opener to those who still belittle what South Africa is doing to try to integrate her sport – especially cricket. There in Johannesburg playing together, staying in the same hotels, attending receptions together, and sharing dressing-rooms were teams from

South Africa white, South Africa black, England, Australia, New Zealand, West Indies and Pakistan. They were all perfectly happy and thoroughly enjoyed the experience, which of course would not have been possible a year or two earlier.

The big crowds enjoyed it too, especially as Eddie Barlow and Barry Richards won it for South Africa white, but only after a tough fight against South Africa black. What a turn-up for the books that would have been had the latter won. But the success of the competition bore out what I have always felt. It is grossly unfair to punish cricketers for apartheid by cancelling their tours, and with boycotts and demonstrations. It is not *their* fault. Blame the politicians but leave sport alone. In the end I am sure it will be the best means of achieving unity between whites, coloureds and blacks – all over the world.

In October I was paid a wonderful and much appreciated compliment by those friendly and generous cricket fanatics – The Wombwell Cricket Lovers Society. They gave a special dinner in my honour and presented me with the 1974 Denzil Batchelor Memorial Award for 'Services to Cricket'. It was totally undeserved because, as I have said so often, I have been lucky enough to earn my living from what is really my life's hobby. But it was a delightful occasion with some excellent speeches by the Bishop of Wakefield and the President of Yorkshire, Sir Kenneth Parkinson.

I have known the latter since before the war, when on my various visits to Yorkshire he used to entertain us at parties with his conjuring tricks. He tells an amusing story of how as an average club cricketer he was called on to open the batting to that very fast bowler, the late Father R. P. H. Uttley of Hampshire. The first two balls which he received both pitched on his middle and leg, and with a loud click the balls shot off to the fine leg boundary. On each occasion there were loud appeals for lbw, but the pace was a bit too fast for the elderly umpire to follow the ball. So hearing the sound of a ball on wood he signalled a four to the batsman each time. A few balls later a very fast yorker from Uttley spreadeagled Kenneth's stumps, and he retired to the pavilion to considerable applause for those two finely executed leg-glides. How was the umpire, or the unsuspecting crowd, to know that Kenneth had a *wooden* left leg, which now had two large dents on it the size of a cricket ball!

My health at the dinner was proposed by Trevor Bailey, who over the past few years has added much wisdom and caustic wit to our ball-by-ball commentaries. He tells a splendid story against himself. In 1954 in the 1st Test at Brisbane, Australia were put in to bat by Len Hutton. They had scored about 300 for 2 when Trevor came on for a final spell. Hot and tired, he ran up to bowl but the ball stuck in his hand, so that although he went through his bowling action, he did not actually deliver the ball. 'That's the best bloody ball you've bowled today, Biley!' shouted a barracker.

Anyway, the dinner was a lovely occasion for me, and Les Bailey, the Society's Poet Laureate, wrote these kind words on the back of the menu:

> *A life full of moment, bonhomie and cheer*
> *Eton to Oxford to a young Grenadier.*
> *Outside Broadcasts and pastures quite new*
> *he even survived being once sawn in two.*
> *A rich sense of humour, an eloquent style*
> *added to cricket a reason to smile.*
> *All the world over where the great game is played*
> *sunshine of commentary is the memory he made.*
> *Cricket, Monte Carlo, or just Down Your Way*
> *We'll remember him always – till the last close of play.*

In December 1974 we had a rather unique gathering of past and present Grenadiers – officers and senior NCOs – to say goodbye and thank you to our much loved Colonel of the Regiment, General Sir Allan Adair. It took the form of a mixed cocktail party in the Banqueting Hall in Whitehall, and there must have been at least a thousand people present. So as you can imagine, there were plenty of reminiscences!

Among these was the tale of a very gallant and distinguished ex-officer who had won the Victoria Cross in Italy. A friend of mine who served with him out there was censoring the letters of the men in his company and one of them wrote: 'Captain – has just been awarded the Victoria Cross. If he was as bloody to the Germans as he is to us he thoroughly deserves it. P.S. Let them keep their f... medals. The only cross I want to see is Charing Cross!' When my friend finished this story someone else asked if we knew that old Major X (a very ugly officer) had been attached to the French in 1940, and had done so well that he was recommended for the Croix de Guerre. Unfortunately they couldn't find a French General who was prepared to kiss him!

But the star of the party was Mr Harold Macmillan, who had served with the Regiment in France during the Great War. He made an excellent speech in praise of Sir Allan and told this story about the war in the trenches.

He and some other officers were sitting in a dug-out near the front line. They were drinking port although their Commanding Officer, Colonel 'Ma' Jeffries, strongly disapproved of drinking and discouraged them from doing so. They had several bottles open on a wooden table, when to their dismay they heard footsteps approaching along the trench, and by the voices realised it was the Commanding Officer making an inspection. They hurriedly got some candles, stuck them in the half-filled bottles, and managed to light them just before 'Ma' Jeffries entered the dug-out. They all got up and stood to attention, and the Colonel seemed quite pleased with all he saw, and after a short chat went on his way. Much relieved, they quickly removed the candles and went on with their drinking.

About six months later one of them met Colonel Jeffries in the Guards Club in London. 'Would you like a glass of port, Colonel?' asked the officer. 'I think I'd prefer a small brandy if I may,' replied the Colonel. 'The port might taste of wax.' I was lucky enough to be introduced to Mr Macmillan later in the evening and he assured me that the story was true.

I had a bit of bad luck myself over the question of drinking in the Grenadiers. When I first joined the 2nd Battalion at Shaftesbury in June 1940 I took with me a dozen bottles of Perrier-Jouet champagne, as I thought I might as well drink it while the going was good. I put it in charge of the mess-sergeant and thought no more about it. One evening one of the officers who had just returned from Dunkirk decided to throw a birthday party and asked one of the mess-waiters to bring in some champagne. This he did, and everyone including myself drank large quantities of it and remarked on its excellent quality – far better than the usual cheap brand we usually had. It soon ran out and yes, you've guessed it. It was *my* precious case which we had been drinking, as revealed by an apologetic mess-sergeant when he returned from an evening out.

Even in retirement I still seemed to be flying all over the world, and after Christmas and New Year's Eve in St John's Wood, I flew off to Australia on the first day of 1975. The excuse was to try and push sales of my book in Australia but I must admit that the main reason was to see another Test at my second favourite cricket ground, Sydney (Lord's must be No. 1). Christopher Martin-Jenkins was now the official BBC Cricket Correspondent and so was covering all MCC tours as I had in the past. So it was just a holiday for me and we pre-recorded three *Down Your Way*s to enable me to be away for nearly four weeks.

While in Australia I appeared on quite a few TV and radio chat shows to talk about the book plus some fruitful interviews with the Press. I stayed with my daughter Clare in a house she shared with some other girls in the pleasant

Woollahra district of Sydney. As usual I had a marvellous time with lots of parties, bathing, harbour cruises and trips up country.

Clare and I gave a small party at her house for friends and some of the MCC party and their wives. We adjudged it to have been an unqualified success when in the early hours of the morning the distinguished cricket correspondent of a top London daily bade us goodbye and instead of leaving by the front door, tottered up the stairs and disappeared into a cupboard!

When I arrived the tour was not going well for Mike Denness and his team. They were having a torrid time against the tremendous pace of Dennis Lillee and Jeff Thomson. They had lost the first two Tests at Brisbane and Perth, but had managed to draw the third at Melbourne thanks to a great innings of 90 by Dennis Amiss, some fine fast bowling by Bob Willis and the usual good-all-round performance by Tony Greig.

Poor Mike Denness was getting the blame for everything and after a succession of low scores he decided to drop himself for the Sydney Test. But to be fair he was not the only one who was failing, and after seeing Lillie and Thomson bowl at Sydney I was convinced that no team in the world – not even the South African or West Indies stars – would have done any better. This was borne out the following year when the West Indies lost five of their Tests.

The Australian opening pair made a fearsome sight. At one end there was the long, classic run up and action, the speed, accuracy and variations in pace of Lillee. At the other, the thunderbolts of Thomson delivered off a shortish run with a slinging action and the right arm coming over *at the very last moment* from right behind his back. Much of his lightning speed was generated by his tremendously powerful shoulders. The Sydney pitch had pace, and even more important, bounce. They did not *have* to bowl short to get the ball to rise, though of course they unleashed a number of bouncers, one or two from Thomson, soaring over the wicket-keeper Rodney Marsh's head, although he was standing at least twenty-five yards back. A good length ball from them was sufficient to force the batsmen to play almost every stroke chest or head high. Batting became a matter of self-preservation.

In spite of everything, England nearly saved this Sydney Test thanks to some typically plucky batting by John Edrich, who after a sickening blow from one of the few balls that didn't rise went off to hospital. But he returned to block for two and a half hours and made 33 not out. Due to him and the tail-enders Bob Willis and Geoff Arnold, there were only five overs and three balls left when Australia won, and so regained the Ashes which had been won by Ray Illingworth's side on the same ground four years before.

Remarkably, a record Sydney crowd of 178,027 watched the match. I say, remarkably, because just as this type of blistering attack is dangerous and unpleasant for batsmen, it is also unpleasant and boring for the cricket-loving spectator. No one, except those who would have got a kick out of the gladiators of ancient Rome, can really enjoy watching batsmen literally fighting for their lives or, at best, preventing serious injury.

Final proof for me of the pace of Lillee and Thomson were the hands of Rodney Marsh. He showed them to me and they were puffy and badly bruised. To protect them he had wound bits of plaster round each finger. I told him it reminded me of an old BBC radio show – *Much Binding On the Marsh!* Unfortunately he had never heard of Kenneth Horne and Dicky Murdoch's show, so my joke (?) fell a bit flat!

Incidentally, if any young wicket-keeper finds that his hands are getting bruised, I strongly recommend something which I always used, and I'm glad to say Alan Knott does as well today. Place a thin layer of plasticine inside the inner gloves. It's amazing how it helps to absorb the shock of the ball thudding into the gloves. But I *don't* recommend the method used by George Duckworth when his hands took such a battering standing up to Maurice Tate on the fast Australian pitches of his day. He placed a thick piece of raw steak inside his gloves, and as you can imagine, at the end of a long hot day in the field, he was given a wide berth by his team-mates in the dressing-room!

I was back in England when Mike Denness led his side to victory in the final Test at Melbourne, and was delighted for his sake that he made his highest first-class score – 188. Admittedly Thomson was not playing and Lillee only bowled six overs because of an injured foot. But losing the series 1–4 was better than the likely result looked at one time.

Nowadays on tour, MCC travel mostly by plane with the occasional coach journey to an up-country match. They rarely, if ever, go by train, unlike the old days, when they used to travel right across Australia for days on end. The trains even had a lounge with a piano to help while away the time. I don't know any modern player who plays the piano, but in the past, Ewart Astill of Leicestershire and Dick Pollard of Lancashire were expert ticklers of the ivories, as of course was Don Bradman. He even made a gramophone record when he was over here in 1930. It may also surprise some people to know that that man with flair for so many things – Ted Dexter – plays the organ and piano extremely well. The Warden of Radley College once told me that often after scoring one of his many brilliant hundreds for the school, Ted would take off his pads and relax by going across to the chapel to play a few fugues!

But back to the trains – because there has long been a story told about an MCC player on tour, though no one seems to know for certain which player it really is. I have heard it told at least half a dozen times. Anyway, let's call him Smith and what is said to have happened is this. A girl was nursing a baby in a carriage, the only other occupant of which was a man who kept staring at the baby. He couldn't take his eyes off it, and the girl became more and more embarrassed and annoyed. Finally she could stand it no longer and asked the man why he was staring so. He replied that he would rather not say. But when the girl persisted, he said he was sorry but he was staring because the baby was the ugliest which he had ever seen in his life. This naturally upset the girl, who burst into floods of tears and, taking the baby, went and stood in the corridor.

She was still crying when the MCC team came along the corridor on their way to the restaurant car. They all passed her except Smith, who being a decent chap, stopped to ask her why she was crying. She told him that she had just been insulted by the man in her carriage. So Smith said, 'Well, cheer up. I'll bring you back a cup of tea from the restaurant car. That should make you feel better.' So off he went and returned in about five minutes. 'Here's your cup of tea,' he said to the girl, 'and what's more, I've also brought a banana for the monkey!' What happened then is not related!

21 Down Your Way

As SOON AS I had returned to England at the end of January 1975, I began to hear rumours within the BBC that *Down Your Way* (from now on *DYW*) was to be taken off the air. For reasons of economy the BBC were having to make cuts and this meant that Radios 3 and 4 and Radios 1 and 2 would have to share programmes at certain times of the day. So something had to go, and it was no secret that Tony Witby, the controller of Radio 4, did not wish to lose a particular favourite of his called *Celebration*. He looked at the tempting time of 5.15 pm on Sundays and decided that it was the right slot for his programme, and that *DYW* would have to be sacrificed.

The news was officially broken to me by producer Richard Burwood as he and I travelled by car during a *DYW* at Sedgefield in County Durham. Even though I had been forewarned, now that it had become definite it came as a bit of a shock. The weekly commitment had become very much part of my life.

The news was given to the Press the following week and I must say they really went to town on our behalf. For a thirty-year-old steam radio programme to hit the headlines in this telly age was a rare and unexpected event. There really was a tremendous outcry against the decision. Somehow the BBC had underestimated the affection with which the programme was held. Not only the nationals but all the provincial papers led the protests and the BBC itself was inundated with letters and phone calls from many devoted followers. The Director-General, Sir Charles Curran, was brought into it when on a phone-in he turned down the suggestion that *DYW* should continue but be presented by the twenty local BBC radio stations.

The real reason for taking it off was never given officially, except to say it was for economy. Some of the Press took this to mean that the programme itself was too expensive, with a producer, engineer and myself travelling to places all over the country every week. But in terms of cost per minute this made no sense at all. With the repeat on Tuesdays, Radio 4 was getting eighty minutes of airtime for about £130 – mere chicken-feed compared with most other similar programmes. In fact, when I read it I immediately told my bosses that I would take a cut in my fee if it would be of any help. But they refused to accept this offer and confirmed to me that there was no question of the programme itself being too extravagant or expensive.

The protests continued to pour in – I admit to soliciting a sister, a brother, an elderly aunt and a couple of cousins! – and some of the letters we received were most touching and rewarding. Many felt they were about to lose an old friend and it was nice to have such proof that we evidently provided some innocent pleasure for so many thousands of people.

Quite a few letters of protest were sent to the newspapers and one of the very nicest was written to the *Daily Mail* by comedian Norman Vaughan. He wrote: 'I don't mind things being changed so long as they remain as good or better than they were before. But *Down Your Way* was as gentle and honest as Sunday cricket on the village green.' Alongside that letter was one from another comedian and friend of mine – Dickie Henderson: 'I'm all for change, but why change something which is successful? I found *Down Your Way* not only interesting but educational.' Gentle, honest, interesting, educational – four very welcome adjectives to have applied to our programme.

The last programme was to come from Painswick in Gloucestershire on Sunday, 20 April, but even before then the planners had gone some way to mollify the protestors. It was announced that *DYW* would return temporarily for six programmes on Saturdays in July/August during the usual repeat time of *Any Questions*, which was taking its annual six weeks' holiday. But unknown to us even more was going on behind the scenes. The pressure from listeners had impressed Clare Lawson-Dick, the new controller of Radio 4.

The first I heard about it was a telephone call from Anthony Smith, the BBC's radio outside producer from Bristol. I knew him well as I had worked with him for many years, contributing cricket reports into his Saturday night sports programme from the West Region. I was surprised and delighted with what he had to tell me. He said he had just been stopped in a corridor by his immediate boss, Michael Bowen, of *Any Questions* fame. Michael had asked Tony whether he would like to produce *DYW*, which was coming back in October on the same regular basis as before, but would in future be produced and run from Bristol. Tony had rung me immediately before I heard it from anyone else, as he wanted to assure me that I would still be the presenter – which was very thoughtful of him.

The announcement in the Press came a month later – appropriately on my birthday, 24 June. In a statement, Clare Lawson-Dick said: 'Fans of the programme wrote to us in large numbers asking for it to be restored. We were also greatly touched and influenced by letters from blind and disabled people who were unable to travel and said that *Down Your Way* had been their only means of getting to know Britain.' I think the BBC deserves credit for admitting that their previous decision had been wrong. By so doing they showed that they *do* try to give listeners what they want. It was quite an exercise for the Press office, who told me that it was the first time that the BBC had *publicly* admitted to bowing to public pressure on behalf of a programme.

But amidst all our jubilation there was one person in particular for whom I felt very sorry – Phyllis Robinson. With Richard Burwood she had produced the programme from London for the past thirteen years. It had become very much her 'baby' and part of her life, since her associations with it started far earlier than that.

DYW began in December 1946, produced by Leslie Perowne and John Shuter, with boxing and ice hockey commentator Stewart Macpherson as the presenter. The very first one came from Lambeth Walk and for the first ten programmes it came from various parts of London. It was all very free and easy with no preliminary research. Stewart just went along with a recording car, knocked on people's doors and interviewed them there and then. It was naturally very much hit and miss in more senses than one. Not only did Stewart have no prior knowledge of the person he was going to interview, but on one occasion he was actually hit under the chin by a man who came to the door and mistook Stewart for someone who had been molesting his wife! Shortly after this Stewart said he had had enough and that he felt that the programme wasn't 'him'.

Lionel Gamlin then took over for half a dozen programmes until the BBC found that one of their wartime reporters was 'available'. In fact he was virtually unemployed. So they booked him in the early spring of 1947 for a trial six programmes. His name was Richard Dimbleby and he (naturally!) did so well that he continued to do it till 1953, when after exactly three hundred and fifty editions he found that his family newspaper at Richmond, and his growing TV work, made the weekly *DYW* assignment too much of a burden. Phyllis Robinson had started with him as a recorded programme assistant, and then took over as producer towards the end of Richard's time. In those days the programme was occasionally done live from places like the Hebrides, Shetland Islands and the Channel Islands. During the six years, Richard only missed one programme when he caught chicken-pox from his eldest son, David, and then Wynford Vaughan-Thomas deputised for him. He did, however, have to link the two hundred and fiftieth from his Surrey home because he had broken a rib falling off his horse.

For some reason *DYW* was rested for two years but returned in 1955 with Franklin Englemann (Jingle) to present it. Previously all the interviews had been recorded on to discs, but now the era of the tapes had arrived and they have been used ever since. The first of the new *DYW* came from Crewe – the theme being 'all change', with Richard making a typical gesture by going up to Crewe to introduce Jingle. From then on Jingle became *DYW*, and *DYW* became Jingle. People will always associate his strong but friendly personality with the programme. Like Richard, he only missed one between 1955 and 1972. He caught 'flu and as it was coming from Cardiff, Alun Williams was able to deputise for him at the last moment.

Jingle had just recorded his seven hundred and thirty-third programme when he died suddenly in March 1972 and I had to take over from him at short notice, and except for two breaks have done it ever since. The two breaks were during the summer of 1972 when, because of my duties as BBC cricket correspondent, Roy Trevivian, Geoffrey Wheeler, Alex Macintosh and Paddy Feeney took over for four weeks each. The other was for four weeks in January 1973 when I went to South Africa as PRO for Derrick Robins on his cricket tour out there. My place was taken by that fact-seeking Scotsman with the querulous plaintive voice – Fyfe Robertson – a complete contrast to me in accent and pace of delivery.

The format of *DYW* has changed from time to time, but has always had the basic idea of a certain number of people being interviewed about their town or village and then each being asked to choose a piece of music. For the first two years after Jingle took over, it only ran for six months each year, but then settled down to a steady pattern of ten months a year, with Jingle doing *Holiday Hour* in January and February. For ten years the programme lasted for an hour with nine people being interviewed. But ever since I have been the presenter it has lasted for forty minutes with six interviews. In Richard's day the emphasis was very much on the music with short interviews but ever since Jingle took over the interview has invariably been longer than the music. Nowadays the average is something like four and a half minutes of interview and two and a quarter minutes of music.

The choice of music is left entirely up to the person interviewed, with two provisos. It must not have been chosen the week before and obviously it has to be available – either in the BBC Record Library or obtainable in the shops, or perhaps the person interviewed has a private recording. At one time, because the programme goes out first on a Sunday, much sacred music was chosen, especially in Scotland. I think people possibly thought that this type of music was what the BBC wanted them to choose. Though there *was* proof in 1958 that even in London the Sunday puritan spirit still existed. When *DYW* visited Oxford Street the proprietor of an umbrella shop forbade any of his staff to take part because it *did* go out on a Sunday.

Over the years the choice has broadened. Although we still get the inevitable favourites, nowadays we do have a few requests for something in 'the charts'. But there *are* some regulars which continually crop up. In Richard's day it was *Bless This House* and *Now is the Hour*. With Jingle, *Jerusalem* and *Stranger on the Shore* were top favourites. Among our most popular ones today are Handel's *Hallelujah Chorus*, Verdi's *Hebrew Slaves Chorus*, the theme tunes from *Love Story*, *Dr Zhivago* and *The Onedin Line*, and the music from Gilbert and Sullivan. And of course there's our distinctive signature tune, which most people know so well but of which they frequently ask the title. It's *Horse-Guards Whitehall*, by Haydn Wood played by the Queen's Hall Light Orchestra.

People also often ask us how we choose the places which we visit. As we are now approaching our fourteen-hundredth town and village, this is getting a little bit harder every year. Stick a pin in a map of the United Kingdom to represent each place and you would find that there's not much space left. But the producers who actually choose the locations follow certain basic rules. First of all we never (with exceptions in Northern Ireland) visit a place twice. Then we must distribute our visits equally over all parts of the country, and ensure that we have the right proportion of big and small towns, villages and industrial, residential or agricultural districts.

Luckily our files are still full of invitations from people asking us to visit them. So once the area is decided, reference to a file usually produces a place within it where we have been asked to go. There are by now very few big towns unvisited by *DYW*. Since 1972 the only really large place I have been to is Blackburn with just over 100,000 inhabitants, and I think the next largest is Harpenden with about 30,000. Our present average is something between 2,000 to 5,000. Sadly, since I took over we have only been to Northern Ireland three times, though since 1947 there have been thirty-nine visits altogether. But with a non-controversial programme like ours it is practically impossible to talk to people about their town or village and ignore all the terrible things that are going on around them. It would put me in the position of being completely insensitive, and out of touch with their real problems, and to appear to be asking inane and pointless questions.

DYW at one time went abroad, mostly to Europe, often to fit in with a Trade Fair or an event like the Olympic Games. But now, except for a short cruise on the SS *Canberra* in 1976, we stay at home, though we are hoping to go abroad again. In addition to geographical locations (as they say in *Twenty Questions*) there have been a number of 'one-offs' such as exhibitions, institutions, hospitals, theatres, schools, charities, museums, the three Services, stations, airports, zoos and even an oil rig.

Most of what success *DYW* has depends on the selection

of the right six people and this is entirely the responsibility of the producer. There are certain obvious ingredients needed to achieve a properly balanced programme – i.e. one person who can tell the listener as much as possible about a place in as entertaining a way as possible. There must be someone to talk about past events and the history of the place. If it is an industrial town then we probably look for someone from one of the factories, or if it is agricultural then a farmer or a shepherd or someone connected with the countryside. Many places have some sort of traditional ceremony, such as an annual traction-engine fair or a pancake race, and a person is needed to explain these. There is the social side of a town with its clubs, institutions, sports complex, and also the 'do-good' side of a community, which is so essential to the happiness of a place. But more important perhaps than any of these, the producer is always on the look-out for a 'character', or the man or woman with an unusual job or hobby. If they have the local dialect and accent so much the better.

We are very conscious of the fact that the majority of the people we interview are on the elderly side. This is inevitable, as in general they know far more about a place and its customs, simply because they have lived there longer. 'Characters', too, develop the older they grow. So whenever possible we do try to include at least one young person to represent the youthful side of a place – this also helps to liven up the choice of music! There is also the need to get as fair a balance as possible between the sexes, though in spite of Women's Lib I would say we still average four men to two women per programme – it just seems to work out that way.

One of the producer's difficulties is to avoid any similarity with the programmes which have gone out in the previous few weeks. For instance, however old or beautiful a church may be, vicars have to be rationed out, so do farmers, good ladies who run Women's Institutes, Old

People's Homes or Meals on Wheels. Everyone naturally wants to mention *everything* which goes on in their town and naturally feels that theirs is better than anyone else's. Quite often we get somebody writing in after a programme asking why we did not include old so and so who is a real character and known to everyone as Mr Whatever the name of the place is. What they don't realise is that the producer has probably visited the person but found that he or she is stone deaf, has a slight stammer or even that we interviewed someone in the same trade or profession only the week before. They may even have refused to take part, though this very rarely happens, and when it does it is usually because of excessive modesty or shyness.

How then does the producer make his or her choice? After selecting the place we are to visit, something like two or three months in advance, a letter is written to the local town clerk (or his equivalent in these complicated days of council reorganisation) saying that we would like to visit the town and asking the clerk to prepare a list of likely people to interview who can best put the town on the map. Any list they send is of great help, but the producers will also have read every guide book available about the place to find out about its industries, history and customs. This will give them a clue as to the type of people they must look for on arrival, when they will not only call on the town clerk, but meet the local press and pick up valuable information in the pubs – often the best sources of all. The producer is also often helped by the original letter suggesting our visit, which may include some possible names.

To be courteous and polite we have always allowed up to one hour for each person so that we don't appear to rush in and out. This still applies today and Tony Smith and I purposely don't look at our watches until we get up to go and it's amazing how often we find that we have taken between fifty-five and sixty minutes. The producer has of course already met the person to be interviewed, but although he has briefed me beforehand, I always spend the first twenty minutes or so over a cup of tea or coffee getting to know them, finding out about their family and interests – in fact gaining their confidence and making friends. I then know roughly the sort of question I will have to ask to draw them out and get the information which we want in a relaxed way.

We record possibly up to seven minutes depending on the interviewee's ability and clarity in answering my questions. We then have time to play back the interviews so that a husband or wife who has been sent out of the room during the recording can hear the result. We find that most people are far less inhibited if they have no one else in the room except for the producer, the engineer with tape-recorder and myself. Sometimes when a wife is the domineering type, if present she can be tempted to prompt her husband with stage whispers – very off-putting! Because some of the people interviewed are busy they can only see us in their factory, office, shop or home at a certain time. So we don't necessarily record the interviews in the exact order in which they will finally go out on the air.

Before the interviews are broadcast on *DYW*, they are edited by the producer and the music is slotted in between each interview. The editing of the interviews is done first of all to 'tidy' up, removing the occasional 'ers' and hesitations, or something which the person regrets having said and would like removed. Or again if the answers given to me are rather monosyllabic, it means I have to prompt and encourage the interviewee with a number of supplementary questions. The whole thing then ceases to be a conversation and becomes just a series of questions and answers. But in the editing it is often possible to take out some of my questions so that the answers are joined up to make a more comprehensive reply.

But basically, it's all a matter of the timing and, as I've shown, unless the person is outstanding, the average interview has to be cut down to just over four minutes. One other thing which has *not* changed is that we choose and interview six people *only* and those are the ones who go out on the air. Some other interview programmes record a number of people and then finally select a few of them. But we don't think that is fair and anyone whom we have interviewed can safely tell his or her friends: 'Listen to me next Sunday at 5.15 pm – I'm on *Down Your Way!*'

The way the programme is recorded and edited has changed since it has been produced from Bristol. When the programmes came from London, they were edited on the Friday and used to go out two days later on the Sunday. It is difficult to believe it now but there was *never* a spare programme in reserve in case of an accident to me or the producer or engineer, or even in case the tape got lost or destroyed by mistake. Phyllis backed her luck and with Richard and Jingle only missing one programme each out of more than a thousand and with me luckily fit, she was proved right. But it was a terrific gamble and I often implored her to record at least one in reserve. But she felt that she gained from the topicality and avoided the risk of any of the people interviewed dying if the programme was recorded too far in advance. But of course this policy was the reason for the hurried selection of myself to replace Jingle. He died on the Wednesday night after recording a programme, which, with the consent of his widow, went out on the following Sunday and Tuesday as usual. But the show had to go on – hence my first *DYW* only six days after Jingle's death.

Partly to avoid this risk, but mainly for reasons of time and money, we now record two programmes in the first week of the month and two in the second, leaving the last fortnight free for editing, in which, by the way, I have no say, I am never present in the studio when it is done. This I think is a good idea as I am too close and involved, whereas the producer has been able to listen to and judge each interview impartially as it's being done. Each pair of programmes are recorded within an area of about sixty square miles to save mileage and time, but they are not put out on the air in successive weeks. For instance, if we record a pair in Oxfordshire and Northants, two programmes, say from Scotland and Wales, would be put on between them.

Tony Smith (or the producer who deputises for him about twelve times a year) leaves Bristol on a Monday, vets one town from Monday evening to Tuesday evening and then travels the sixty miles or so to the next place. By the time the engineer and myself have arrived on Wednesday evening he has made his selections. We sometimes do one interview that night and five the next day before setting off for the first town which Tony vetted on the Tuesday. We finish sometime on Friday afternoon ready for a nice peaceful weekend.

It's a tightly-timed but well-organised timetable and we still find that each place takes around six hours to do, though the kind hospitality of people does sometimes mean that we get behind the clock. It's not unusual to be offered tea or coffee, biscuits and home-made cakes at all four houses or offices which we visit in a morning. We have learnt to say 'no thank you' politely, but sometimes when the tray is laid out ready we don't have the heart to do so, no matter how much our stomachs complain. We appreciate that although it's just another pleasant day's work for us, *DYW* only visits a place once in a lifetime, so in a small way it's quite a big day for the 'victim'. Luckily I have never had the same experience as Richard Dimbleby, who once had to squeeze in three interviews in one evening. As a result, in each house he visited, the table was laid either for high tea or supper and he bravely did justice to all three! But he did have more room for it than me!

It's the same everywhere we go. We invariably get a very warm welcome and this really does make my job rewarding. I was, however, once slightly surprised by a greeting from an effusive and friendly lady. She flung open her front door and said: 'Oh, Mr Johnston, how nice to see you. I have always wanted to meet you. And do tell me – how big is your apparatus?'!! I can only think that she was referring to our engineer's equipment – if you see what I mean!

As you can imagine, *DYW* involves a lot of travelling and I usually go by car except to Scotland, when I either fly or use the train. Trains have a funny effect on me. I hope I am a fairly gregarious and friendly person, but once inside a railway carriage I shut up like a clam. Even if there's only one other person I never say a word but just slump behind my newspaper. It sounds dreadfully unfriendly, but I find there are quite a few people who do the same.

While on the subject of trains, there was the bishop who was sitting in the corner seat of a crowded carriage doing *The Times* crossword puzzle. He seemed to be getting on pretty well and filling in a lot of the answers. But he began to look puzzled and putting down his paper asked the other passengers: 'Could any of you kindly help me? I want a four-letter word with female affiliations ending in UNT.' There was a slight pause and then a young man suggested: 'What about Aunt, sir?' 'Ah,' said the bishop with relief, 'that's it. I thought I must be wrong. Have any of you got a rubber?'

But, as usual, I have digressed, and now a final word about *Down Your Way*. As this book goes to press I have recorded two hundred and fifty-five programmes and interviewed more than fifteen-hundred people.[1] It is a wonderful programme to do and as with so much of my life I have been unbelievably lucky to get the job. We are

[1] Brian continued to present *Down Your Way* for a further ten years. He retired after 733 programmes, exactly the same number as his predecessor Franklin Engelmann, and by then he had interviewed some 4,500 people. His final programme was recorded on 20 May 1987 at Lord's Cricket Ground and his last interview was with his old friend, Denis Compton.

unashamedly square and uncontroversial. We go to a place to find out the good things about it, and never look 'under the carpet' for the sort of things which hit the headlines in the popular press. We just try to find nice people who will reflect all these good things. It is one of the satisfying features of *DYW* that there *are* so many nice people about. We are told *ad nauseam* of the terrible things which go on in our society and how mean and self-centred people are. Up to a point this is obviously true. On the other hand you come round the country with me and it really will cheer you up to meet so many people who are devoting so much of their lives or leisure time to helping others. Call them do-gooders – or what you like. But their numbers are legion and they are the salt of the earth. I like to think that they are the true heart of Britain. It all sounds terribly old-fashioned and patriotic – but I *do* mean it. In addition of course I learn a little about a lot, and discover old buildings, customs and traditions which have been in existence for centuries. There's also the joy of journeying all over Britain, which in spite of the growth of towns and the spreading tentacles of industry still remains to me the most beautiful country in the world.

22 Nice people

THE MOST IMPORTANT part of *Down Your Way* to me is the memory of the people whom I have interviewed. There have been so many now that I can obviously only mention a fraction of them. I suppose pride of place must go to the only centurion whom I have so far interviewed in the programme – Mrs Emma Brewster of Radcliffe on Trent. She was as bright as a cricket and looked wonderfully fit and alert as she sat in her armchair by the fire. She had goodness knows how many great-grandchildren and was lovingly looked after by one of her granddaughters. During the interview I asked her whether she had received a telegram from the Queen on her hundredth birthday. 'Oh, yes,' she said, 'I did, but I was very disappointed. It wasn't in her own handwriting. I think she must be getting old and bored with doing it so often. I know I would be!'

Then there was the vegetarian from Usk in Wales, who during the war was sent out to India to run the mule transport. Knowing he would be short of the green stuff out there he took with him a lot of mustard and cress seeds. Each night at the end of a hot sticky day he would take off his wellington boots and plant some seeds inside them. By next day he had some fresh(?) mustard and cress to eat with his curry for lunch.

Talking of wellies – when we went to Presteigne in Powys, a young farmer called John Davies, who was a champion sheep shearer, told us about an unusual competitive sport which was very popular in those parts. It was welly-wanging, and it used to take place at all the local fairs and fêtes. It is very similar to throwing the javelin except that you hurl a wellington boot instead. The good throwers get quite a good distance – something in the region of forty yards. John told us with delight that the ladies also ran a competition and that the local lady welly-wanging champion was a Mrs Woolley from Willey!

There was a lovely old lady of well over eighty in the small town of Penkridge in Staffordshire. She was a farmer's daughter and still delivered milk round the town each day. She lived in her father's old house where she had been born. It had been a farm but was now a terraced house in a street. The remarkable thing she told us was that in all her life she had never spent *a single night away from the house*. She had been to London for the day and on several coach trips to the seaside, but had always returned at night to sleep in her own house. The only concession she made in this extraordinary tale was that she had not always slept in the same room. I found it very difficult to take in when I thought of the many hundreds of nights I myself have spent away from home either on my job or on holiday.

When in Buckfastleigh for *Down Your Way* I was told the following story of a new vicar at the parish church on the top of the hill above the town. He was being taken round the churchyard by the verger who was giving him a potted history of the various people buried there. When they came to one tombstone the verger said: 'This was Harry – I warned him but he wouldn't listen. I told him that the cider would be the death of him and would get him in the end. And it did. He went on drinking it in spite of all my warnings.' The vicar stooped down to read the writing on the tombstone, and read: 'Harry––, who died aged 96 years on –.'

In St Davids Dyfed – the smallest cathedral city – we came across the local baker, a great talker and character called Dai Evans. He kept a donkey which drank beer and was famous for miles around for his home-made bread and cakes. Inevitably he was called Dai 'the Crust'. His greatest triumph was on a visit to the district by Prince

Charles. Dai had the honour to present one of his special loaves personally to the Prince of Wales. From then on he assumed the title of Dai the *Upper* Crust!

Anthony Beard was a young farmer at Widecombe-in-the-Moor in Devon, of Uncle Tom Cobley fame. He did a milk round in the local villages, and, incidentally, used plastic instead of glass milk bottles and so saved himself the time and labour of having to collect and wash them. In his spare time he was an entertainer, singing West Country songs and telling stories in the Devonshire dialect. He even yodelled and composed his own songs. One of the stories was about a farmer who often milked the cows in the open fields to save bringing them back to the farm. One summer evening he was milking away when a holidaymaker leant over the hedge and asked him if he knew the time. The farmer put his hand under the cow's udder and replied: 'Ten minutes to six, mister,' and went on with his milking.

The holidaymaker was amazed and rushed off back to the village to fetch his wife to see this extraordinary countryman who could tell the time by putting his hand under a cow's udder. The couple came back in about twenty minutes and found the farmer milking another cow at the same spot by the hedge. The holidaymaker persuaded his wife to ask the time. Once again the farmer put his hand under the cow's udder and replied: 'Just on ten minutes past six.' The couple thanked him and went off dumbfounded at what they had seen. In explanation Anthony added: 'What the farmer didn't tell them was that each time he lifted the cow's udder, he could see the clock on the church tower.'

When we visited North Berwick – that mecca of golfing – Mrs Doreen Stevenson told us about the old professional, Ben Sayers, renowned maker of golf clubs and with a great reputation as a teacher. At one time North Berwick was very fashionable with politicians, who went there to breathe the invigorating air and, of course, to play golf.

Lord Balfour and Sir John Simon were frequent visitors and one day Ben was partnering Lord Balfour in a foursome. They were playing on the No. 1 links which run along by the sea, and on which in the old days the local farmers had grazing rights.

At one hole Lord Balfour drove off and his ball went straight down the middle but landed slap in the middle of a juicy cow pat. Lord Balfour thought this was very funny and laughingly apologised to Ben, but said it was his shot and that he would have to 'get out of the mess'. But the wily Ben took a mashie and after taking deliberate aim played a complete air shot. 'I'm sorry, m'lord,' he said with a cunning smile, 'I'm afraid I got a fly in my eye, which made me miss it completely. Now it's *your* turn to get it out!'

One of the most cheerful people I have ever met in *DYW* was Syd Hart who had spent most of his life in the Cheshire Home at Ampthill suffering from multiple sclerosis. In spite of all his trouble, life seemed to be one big joke to him, and he apologised during our interview for not speaking too clearly. He explained that in his hurry to get ready he had put in someone else's false teeth by mistake!

Then there was Arthur Roland of the little village of Alston in Cumbria. He kept – of all things – a bottle shop. Just rows and rows of empty bottles – eight thousand of them, of all shapes, sizes and colours. Some were worth £20 or more, and people from all over the world descend on Arthur to add to their own collections. The surprising thing about Arthur was that he did not drink anything except tea.

In Ruthin, North Wales, we discovered a young girl called Patricia Evers-Swindell who remarkably painted on *cobwebs*. She lived in an old house with some old stables attached. She collected the cobwebs from these, some still with the spider and dead flies in them. She then covered them thinly with milk to take some of the stickiness out of them and then painted on them with ordinary brush and paint. Dogs' heads were her speciality and by framing the web between two pieces of glass she obtained an excellent three-dimensional effect.

The great thing about doing *DYW* is that we are always learning something new. I personally had never heard of a Foaling Bank but we came across one in Newport, Shropshire. It had been started by Joanna Vardon as a completely new idea, and was the only one in the world. It was really a sort of swap shop. All over the country a number of mares die giving birth to their foals and so leave orphans to be looked after. Alternatively a number of foals die at birth or are stillborn, leaving an unhappy mother with lots of milk and no foal to drink it.

So Joanna Vardon had what was really a very simple idea, but a very difficult and complicated one to carry out. She thought what a waste it was of foal-less mares and motherless foals. So why not bring the two together? This she has done in a remarkable way and people from all over the country – and even from abroad – arrive at all times of the day or night with horse-boxes – or even a mini in the case of one tiny foal lying on the back seat! Speed is the essence of the operation as a mare's milk dries up in about twenty-four hours if there is no foal to suckle her. There is also the problem of a mare accepting a foal which is not her own. Joanna found that she had to skin the dead foal and wrap its skin round the orphan foal before the mare would accept it. A rather gruesome business but carried out cheerfully by Joanna Vardon and her band of lady helpers. It should also be pointed out that the whole scheme is non-profit making and people pay what they can afford. Since the bank started in 1966 Joanna and her staff have dealt with well over five thousand cases.

At Budleigh Salterton we had the pleasure of meeting 'Golden Voice' – alias Stuart Hibberd, the first-ever BBC radio announcer. Now aged eighty-four, he was amazingly hale and hearty and entertained us before the interview with songs and recitations without any music or notes. He recalled the early days at Savoy Hill when all the announcers had to change into dinner jackets at 6 pm. At first he wore a stiff shirt but the engineers complained that it made crackling noises into the microphone, so from then on he had to wear a soft one.

He denied making some of the well-known gaffes which are generally attributed to him, such as:

'There'll now be an interlush by Ernest Lude';

'We are now going over to the bathroom at Pump';

'You will now hear the bum of the flightlebee.'

But he *did* admit to two. During a weather forecast he once said that there would be 'heal and slate' instead of 'sleet and hail'. And when introducing a programme of American music he announced that the next piece would be *The Star Bangled Spanner*!

He made one amusing slip during our interview. I said that I understood that he still played a part in the life of the church at Budleigh. 'Yes,' he said, 'I still read the news – hmm lesson, every Sunday evening.'

At Goring on Thames I interviewed the wartime Commander-in-Chief, Bomber Command, Marshal of the Royal Air Force, Sir Arthur Harris, nicknamed 'Bomber'. I was a bit apprehensive as I had never met him before and outwardly he had always seemed to be a tough stand-no-nonsense sort of character. He had certainly had to fight hard throughout the war on behalf of his Bomber Command, and had a reputation of speaking his mind, with no fear of anyone. Anyway, we thought we must make sure to be punctual for our interview and so get off to a good start.

As a result, we were in fact a few minutes in advance of the time arranged. After we had rung the bell of his charming riverside house, the well-known figure opened the door and in a gruff voice barked out: 'You're early,' in such a way that it appeared to be a bigger crime than being late. However he soon smiled and welcomed us and we spent a delightful hour with him in his study. There were pictures of all types of aeroplanes dating from the early days of the 1914 war and signed photographs of all the great war leaders, from Sir Winston and General Eisenhower downwards. There were letters and memos written on paper with headings of No. 10 Downing Street or SHAPE headquarters.

I asked Sir Arthur why Bomber Command never got the full appreciation and recognition which it undoubtedly deserved. He thought that it was because people, having been bombed themselves, disliked bombs. The public also never saw the direct results of his bombers' work whereas the more glamorous Fighter Command could be seen in action in the skies defending our homes. I also asked him why he was not given a peerage like all the other war leaders. He said that after the war, Winston had said he would ask Mr Attlee to give him a peerage but that he, Sir Arthur, had refused and was content to accept a baronetcy in 1953. But he seemed to have no bitterness and to be living a happy and contented life among the friendly people of Goring. He had obviously lost none of his guts and determination because on the day before I saw him he had judged the local Jubilee Baby Competition in the town – and that *does* take courage.

Incidentally, Sir Arthur was not like Monty, who during a battle went to bed as usual at 10 pm and woe betide anyone who disturbed him. Sir Arthur admitted that whenever his bombers were out, except for the odd cat-nap he never went to sleep and was available for instant decisions at any time of the night. He was never made into a war hero like some of the others, but after meeting him I am convinced that Bomber Command and the nation owed him much gratitude and possibly a slight apology for the somewhat churlish way he was treated.

At Coldstream in Berwickshire, I interviewed Henry Douglas-Home, brother of Sir Alec, now Lord Home, and a well-known ornithologist and broadcaster in Scotland. I talked to him in a glade of a wood on the Hirsel Estate – family home of the Homes. It was from here that he used to compete with *his* birds against me with *my* birds from a wood at Hever in Kent. These friendly competitions were great fun to do and were done live. We both had microphones placed strategically throughout our woods to catch the song of as many birds as possible. Percy Edwards was the judge and noted down all the different birds he heard, each side taking it in turns to broadcast, and the one with the most species of birds heard was the winner. The results were always very close, though on one occasion Henry did accuse me of cheating! I must say I was once very suspicious of him, too, when, with the scores level, we suddenly heard a cuckoo from his wood – a most unlikely bird to hear at the time of the year when we were broadcasting. There is in fact the hoot of an owl in the archives in Scotland which Henry recorded, saying it was the most perfect reproduction he had ever heard. It was only years later that his brother William admitted that it had been him hooting behind a bush! No wonder I was suspicious about that cuckoo!

Henry told us a delightful story about the Home family. They had a wonderful Jeeves-like butler called Collingwood, and one day before the war someone said to the old Lord Home: 'I'm sorry to tell you, m'lord, but I think Collingwood is going mad. Early this morning at 7 am I saw him walking over a ploughed field in full butler's rig. Black coat, striped trousers and all, talking and singing to himself.' On investigation Lord Home discovered what had happened. His youngest son, George, was a very keen birdwatcher and used to go off at 5.30 am to a hide to watch the birds through binoculars. But he found that the birds, having seen him arrive, were aware of his presence, and stayed quietly out of sight. So George persuaded Collingwood to go with him one morning, much against Collingwood's will. He finally agreed but said he would have to come fully dressed as he had to be back in time to take up early morning tea to Lord and Lady Home. The idea was that the birds would see George and Collingwood go together into the hide, and that after a short time Collingwood would ostentatiously leave it, singing and talking to himself to attract the attention of the birds. The hope was that the birds would be fooled into thinking that the 'enemy' had now gone, not noticing that although two had arrived only one had left. Anyhow, that was the explanation of the singing butler.

One of the most unusual and eccentric people I have ever interviewed was Richard Booth of Hay-on-Wye. He was unusual because he has turned Hay into a book town. He has six second-hand book shops with over two million books on about fifteen miles of shelving. His object is to have as many books as possible on each subject, so that someone who is, say, interested in bridge or gardening can go to Hay and be directed to shelf after shelf on his or her subject. In no other bookshop in the world would it be possible to find such a concentration of books on so many different subjects. Visitors come to Hay from all over the world and there is an annual book week with lots of celebrations.

Richard buys his books in vast quantities, and when I went to see him he was just back from America where he had bought up a hundred thousand second-hand books. Just think of the job of sorting that lot, and then the even more difficult task of deciding on the right price for each one after buying them in bulk. He admitted that he must sometimes unknowingly buy up a rare first edition and let it slip through his fingers.

He was eccentric because on 1 April 1977 he declared Hay-on-Wye independent and indeed I received an invitation to the opening ceremony. He was also in the process of appointing his own ambassadors to various countries.

It was, as you can imagine, a fascinating interview to do and it had a most surprising and hilarious ending, which alas the listeners never heard. When I asked Richard for his choice of music I caught his eye and for some unknown reason he got the giggles – or in theatrical language he 'corpsed'. So did we all, but luckily the engineer kept recording and I often play the tape when I want a good laugh. It's quite hysterical. He was laughing so much that to start with he couldn't get a word out. So I kept on repeating my question in between my own laughs. Gradually through his chokes and sobs he managed to blurt out that he wanted *Golden Years* or anything by David Bowie.

I must have asked him at least ten times for his music before his answer was considered good enough to go in the programme. Although they did not hear the laughing tape on *Down Your Way*, listeners did hear it at the end of a programme I did with producer Michael Craig called *It's a Funny Business*. I explained what had happened and then we just played the hoots of laughter. Jimmy Tarbuck told me sometime afterwards that he was motoring along listening to the programme, and began to laugh so much that he had to pull into the side of the road until it had finished.

And then there was a young chap called Chris Fleming at Wem in Shropshire. He played a big part in organising activities in the town and also ran a disco. He advertised it as 'the most boring disco in the world', chiefly because his Shropshire customers demanded a squarer type of music than is normally played in discos. He wore an earring on his left ear. I asked him why only *one* earring and not one on his right ear. 'Well,' he replied, 'I would look an awful fool if I wore two, wouldn't I?'

Jack Pharoah of Ravenglass was an amusing character and one of those people who seem to be able to turn their hands to anything. When I interviewed him he had a cobbler's shop and kept a garage. But he had been a fisherman, a ferryman and a guide to the local bird sanctuary, among other things. He was not above a bit of subterfuge to help to boost trade. As a ferryman he used to ferry visitors across to the sanctuary. But at low tides it was just possible for them to walk across if they so wished. So to discourage them he used to get his son to walk across the sands in full view of the visitors. Then suddenly his son would pretend to be sinking into the sand and mud, as if caught in some quicksand. Naturally enough after that, most visitors opted to go across by boat!

Jack also once worked quite a clever trick on the owner of a Rolls-Royce. The man drove up in his Rolls and asked Jack to fill it up, while he went across the road to get some cigarettes. He was in such a hurry that he left the engine of the Rolls running. When he got back he asked Jack how many gallons he had put in. 'Seventeen, sir,' said Jack. 'But,' protested the Rolls' owner, 'the car only holds fifteen gallons.' 'I know,' said Jack, thinking quickly, 'but as you left the engine running it used two gallons while I was filling the car up!'

We received a double bonus when we visited Harpenden in the shape of Lord Hill and Eric Morecambe. Lord Hill, the former Cabinet Minister and, uniquely, chairman, in succession, of both ITA and BBC, was still best known to many people as the wartime 'Radio Doctor'. He told me how he was the first man ever to mention the word 'bowels' on the air with that deep bedside voice of his. His philosophy in his radio talks was to give confidence to his listeners and discourage them from worrying about their health. 'Leave it alone. It won't get better if you pick it,' was a typical bit of advice.

As for Eric, what a lovely person he was. Modest, kind, friendly, a great worker for charity but perhaps most important of all, a naturally funny man. He didn't have to try to be funny. He just was. Jokes came automatically to him no matter to whom he was talking. During our interview, which was completely unrehearsed, I asked him why he came to live in Harpenden. 'Oh, we came here one day to sell my mother-in-law . . .', or again when I asked him about the running 'feud' between him and Des O'Connor, 'Oh, we're great friends really,' he said. 'He even came to my daughter's wedding – he wasn't asked, but he came.' Eric was a keen ornithologist, so I asked him if he went out walking with big binoculars. 'Oh, no,' said Eric, 'I leave Big Binoculars behind. He's not too keen on birds.' And so on.

Eric was a most rewarding person to talk to, and genuinely fond of Harpenden and its inhabitants. They all knew him by sight of course and he said he enjoyed going shopping and talking to them. 'It's only when I go to Luton,' he said, 'that I put on dark glasses and a limp . . .'

Inevitably, as I've said, we tend to talk to a good many elderly people on *Down Your Way*, and a friendly colleague warned me of one pitfall into which he had fallen. He was interviewing a very old lady who was ill in bed. Sitting by her bedside he asked her. 'Have you ever been bed-ridden before?' 'Yes, young man,' she replied, 'I have many times. And I've got ten children to prove it!' So that is *one* question I never ask!

And another warning to would-be interviewers. Never judge people's age by their appearance, as a mythical broadcaster is 'reputed' to have discovered to his cost! He was visiting an old people's home to find out why some people live to such a ripe old age. He picked out the three oldest men he could see, and asked each one the same questions. How old are you, and to what do you attribute your old age?

The first old man said he was a hundred and two and had never smoked in his life, had always gone to bed at ten o'clock every night and had been happily married for sixty-five years.

The second said he was a hundred and six, had never drunk, took a long walk every day and although a bachelor had enjoyed a healthy sex life as a young man.

The third old man looked particularly frail and wizened. He said he had never gone to bed before 2 am, drank at least two bottles of whisky and smoked sixty cigarettes a day. But most important of all he had enjoyed sex at least three times every night with any woman he could find.

The interviewer was flabbergasted as he gazed at the wrinkled old face ravaged by time. 'Well,' he said, 'I don't know how you've done it. Remarkable. But I don't think you said how old you are.' 'Twenty-eight next birthday,' replied the 'old' man.

All this travelling round the country staying in different hotels can have its complications – as my friend Henry Blofeld, the cricket writer and commentator, once found to his cost. He was reporting a county match at Nottingham and for the first night stayed at the Bridgford Hotel. But because they were booked up he had to move to the Albany Hotel for the next two nights. He had a good dinner with a few aperitifs and a bottle of wine and then went up to his room for an early night feeling 'nicely thank you'.

As he always does, he slept in the nude, and woke at about 2 am wanting to spend a penny. So in a sleepy, bemused state he got out of bed, groped his way round the room and found a door which he thought was the bathroom. He went through it and it shut with a click behind him. He then looked for the loo but to his horror found he was standing in the brightly-lit corridor outside his room, without a stitch of clothing on and without his key. He was by now wide awake and quickly spotted a tray on the floor outside the next-door room. He whipped the paper napkin from under the plates and held it in front of his vital parts.

He realised that he must get hold of the night porter to open his door for him with a pass key. So he crept along the deserted corridor to the lift, which to his relief started coming up when he pressed the button. When it arrived he got in and pressed 'Ground Floor', intending when he reached there to call out to the night porter for help. The lift began to descend but to his alarm he felt it slowing up as it approached the second floor. Someone had obviously pushed the button and sure enough as the lift stopped at the gates there waiting to get in was a party of men and women in evening dress, laughing and joking after what had obviously been a very good evening.

The laughter stopped for a second as they saw Henry crouching at the back of the lift desperately clutching the inadequate napkin against himself. Then of course there was uproar, with roars of laughter, and a few shrill squeaks from the ladies. Luckily they had not opened the gates so Henry quickly pushed the ground-floor button again and the lift shot down out of sight of the party. He explained what had happened to a surprised night porter, not used to seeing naked men approaching his desk in the middle of the night. He gave Henry a pass key and saw him into the lift, which luckily raced up past the party on the second floor still recovering from shock. So Henry slunk back to his room and ever since has made sure that he knows the geography of every hotel room before he goes to sleep. A lesson for us all!

23 All's right with the World Cup

WHETHER OUT OF kindness or not, I don't know, but within a few days of learning that *Down Your Way* was coming off, I was asked to become a member of a new *Twenty Questions* team. This, too, caused quite a furore as, except for Anona Winn, all the members of the old panel were to be discarded. It seemed bad luck on them, especially Joy Adamson who had been on the panel for twenty-five years and Norman Hackforth, who for eighteen years had been either the mystery voice or one of the panel. The new Question Master in place of Peter Jones was to be Terry Wogan, and in addition to Anona and myself our panel was completed by humourist Willie Rushton and a charming actress, Bettine Le Beau.

But of course as a professional broadcaster one must accept any opportunity which is offered, without allowing one's feelings to interfere, and I'm sure the old panel understood this. Anyway, we were on a hiding to nothing because in fact *Twenty Questions* is not an easy game to play. In order not to waste questions team spirit is essential and this can only develop after several series together. There is the knack of knowing the right questions to ask early on to establish in which area the object is. For instance, if it is 'Animal' someone must ask: 'Is it human?' If so, then: 'Alive or dead? Fact or fiction? Are there lots of them? Only one,' and so on.

If it is *not* human then: 'How many legs? Domestic or wild? Do you eat it? Is it something made from an animal?' For 'Vegetable' you obviously start with: 'Can you eat it? Is it a growing plant? Can you wear it? Is it wooden, rubber etc?' And for 'Mineral' you have to establish whether it is wet or dry, metal or stone, natural or handmade. That leaves the hardest of them all, 'Abstract', which can be almost anything and the recognised first question here is: 'With what sense do you recognise it?' After that the best of luck! It's hit or miss.

So you can realise that there is a lot of skill needed which is only acquired by practice and knowing what the other team members are thinking. Plus of course that unbelievable intuition with which Anona Winn seems to be gifted. Willie Rushton proved to be a splendid guesser, keeping quiet for possibly two-thirds of the questions and then suddenly popping up with the correct answer – which proves the value of listening carefully to the answers given by the Question Master. Bettine with her broken accent and innocent charm managed to inveigle far more helpful answers from Terry than any of us.

We did thirteen programmes altogether during the summer, recording two in an evening or at lunchtime in front of an invited audience at the old Playhouse Theatre near the Embankment. We were nowhere near as good as the old panel, not surprisingly in my opinion, which I hope was some small comfort to them! We got a little better the more practice we had, but our producer, Alastair Scott-Johnston, did not make it easy for us. He had a special delight in giving us the dreaded Abstract objects so that our percentage of victories over Terry was not as high as it should have been.

Just to show what people thought of us, two old ladies were leaving the Playhouse after two of our recordings. Someone heard one of them ask the other: 'Did you enjoy it dear?' 'Yes, I did,' the other replied, 'very much indeed. But you know I *still* prefer *Twenty Questions!*'

But it was all great fun to do and under Terry's cheerful guidance we were a very happy team. The only thing I did *not* look forward to was the solo spot which really was rather frightening. You are out on your own with no help from the rest of the team. Often your mind goes a complete blank when it is quite obvious to everyone else what the object is. For instance, for one of my solos, the object was Animal or Vegetable. By the applause and laughter of the audience when they read what the object was, I suspected it would be something personal. After a few questions I established it had to do with cricket but failed to get it in twenty questions. I could have kicked myself afterwards. The answer was – a bat.

The year 1975 was a great summer for cricket. The sun shone, there was the first-ever World Cup Tournament, the Prudential Cup, and the added bonus of a four-match Test series against Australia.

The Prudential Cup was an unqualified success. Eight countries took part and during an unbelievable fortnight of uninterrupted blue sky there were fifteen matches played of one innings each with a maximum of sixty overs. Naturally the two junior members of the International Cricket Conference – Sri Lanka and East Africa – were outclassed, but there was some thrilling cricket watched by large crowds everywhere.

The teams were divided into two groups. In Group A, England and New Zealand got through to the semi-final, and in Group B, West Indies and Australia. So England played Australia, but lost by four wickets, while in the other semi-final, West Indies beat New Zealand easily by five wickets. That meant West Indies would meet Australia in the final at Lord's and what a match it proved to be, watched by 26,000 with the gates closed.

It continued uninterrupted except for the intervals from 11 am to 8.43 pm. This made it probably the longest-ever day in cricket of this class. The famous Gillette semi-final between Lancashire and Gloucestershire at Old Trafford in 1971 started at the same time and didn't finish until 8.50 pm. But this included an hour's delay because of rain at lunchtime. But luckily the Prudential final was on 21 June – the longest day in the year – so the light held and

Prince Philip presented the Prudential Cup to the worthy winners – West Indies.

Thanks almost entirely to a superb innings of 102 by their captain, Clive Lloyd, they made 291 for 8 off their 60 overs. In reply Australia were 274 all out off 58.4 overs, but when all seemed inevitably lost they nearly brought off a dramatic victory thanks to a last-wicket stand of 41 between that dynamic speed-duo Lillee and Thomson. It really was a wonderful match and set the seal on the competition, which was such a success that there was universal clamour for a repeat as soon as possible. It also gave me an opportunity for a nickname which I could not resist. Eighteen-year-old Javed Miandad just had to become Javed 'Mumandi'.

After the severe drubbing which England had received during the winter in Australia, not even their most optimistic supporter could have expected them to win the four-match Test series against Australia, which had been laid on at short notice to fill the gap after the Prudential Cup was over. In fact Australia only won 1–0, and their victory in the 1st Test at Edgbaston was largely due to Mike Denness' decision to put them into bat when he won the toss. Poor Mike! He had seemed to have salvaged some of his reputation as a captain and player after England's Test victories at Melbourne and Auckland, to which he contributed scores of 188 and 181.

But the morning of 10 July at Edgbaston was dull and grey, and after consultation with his team Mike took a gamble and lost. The gods don't like captains who put the other side in. As it turned out, the England bowlers got no movement off the pitch nor in the air and though at one time Australia were struggling a bit, they reached 359. Then as soon as Edrich and Amiss opened for England, so did the heavens for Australia, and a terrific thunderstorm flooded the ground. On a damp pitch England were all out for 101 and had to follow on.

After further thunderstorms on Monday, England were

all out 173 – beaten by an innings and 85 runs with a day and a half to spare. Mike Denness of course became the scapegoat and the media brayed for his blood. In fact by the Friday evening he had already told the selectors that he was ready to stand down in view of what had happened.

Naturally the statisticians had a field day. At least so far as England is concerned W. G. Grace seems to have been right, when he once said, 'After winning the toss, by all means think about putting the other side in. Then think again and invariably decide to bat.' Including Edgbaston, England captains have put Australia in to bat on eleven occasions, and have only won once – in Melbourne under J. W. H. T. Douglas in 1912.

Before leaving Edgbaston I must relate an amusing experience we had in the commentary box there. During one of the breaks in play due to the thunderstorms, we were having one of our usual discussions in the box rather than return to the studio for music. It was a hot sultry afternoon and for some reason we were discussing how cricket seemed to run in families. I suggested that this was often due to an enthusiastic mum who was prepared to play cricket in the garden with her sons. I quoted Penny Cowdrey, whose three boys are all following in Colin's footsteps. I said that only the week before she had taken five wickets against the Junior Boys XI of her youngest son Graham's preparatory school at Broadstairs. I then added mischievously: 'Yes, they tell me that on that day her swingers were practically unplayable.'

As I had suspected, this remark started everyone in the box giggling. Under some difficulties we continued the discussion and mentioned Vic Richardson's daughter who for years bowled for her three sons Ian, Greg and Trevor Chappell. Don Mosey said Trevor was having a wonderful season in the Lancashire League and that people were saying he would eventually be better than either Ian or Greg. I added that he had already played for South Australia, but that I thought he had lost his place in their side last season. 'Anyway,' I went on with confidence, knowing that Alan McGilvray was at the back of the box, 'we've got just the chap to confirm this. Alan . . .'

I turned round and saw that Alan was fast asleep, chin resting deep on his chest, with a slight whistling sound coming down his nose. This set us all off laughing again, but to cover up and save Alan any embarrassment I managed to blurt out: 'I'm sorry, I'm afraid Alan must have left the box.' With that Alan woke up with a snort and a start and said: 'What's going on? What do you want to know?' But by then we were helpless with laughter and couldn't tell him. All the listeners could hear was a gentle hissing and sobbing as we tried to stem our laughter. Nobody spoke for at least ten seconds, and that is a long time on the air. Don Mosey, who is the worst giggler of the lot, managed to make a bolt for the door, and collapsed outside, leaving me to hold the fort. When I was able to talk I came clean with the listeners and admitted that Alan had indeed been caught napping!

For the Second Test at Lord's Tony Greig was appointed captain, and the selectors decided to try batsmen known to be good against fast bowling – somewhat obvious perhaps! The match produced good performances from both sides – including 175 from Edrich – and ended in an honourable draw. Greig's flamboyant captaincy seemed to give new spirit to the England team and he personally got off to a great start. After four wickets had fallen to Lillee for only 49 runs, he made an aggressive 96. His first partner in this rescue act was the newcomer David Steele.

With his grey hair and steel spectacles, Steele was a most unlikely figure to bat No. 3 for England, and to have to face the speed and fire of Lillee and Thomson. But in addition to his normal forward defensive stroke, he attacked anything short with superb hooks and cuts. He made a fine 50 before being bowled by Thomson, and the crowd rose to him. They had taken him to their heart and in this one short innings he suddenly became a national hero – the plain Mr Everybody who dared to stand up to Lillee. People felt they could identify themselves with him, since in his appearance he was more like someone you'd expect to see in a solicitor's office than a Test cricketer.

Amiss, alas, failed again and this was to be the end of the road for him – temporarily only as it turned out. He obviously needed a rest from the battering of Lillee and Thomson, who always seemed to keep something especially nasty up their sleeves for him. Equally sad was that Graham Gooch, in spite of 31 in the second innings, was dropped by the selectors for the 3rd Test. To many it seemed a cowardly and retrograde step. Admittedly Gooch had picked up a 'pair' in his first Test at Edgbaston, but if he had been good enough to be chosen it was surely much too early to discard him after only four innings.

It had been mighty hot at Lord's with the temperature in the nineties. In the Long Room of the pavilion even the most traditional members removed their jackets and ties, much to the 'distress' of the Secretariat. But they did not go quite as far as a gentleman in front of the Tavern. For a bet he removed all but his plimsolls and socks and 'streaked' on to the field during a break in play. He ran across towards the grandstand, and then turned right-handed and ran down the length of the pitch towards the Nursery End, doing the splits over both sets of stumps. It was of course a 'first' at Lord's, which was the last place one would have expected it to happen. I suppose I should have disapproved, but I must admit I thought it gloriously funny and that it fitted into the gala atmosphere of the packed, sun-drenched Lord's. The streaker did it very delicately and no play was interfered with. The police led him gently away to loud applause and much laughter from the huge crowd.

The next day, the magistrate fined him the amount of his bet, which left him with a small profit from what he got out of interviews with the Press. They splashed his photograph across their front pages, showing his backside as he cleared the stumps. In private I was shown the full frontal photograph which the Press did NOT publish! Alan Knott was batting at the time and standing down by the stumps at the Nursery End. He told me later that as the streaker ran towards him it was the first time he had ever seen *two* balls coming down the pitch at him! Needless to say my poet friend, Les Bailey of Wombwell, turned up trumps and sent me this poem:

> *He ran on in his birthday attire*
> *Setting the ladies aflame with desire.*
> *But when he came to the stumps*
> *He misjudged his jumps –*
> *Now he sings in the Luton Girl's Choir!*

In between the Tests I took part in two unusual events. First of all Guinness sponsored a competition for throwing the cricket ball, which was televised by London Weekend. It took place after a day's racing in front of the grandstand at Sandown Park. A number of first-class cricketers and club cricketers took part, and the object was to see if anyone could beat the ninety-one-year-old record made by Richard Percival in 1884. He threw a ball 140 yards 2 feet – an incredible distance, and funnily enough he also did it on a racecourse at Durham.

Everyone had three throws but no one got anywhere near the record. The winner was John Lever of Essex with 107 yards 8 inches, second was Majid Khan 106 yards 1 foot 3 inches and third Keith Boyce 106 yards 1 foot 1 inch. Boyce in one of the practice throws the competitors were allowed before racing began actually threw 120 yards, but possibly the long wait affected him and the others. But whatever the reason I was surprised that no one could get nearer than 34 yards to the old record. In almost all other athletic sports such as running, jumping, swimming and so on there has been regular improvement in performances, with records being smashed year after year. Perhaps

– dare I say it – Mr Percival's record was not made under such close and careful scrutiny as we had at Sandown Park.

The other event was a nostalgic one for me and I hope for quite a few listeners too. Aeolian Hall in Bond Street, which had been the home of BBC Radio Light Entertainment for many years, was being closed down. To mark the occasion Radio 2 decided to mount a special edition of the old *In Town Tonight* programme. It was broadcast live in the actual studio from which *In Town Tonight* used originally to come, and in addition there were three or four points outside in various parts of London. John Ellison – the old presenter of *In Town Tonight* – was in Piccadilly Circus doing interviews with passers-by, Pete Murray was up in Big Ben and I was in a sauna bath in Kensington. It was quite like the old days of *Let's Go Somewhere*, the spot I used to do in the programme from 1948–52. Radio 2 paid me three visits – in the hot room, under the cold shower, and being 'slapped' on the massage table – all of them naturally accompanied by my usual giggles and shouts. It was twenty-three years since I had done a similar programme, and I must admit at least *I* enjoyed it.

At the time, too, it was a happy occasion for my old friend John Ellison. He had been seriously ill for the past year or two and came back especially to do this broadcast, in the programme which he had introduced for so many years. But sadly it was his last broadcast as he died a short time later. Besides being a great friend of mine, John had taken me under his wing when I first joined the BBC in 1946, and I learnt much of what I know today about radio from him, especially in the art of interviewing. He was a really professional radio performer with great charm and an ability to get on with people. Someone once described him as the commentator with the smile in his voice – a well-deserved epitaph.

*

The 3rd Test at Headingley in August made cricket history. It was the first Test ever to be abandoned because of vandals as opposed to rioters or bottle-throwers. England went into the match greatly heartened by their performance at Lord's. The selectors made four changes and poor Amiss was replaced by John Hampshire on his home ground. Keith Fletcher was picked instead of Graham Gooch – an astonishing choice if you believe in the concept of horses for courses, because Headingley was known to be Fletcher's unlucky ground.

Greig won the toss and England struggled to 288 thanks to the doggedness of Edrich and that man Steele again with 73. Australia could only make 135 in reply, thanks to a sensational Test debut by Phil Edmonds, who in his first twelve overs in Test cricket took 5 for 17.

In their second innings England managed to muster 291, thanks inevitably to Steele, who scored 92 and once again combined grim forward defence with the occasional four off the shorter balls. Incidentally, his runs for England earned him a lifetime's supply of lamb chops and steaks from a local butcher, who sponsored Steele with a chop for every run up to 50, and a steak for each run after that. The failures of Hampshire and Fletcher confirmed that the selectors' policy of chop and change in order to follow the men in form seldom pays off.

Australia were set the 'impossible' task of scoring 445 to win. At that time only Australia with 404 in the Headingley Test of 1948 had made more than 400 to win in the fourth innings of a Test. But by close of play Australia were 220 for 3, and so only needed 225 to win with seven wickets in hand. The game was beautifully poised, with both sides having good reason to think that they could win.

This made the abandonment of play on the last day all the sadder at the time, though as it turned out heavy drizzle from mid-morning onwards would have prevented play anyway. The first I heard of the vandalism was when I was woken up at my hotel by a telephone call from the

Today programme. They told me what had happened and asked me to comment. Naturally I was disgusted and angry that cricket had once again been made the scapegoat of politics.

The damage to the Headingley pitch was not severe. There was some crude oil on a good length and some holes dug with a knife near the batting crease. But it was sufficient to make play out of the question, as it would have been grossly unfair to restart the match on a newly-cut pitch, unaffected by the wear and tear of four days' cricket. The culprits were caught and one of them served a thirteen-month prison sentence. Ironically, as I've said, because of rain their action had no affect on the result of the match but it did give them the publicity they wanted for their cause – the release of a colleague from prison. Unfortunately, it cost cricket several thousand pounds and could have ruined what was certain to be a really exciting Test.

The 4th and final Test at the Oval also earned its place in cricket history. It was the longest game of cricket ever played in England, lasting the full six days and ending as late as 3 September – the only time I can remember a Test match in September. Our selectors admitted their mistake at Headingley and dropped Fletcher and Hampshire, bringing back allrounder Bob Woolmer and re-introducing Graham Roope to Test cricket after an absence of two years. Ian Chappell won the toss for the first time in the series on what was to be a slow pitch throughout. After being robbed of his hundred by the vandals at Headingley when he was 95 not out, Rick McCosker made his maiden Test century and Ian Chappell, in his last Test as Australian captain, made a typically aggressive 192 and was able to declare at 532 for 9.

England as at Edgbaston got the worst of the weather, and during their first innings of 191 had to struggle against drizzle, interruptions, heavy cloud and bad light. Following on, there was only one thing for England to do – to get their heads down and fight for a draw. And this, with grim determination and plenty of guts, they proceeded to do. The newcomer Roope with 77 and Woolmer with 149 justified the selectors' choice, and need I say it Steele again 'came good' with 66 and brought his final figures in his first ever Test series to:

Inns	NO	Runs	Top Score	Average
6	0	365	92	60.83

Remarkable. Those two great England stalwarts Edrich and Knott also made big contributions to England's second innings' score of 538. There were only eighty-five minutes left for Australia to try to make 198 to win, and they made 40 for 2 before stumps were pulled up half an hour early.

The short series of four Tests had been a great success, the cricket, the crowds and the weather all helping to make the 1975 cricket season one to remember. Australia deserved to win the series, because they took their chance when it was offered them at Edgbaston. England could console themselves that thanks largely to the lack of pace and bounce in our pitches they had wiped the slate clean after their annihilation in Australia, and but for the weather might have squared the series.

Just two last memories of the Oval Test. Bob Woolmer's hundred was the slowest ever by an England batsman against Australia. It took him 6 hours 34 minutes against the previous slowest 6 hours 2 minutes by Colin Cowdrey at Sydney in 1959. And I was given an opportunity for one of my more preposterous puns. Trevor Bailey was discussing whether England should have taken more risks in their second innings in order to score more quickly. If they did, of course, there was the danger of their losing wickets. 'It's very difficult to strike a happy medium,' he said. 'You *could* go to a séance,' I butted in, ducking the sweets and bits of paper flung at me by my long-suffering colleagues.

In September 1975 Pauline and I went to Corfu for a fortnight's holiday and were lucky enough to enjoy cloudless blue skies and hot sunshine throughout our stay. We went with a party organised by *Cricketer* magazine and stayed in the Cricketer Taverna situated among the olive groves and cypress trees on the west side of Corfu. It is a beautiful island, far lusher and greener than we had expected with majestic mountains and quiet secluded beaches and coves. We visited these in a caïque belonging to Ben and Belinda Brocklehurst – the *Cricketer* hosts. We used to chug our way along the deserted west coast until we found a peaceful spot with not a living soul in sight.

When we were not swimming or sunbathing we went to the picturesque cricket ground right in the centre of Corfu Town. Cricket has been played in Corfu for over 160 years and was first introduced there by the Royal Navy. The ground has been greatly improved in recent years and the outfield is now of coarse grass with a matting pitch. The Greeks are up to good club standard in bowling and fielding but their batting would be no good on an English grass pitch. But out there on the matting with its bounce they get away with some crude cross-batted strokes. What they lack in skill they make up for in enthusiasm and courage, cheered on by the shouts and applause of the large crowds which sit under the trees around the ground, sipping cool drinks brought by waiters from the nearby cafés.

There are usually matches every Wednesday, Saturday and Sunday, and at the weekend there are often three to four thousand people watching. There were two local Greek teams when we were there, now there are three. Our two were Gymnasticos and Byron, who play each other and visiting teams from England and Holland, who usually spend a fortnight on the island. There are also occasional matches against British Airways and the Royal Navy. Somehow there always seemed to be exciting finishes with the excitement and uproar worthy of a Wembley

Cup Final. I was persuaded to play in one match for the *Cricketer* against Gymnasticos and going in No. 11 made a stylish single down to third man before being caught in the gully. But at least I can say I have played in Corfu.

Although extremely brave when batting – often without gloves – and in attempting impossible stops or catches, the Greeks tend to kick up a tremendous fuss when they *are* hurt. A batsman hit almost anywhere will lie down moaning and drumming his legs on the ground. One of their batsmen was hit in a match against the Old Wellingtonians who, with a team made up from the *Cricketer* readers, were staying at our Taverna. The bowler was their volatile captain – Christopher Brown, son of Freddie Brown and a fast and highly dangerous bowler on the matting. As usual the batsman collapsed groaning on the ground, and various spectators rushed out to attend to him. But he lay there writhing in apparent agony, so a call was made for any doctor in the crowd.

In the Old Wellingtonian party was a young medical student in his first year at a teaching hospital. He wasn't selected for this match, so got up from his deck-chair in the shade and went out to try and help. He approached the injured man, knelt down and asked him where he was hurt. Between his groans the man muttered something in Greek and pointed to his left ankle, which when the sock was rolled down, was sure enough badly bruised and looking a nasty mess. But the young Wellingtonian rose to his feet without doing anything. 'I am sorry,' he said, 'I haven't got down that far yet in my studies,' and walked back to his seat.

One day, when watching, I was looking through an old scorebook on the scorers' table. You won't believe this, but I do assure you the Greeks have some rather unusual names. I found that in one match a batsman from a visiting English team was out: stumped Penis bowled Crabsarse!

24 The sun shines on cricket

THE YEAR 1975 had been hailed as the golden summer, with its glorious weather and champagne cricket provided by the World Cup and the Australian tour. However, 1976 did even better. The series against West Indies inspired brilliant stroke play and devastating fast bowling, which those lucky enough to see will never forget. As for the sunshine, the weather beat all records, and needless to say that indispensable Bible of Cricket, *Wisden*, gave us all the details. A spell of fifteen days in June/July was the hottest and longest over the previous two hundred and fifty years. Up to the end of August there was the driest sixteen-month period since records for England and Wales began in 1727. Whew! It makes one sweat just to think of it. But the cricketers revelled in it and cricket itself prospered as a result. There were record crowds and receipts and increased sponsorship and membership.

In the Test matches England were outclassed and the West Indies won the Wisden Trophy 3–0. Their batting line-up was possibly the strongest I have ever seen in Test cricket and they were all magnificent stroke-players – not a dawdler among them. Just look at this for a batting order: Fredericks, Greenidge, Richards, Kallicharran, Lloyd, King or Rowe. And to support them a terrifying trio of fast bowlers: Roberts, Holding, Daniel, plus Holder for good measure. It's not surprising that this was the most successful West Indies team ever to tour England, winning eighteen of their twenty-six first-class matches, including three Tests, plus all three of the Prudential Trophy matches.

England could do little to counter this great side except

to bring back Brian Close in his forty-fifth year, knowing that he would present a valiant and immovable target for the West Indian bouncers. These they bowled to excess in the 3rd Test at Old Trafford. It made a travesty of the new experimental law that the two umpires did not inter-vene as bouncer followed bouncer, until finally Bill Alley did warn Holding after he had bowled *three in succession* to Close. The combined ages of Edrich and Close was eighty-four and their batting at the start of England's second innings was the most courageous I have ever seen.

England had to bat again for eighty minutes on the Saturday night and it was then that the West Indian fast bowlers seemed to go mad. They hurled bouncers indis-criminately at Edrich and Close, who resisted with tremendous bravery and somehow avoided serious injury. There was uproar in the Press over the weekend and I hope we on radio and TV spoke out against it as strongly as it deserved. Anyhow, on the Monday, although still bowling very fast, the bowlers pitched the ball up on a length and Roberts took 6 for 37. England were all out for 126 and so were beaten by 425 runs. A moral here surely. Good bowling will always take more wickets than the loathsome short-pitched stuff, which is not only dangerous but ruins cricket as a spectacle.

England lost the 4th Test at Headingley – and with it the series and the Wisden Trophy – but they had fought back magnificently after a disastrous first day. They showed that given the right conditions to produce swing and seam, the brilliant West Indian stroke-makers could be contained and bowled out.

The return of Alan Ward to the England side after an absence of fifty-one Tests revived the old story of how he had once gone on a club tour of Germany, during which he took a hat-trick against a team of Germans. From then on he was known as 'Jerryatric Ward'!

West Indies' easy victory in the 5th Test at the Oval by the huge margin of 231 runs after declaring twice, merely emphasised what a great side they were. It also made it all the more difficult to understand how they had succumbed so easily to Australia during the previous winter. Was the partnership of Lillee and Thomson on their own bouncy pitches practically unplayable? I myself suspect that it was, and that not too much blame can be attached to either Mike Denness' or Clive Lloyd's batsmen.

Anyway, at the Oval all the West Indies' batsmen prospered. Viv Richards scored a superb 291 and, until tiredness overtook him, looked as if nothing could stop him beating Gary Sobers' record Test score of 365. He finished the series with the fantastic average of 118.42 for his 829 runs. On this form he must soon be toppling Barry Richards off the throne of No. 1 batsman in the world.

So the West Indies won the series 3–0 and must rival the 1950 side as the best ever to tour England from West Indies. It may be many years before we shall see again such a superb combination of brilliant stroke-makers and lightning-fast bowlers. It may also be many years before we enjoy another such hot, dry summer, which of course was just what the doctor ordered for the particular talents of this West Indian side. As for England, they were simply beaten by a far better side in the conditions.

One amusing incident occurred during the West Indies second innings. For many years now I have written short articles for the benefit brochures of players. I have naturally done it for nothing as part of my contribution to their well-deserved benefit – that is all except once. When Alan Knott had his benefit he asked me as usual to write something for him. I replied that I would be delighted, but for the first time ever I was going to charge him for my work. This shook him a bit but he bravely asked me what my fee would be. I told him that my payment would be a promise from him that, if Bob Woolmer played in a Test during the summer, he would stand up to the stumps for at least one over.

This business of standing up happens to be a hobby-horse of mine, since the days when Godfrey Evans stood up to Alec Bedser and kept so brilliantly. Nowadays all Test wicket-keepers stand back to every bowler other than the all too rare spinners. Farooq Engineer was an honourable exception. I think Gil Langley probably started it when he began standing back to the medium pace of Ken Mackay. Even that superb wicket-keeper Wally Grout did so too, encouraged I believe by his captain, Richie Benaud.

I've had a friendly running argument about it with Knotty for years: he maintains that if he stands up he runs the risk of dropping a vital catch, and that it is not worth it for the few stumpings which might result. He and others also claim that they might unsight the leg slip, who is placed there to take the sort of catch on the leg-side which a wicket-keeper standing up would try for. This is possible. But the use of a leg slip is becoming rarer and rarer. Anyway, I have always felt that such a brilliant wicket-keeper as Knotty would be very unlikely to miss a chance, however difficult, and that the benefits of standing up far outweigh the risks. One of the most important benefits being the increase in entertainment value of a brilliant take or stumping on the leg-side by a wicket-keeper standing up.

But back to Knotty and the payment of my fee. When Bob Woolmer came on to bowl in the West Indies' second innings, Knotty turned round to the commentary box, gave me the thumbs-up and went right up to the stumps. And of course it *would* happen. Bob's first ball was a near-wide outside the leg stump of left-hander, Roy Fredericks. Knotty only just managed to get a right hand to it, so saving four certain byes. He turned round and gave me a 'there you are I told you so' sort of look. But he gallantly stood up for two overs and made some brilliant takes. I am sure that if Knotty had stood up more often he would have proved that he is possibly the greatest wicket-keeper ever. It is only the lack of proof that he *can* match Godfrey

Evans' brilliant keeping when standing up to the quicker bowlers that leaves a question mark.

By the way, my TV colleagues were not in the know about what was going on, and were speculating that Knott and Woolmer were plotting some trap like a leg-side stumping. Incidents like this surely prove that even in Test cricket there is room for a bit of fun.

I know that I am biased but I have always found that cricketers in general are very nice people. There's something about the game perhaps which helps to build character, tolerance and humour. The modern first-class cricketer is no exception and I am extremely grateful to them all for the way they have always given me – and continue to give – their friendship.

But having said that, I have only one complaint against them. I wish they could look as if they were enjoying themselves more. How seldom do you see them smiling or laughing *on* the field. Yet I know that almost all of them love cricket and are sacrificing quite a lot of money to play it. But I fear the pressure and the pace of the present crowded season has made their cricket too much like a job of work. For them it's like going to the office or factory every morning. It's not that they really *play* too much cricket. But the constant dashing from place to place up the motorways is an exhausting business. They have to do it to fit in all the different types of competitions.

However much anyone loves cricket it is not surprising that it sometimes seems too much of a good thing to the county cricketers. But of course this applies to almost everything in life. The less you have the more you appreciate it when you do have it, as this following story illustrates:

There was a professor lecturing to a group of men on the subject of sex, and he asked his audience if they would help him. Would those who made love to their wives *every* night please hold up their hands? Then those who made it every other night, twice a week, once a week, once a month and so on. Each time the men rather sheepishly held up their hands at the number which concerned them. Finally, after he had counted each category, the professor said, 'Thank you for your help. That's all.' But a small man right at the back of the hall held up his hand and with a cheerful smile said, 'Excuse me, sir, you haven't asked me yet.' 'All right,' said the professor impatiently, 'how often do *you* do it?' 'Once a year,' replied the small man still smiling. 'Well, what are you looking so pleased about?' asked the professor.

'It's tonight,' replied the small man. See what I mean?

During the summer of 1976, I was lucky enough to be asked to commentate on one of the three women's Test matches in the series against Australia. It was the Golden Jubilee of the Women's Cricket Association and though the three Tests were all drawn, England won the limited-over one-day matches, 2–1. Furthermore, their jubilee was celebrated by a unique and memorable occasion. The second of these matches was played at Lord's on a pitch in the centre of the ground, on a flawless day before a remarkably large and enthusiastic crowd. So after much propaganda, lobbying and arm-twisting the ladies had at last been allowed to enter the Holy of Holies even to the extent of using the dressing-rooms and baths, hitherto exclusive male preserves. So far as I was concerned, as a member of MCC, it was a most welcome invasion. Everyone present at Lord's on that day was, I'm sure, grateful to the good sense of MCC, and to the enthusiastic, untiring and witty vocal efforts of England's captain, Rachael Heyhoe-Flint, which had brought it all about.

I am seldom so presumptuous as to disagree with an opinion expressed by a revered England cricket captain, but I did so once. The occasion was a match on Chislehurst Green between Colin Cowdrey's XI and the Women's England XI of that time. I was keeping wicket and Len Hutton was at first slip. So I asked him what he thought of women playing cricket. He gave me a funny look and answered: 'It's just like a man trying to knit, isn't it?' But as I've said I disagreed – and incidentally the women won the match.

In fact I have always supported the girls, and think that they've got quite a bit to teach us men. First-class cricket nowadays tends to be rather scientific or 'professional' as it's so often called. The ladies bring a touch of grace into what is essentially a graceful game. Anyone who has watched women play recently will know that as *batsmen* they use their feet to the slow bowlers. They have all the strokes and run like hinds between the wickets. In the old days if you wished to insult a fielder you told him that he threw like a girl. Nowadays their returns from the outfield come whistling back over the top of the stumps. Their fielding is remarkably keen and their bowling subtle and steady, though lacking in pace.

I have played quite a bit of cricket with women. At my private school, the headmaster's daughter, Kitten, bowled a nifty leg-break and in the holidays we used to play a mixed match in the village of Much Marcle in Herefordshire. The star was a retired bishop's wife called Mrs Whitehead. She was a left-hander and defended dourly, and usually carried her bat. In later years I saw her exact replica in Test cricket – Slasher Mackay, the impassive Australian – though Mrs Whitehead did not chew gum!

Mothers, too, have played an important part in cricket. Perhaps the best example, as I've mentioned before, was in Australia where Vic Richardson's daughter, Mrs Chappell, coached her three sons, Ian, Greg and Trevor in the back garden with results which we in England know all too well. Even more important to me, personally, was the fact that early in our courtship I discovered that my wife Pauline could throw a cricket ball really well. I won't pretend that it was a vital factor in our romance, but it helped!

I hope by now it is obvious that I am one hundred per cent in favour of women's cricket, and wish them success in the years ahead, though unlike the lady jockeys they will never be strong enough to compete on equal terms with men.

There is one small change which I would like to see. I wish they would wear trousers instead of those divided skirts. I'm always worried that the pad straps will chafe the back of their knees. I also think they deserve to get more coverage on radio and TV, though I can see one or two pitfalls for commentators. What girl would enjoy hearing that she had two short legs? On the other hand I suppose none of them would object if they heard that they had a very fine long leg. And finally, since they bring such glamour and a sense of chivalry and good manners into the game, isn't it about time they were called 'ladies' instead of 'women'?

It was with much sadness that in September 1976 I heard of the death of Arthur Gilligan at the age of eighty-one. I had seen him at Lord's earlier in the summer, looking and sounding as well as ever, and telling me about his skiing holiday in the winter. For years he and I used to swap stories, and it was my great pleasure when one of mine was rewarded by his cheerful laugh.

Arthur was an old friend of my father-in-law in the twenties and used to stay with him when Sussex were playing Yorkshire. Just after I had married Pauline in 1948 I was looking through her family scrapbook and saw a photograph of Pauline as a very young girl sitting on Arthur's knee. So the next time I saw him I said that I had a bone to pick with him. He looked somewhat perturbed and asked me what it was.

'Arthur,' I said, 'I see that you have been dangling my wife on your knee, and I'd rather you didn't do it again.' He looked so puzzled and upset that I quickly explained to him what I was referring to.

I used to see Arthur play at the Saffrons when I was at my preparatory school at Eastbourne. He was then – in the early twenties – a very fast bowler, magnificent mid-off and a dashing hard-hitting batsman. His 1924–5 side to Australia was probably the most popular to go there that century, though admittedly they did lose and that always helps! But there is no doubt that ever since, he was one of the best-loved Englishmen in Australia. Not just because of his sporting captaincy but because of his great popularity down under as a cricket commentator. He spoke in a natural, friendly way and even when he could bring himself to criticise, he did it kindly. He formed a famous double act with his old adversary and great friend, Vic Richardson. They always backed each other up and never disagreed with what the other said. 'In my opinion he was plumb out. What do you think, Vic?' 'I quite agree Arthur.' Or, 'I'd say the pitch is taking spin now, Arthur.' 'Yes, I quite agree, Vic.'

It may sound trite now but all I can say is that it created a very friendly atmosphere and made pleasant listening. Arthur knew he tended to agree with everyone, but told me how on one occasion it had helped him out of a mess. Once on a hot day during a Headingley Test he fell asleep after lunch and as he dozed he vaguely heard Rex Alston's voice droning on without taking in what he was saying. Suddenly he woke with a start as Rex nudged him in the ribs and said: 'That's how I saw it. What do you say Arthur?'

Arthur reacted quickly for one who had only just woken up. 'I entirely agree with everything you have just said, Rex,' he replied, as his chin sunk once more into his chest. Being Arthur, no one saw anything funny in his reply.

He also swore it was true that a lady once came up to him at a Test and gave him a packet of indigestion tablets. 'Will you please give these to Brian Statham, Mr Gilligan?' 'Yes, of course I will, but why?' replied Arthur. 'Oh,' said the lady, 'I heard you say on the radio that Statham wasn't bowling as fast as usual as he was having trouble with the wind'!

At the end of October for the first time in my life I was asked to give the address at a memorial service. It was for a unique and remarkable character called Buns Cartwright, who for forty years had been secretary of the Eton Ramblers, and their president for another twenty-one. I had known him since the early thirties when I first played for the Ramblers, and had been his friend ever since. I approached this daunting task with great trepidation because he had so many friends and acquaintances in every walk of life. They knew all about him – his many good points and the inevitable few which were not so good, which we all have.

He was an eccentric, especially in his dress, which was usually a blue pin-stripe suit with carnation and blue plimsolls, topped with a brown cap, or one of his many sombreros with the Rambler ribbon around it. He was one of a dying breed – man about town, clubman, sportsman and *bon viveur*. He never owned nor drove a car, but could be seen at nearly every big sporting occasion, with cricket, tennis, golf and racing taking priority. He was irascible, gruff, critical, but underneath it all was a kind man with a sharp wit and keen sense of humour. He was also an inveterate gambler and when my wife Pauline went to see him in hospital he even offered her odds of 7–4 against his own recovery.

It was obviously no good giving a solemn oration full of false praise and sentiment about such a character. So I decided to recall him as we all knew him and included one or two of the more respectable stories about him. Buns had always been a bachelor, but never let that state interfere with his pleasures. On one occasion a friend of mine said he had met a Colonel Cartwright on holiday in Yugoslavia. He thought he was good value and added . . . 'and what a charming lady Mrs Cartwright is!'

On a cricket tour with the Eton Ramblers we were all staying in a private house for the weekend. At dinner we placed a 'whoopee' bag under the cushion of his dining-room chair. We arranged for everyone to be quiet when our hostess asked us to be seated. The explosion as Buns sat down was shattering. But our hostess (duly rehearsed) remained calm. She summoned the butler and said: 'Meadows, would you please open the window. Colonel Cartwright has . . .' Then there was uproar.

The Guards Chapel was absolutely packed and it was the first time I had ever heard laughs at a memorial service. But I am certain that it was what he would have wanted, and in a strange way showed our love and friendship for him, and our gratitude for all he had done for us. But it is not a task which I want to do again.

In the New Year 1977 we went down to the delightful Theatre Royal at Windsor, to see a new play by William Douglas-Home, one of three which eventually ran simultaneously in the West End. It was called *In the Red* and was all about a popular playwright who lived entirely on a vast overdraft at his bank – I wonder where William got all the necessary background information! I thought the play very funny and so did all the provincial audiences. But it failed when it came to London, possibly because the audiences looked on it as a fantasy, just not believing that anyone could really live like that.

There were some very good jokes in *In the Red* and I suggested another to William – I am not sure whether he put it in or not. It was the old one of the client who was being persistently pressed by his bank manager to pay off his overdraft. The client finally got fed up. 'You remember, two years ago, when I was in credit with you for five hundred pounds?' he asked the bank manager. 'Yes, I do,' replied the bank manager grudgingly. 'Well,' said the client, 'I didn't go on badgering you to pay *me* back, did I?'

Incidentally, I must try that out on *my* bank manager some time. The trouble is you have to be in credit first!

25 'I want to be a cricket commentator'

I THINK THIS WOULD BE a good place in which to say a few words about cricket commentary. I get lots of letters from young boys who say that when they grow up they want to be cricket commentators (in my day it was engine drivers!). They usually ask how to set about it, how can they learn, and what qualifications ought they to have. It's very difficult to give a satisfactory answer, because so far as cricket is concerned, there is only ONE staff job on the BBC – that of BBC Cricket Correspondent. I was the first one appointed in 1963 and then after my retirement from the staff in 1972 I was succeeded by Christopher Martin-Jenkins. All the TV commentators are freelances and only Christopher and Don Mosey of the radio commentators are on the staff. The rest of us are freelances.

Any budding young commentator should read every book which he can get hold of about cricket. He should try to learn its history and absorb its atmosphere and do his best to understand all the laws and regulations. He should watch as much good cricket as possible and of course play it himself. If he can borrow a tape-recorder he should go to any match where he knows most of the players and practise talking about the game as far away from the other spectators as he can get. He should try to describe exactly what is going on and keep going for at least fifteen minutes without drying up. It won't be easy at first but he will find that as his confidence grows it will become easier to keep the flow going. The secret is practice and he mustn't mind if the other spectators think that he is mad chatting away to himself!

Another stepping stone to the commentary box is a job on the local paper or at the local radio station. The paper will help him put his thoughts into words and the radio will teach him the art of projecting himself into the microphone – i.e. broadcasting. The snag is, of course, that it's not easy to get jobs in either of these media, but it is something well worth trying. In fact commentators on local radio do by far the longest stints of commentary these days except for the Test match commentators. Another possible training ground is the hospital broadcasts which take place from so many county grounds. I'm never quite sure how the admirable people who give up so much of their spare time manage to learn to commentate in the first place. Perhaps they just practise on the poor patients right from the start!

And now for the art of cricket commentary itself. It is an art for which there is no real school, except experience at the microphone at the expense of the listener or the viewer. This is one reason why cricket commentators tend to be mostly in the thirty-five to sixty-five age bracket. It takes that long to learn! Nowadays, except for the ball-by-ball Test match commentaries, there is little opportunity to practise commentary. Up to the mid-sixties there were regular broadcasts of twenty- to thirty-minute periods from county matches. Now it is usually only one- to three-minute reports, so that the budding commentator has no chance to test his ability to keep going for long periods, which is what the top commentators have to do. In addition, a young voice lacks the authority of an older one and because of cricket's slower tempo this is more noticeable than with other games.

So, it's not easy to become a cricket commentator and more or less impossible without a large slice of luck, such as being available at the right place at the right time when the opportunity occurs.

Now for the qualifications:

1 Good health – 'the show must go on'.
2 A gift of the gab and the ability to keep talking.

3 A clear, strong voice, which must sound confident. The accent doesn't matter, though in fact a dialect comes over particularly well in cricket. But personality is important and can 'come through' in a voice.

4 The ability to put into words what he is seeing, which means that besides being observant he must have a varied and colourful vocabulary and a sound use of good English. The long periods of comparative inaction during a cricket match give the listeners an all too easy chance to notice imperfections in syntax or language.

5 And most important of all – for without it he can never become a cricket commentator – he must have a deep knowledge of the game, its laws and regulations, its customs, its record, its history and its players.

Acquaintance – or even better – friendship with the players is a tremendous asset and helps give an understanding of what goes on 'in the middle'. A commentator should have played the game himself, though not necessarily in the highest class. TV commentators these days are usually ex-Test cricketers, whereas on the radio they are professional broadcasters supported by ex-Test players as summarisers. But then there is a great difference in the commentary techniques of TV and radio and there is no doubt in my mind that television is the more difficult.

Television Commentary

The first thing for a TV cricket commentator to realise is that he can never hope to please *everybody any* of the time. In fact he will be jolly lucky if he manages to please *anybody all* the time. Cricket, like golf, is a game played at a much slower tempo than most of the other televised sports such as football, racing, athletics, etc. There are, of course, many moments of excitement and tension but they are spread out over a whole day, and the action is anyway much slower. This means that the commentator's remarks drop like stones on a still pond. The viewer has time to listen and digest them and to weigh up their meaning and their accuracy. In the faster games a slight fluff or inaccuracy by the commentator is soon forgotten within a few seconds as a new situation develops on the screen. So the cricket commentator's comments must be concise and fit the picture exactly, and be well thought out and accurate while having to be made spontaneously at a moment's notice. This means that he must have a complete and expert knowledge of the game. He has to comment rather than give a running commentary, which is basically what happens with football or racing on TV.

So the cricket commentator always has to ask himself the vital question: 'When to talk and when not to talk?' It's easy to trot out trite instructions such as: 'Only talk when you can add to the picture', but it isn't as easy as that. First of all there is the expert viewer who plays or has played the game. He knows the laws and regulations, and all the players by sight. On switching on he only wants to hear who won the toss, the score, a report on the weather and an opinion about the pitch. After that he just wants to be kept up to date with the score and to make his own judgements on the playbacks after an appeal or a wicket has fallen.

I can understand this. A commentator on TV should, in my view, be like a knowledgeable friend who sits alongside you at a sporting event, and who fills in the details which you don't know. I enjoy watching cricket with a friend, but if he starts to tell me what is happening, who so-and-so is or why the captain has moved a certain fieldsman, I feel like crowning him. I think I know and just don't want to be told.

But sitting alongside me there may well be someone

who welcomes all this sort of information, and wants help with identity of the players and explanations of the laws. And so it is on TV. A large majority of the viewers are not cricket experts. I should know from some of the letters I have received in the past. What is a 'chinaman', 'silly mid-off', or a 'googly'? How is someone out 'lbw'? So, the TV cricket commentator has to try to strike the happy medium, knowing that there is really no such thing. He will always have irate and dissatisfied viewers who will say either: 'Why on earth can't he stop talking?' or 'Why can't he tell us more?'

Radio Commentary

As he has no camera to help him, the radio commentator must paint the picture himself – with words. He is the eyes of every listener and must describe in as much detail as possible everything he sees. As opportunity offers he should describe the features of the ground so that the listener who has never been there can conjure up his own idea of what it is like. It also helps if the commentator explains the exact position from which he is broadcasting in relation to the play. A brief description of the main features and characteristics of the players bring the game to life – 'he has red, curly hair, wears size 14 boots, scratches his nose before every ball . . .', etc. There is also more time on radio for details and records of players' careers.

All this information is useful to fill in the gaps which do occur during a game of cricket – when the fast bowlers are walking back to the start of their long runs, during the drinks interval or when the umpires go off to search for a new ball. But there is one cardinal rule: NEVER MISS A BALL. All this information must stop as soon as the bowler starts his run. The commentator must then describe in detail exactly what is happening until the ball becomes dead.

The art of good commentary is to get into automatic rhythm with a description of:

The bowler running up.
His approach to the umpire and the wicket.
The delivery, the type of ball and where it has pitched.
The batsman's stroke.
Where the ball has gone.
Who is fielding or chasing it.
How many runs the batsmen are taking.
And finally, when the ball has been returned to the wicket-keeper or bowler, say how many runs have been added to the team's and batsman's score.

Only then is it permissible to leave the action and talk about something else, until the bowler returns to his mark. Then back to the rhythm again to describe the next ball.

Some Hints to Budding Commentators

1 Have light and shade in your voice, so that during quiet periods you can talk normally and not too fast. Then when there is sudden action or excitement you can increase your tempo and raise your voice, though of course, without shouting.
2 Always think of yourself as speaking to ONE person, not to millions. You are that person's friend and guide. Tell him or her what you yourself would like to hear if you were not at that match.
3 Try not to talk over applause, especially when a batsman is returning to the pavilion after a big score. Let his reception register. This is often easier said than done, as there are many details about his innings to give to the listener before the new batsman comes out.
4 Try not to describe in too much detail how a batsman is out. Leave that to the expert summariser.

5 Remember that you are a commentator not a critic. So don't criticise an umpire's decision. Whatever you may think about it, he is in a better position to judge than you are.

6 At the end of each over, give the bowler's analysis, the total and the scores of the two batsmen. Then shut up, so that the summariser can come straight in.

There is one problem which is common to both TV and radio commentators – when to give the score. The answer is as often and as unobtrusively as possible without interrupting the action, and at the very least whenever a run is scored and at the end of each over. This may be annoying to the lucky viewers or listeners who stay switched on for the whole period. But tens of thousands are switching on every minute and there's nothing more infuriating than having to wait for five or ten minutes before hearing the score. That's why in these days of an over taking up to five minutes it's a good idea to slip in the score during an over even if a run hasn't been added. In addition, of course, newcomers will want to hear details of what has happened before, so the scorecard should be shown on TV or read out on radio at least every ten minutes.

There remains one fundamental difference between the TV and radio commentators today. On TV with their galaxy of ex-Test players they nowadays concentrate solely on the cricket. They give an extremely expert and professional analysis of the play, with critical opinions on the captains' tactics and the skills of the batsmen and bowlers. But they are not encouraged to be humorous about the fringe aspects of cricket, which provide so much of the colour and fun – the fat member asleep in the pavilion, the bored blonde knitting in the crowd, the umpire's funny hat and so on. But, probably because they have more time to fill, radio commentators are given a freer rein, and indulge in more light-hearted descriptions and reminiscences, and a certain amount of friendly banter in the box.

But whatever the style of commentary one final word of warning to ALL commentators – NEVER MISS A BALL. If you do it's sure to be the one that takes a wicket.

One of the hazards of being a cricket commentator is that even the most innocent remark can have a double meaning – *if* you have that sort of mind! I have already mentioned some of the unfortunate gaffes which I have made during cricket commentaries. Not only do they still happen, but people keep reminding me of ones which I had forgotten all about. Such as a few years ago, when a mouse ran across the pitch during a Test match at Edgbaston. Play was held up while players tried to catch it, and the poor little mouse showed up beautifully on our TV zoom lens. I was doing the commentary on TV and when describing the chase said: 'They are bound to catch it soon – it's got no hole to go down.' I then unfortunately added: 'Lucky it's not a ladies' match.' All I meant was that they would be rushing about screaming as they are always meant to do when they see a mouse. But Denis Compton especially thought it was very funny!

The cricket commentators, however, are not the only ones who drop clangers, and the 1976 Olympic Games at Montreal produced one or two good ones. During the swimming, Peter Jones on the radio said: 'It's the pool that sets the spectators alight', and Alan Weekes on TV: 'If Wilkie goes on like this he'll be home and dry!' It seems uncertain whether it was David Coleman or Ron Pickering who during the 800 metre-final talking about Juantorena the eventual winner commented on TV: 'Every time the big Cuban opens his legs, he shows his class!'

Frank Bough has admitted he once said as he handed over to a boxing fight, '. . . and your carpenter is Harry Commentator'. But it was the golf commentators who had the biggest nightmare of all, and nightly went down on their knees and prayed that Coles would not be drawn to play against Hunt.

Two more gaffes are attributed to David Coleman. The first at the Montreal Olympic Games where he said: 'To win a gold medal you've GOT to come first.' The second was at a League match in which Manchester United were playing: 'United are buzzing around the goal mouth like a lot of red blue-bottles.'

Another good soccer one came from John Motson during the 1977 FA Cup Final. 'If Liverpool lose today it will cast grave doubts on their ability to win the treble.'

But poor Hugh Johns made a perfectly innocent remark on ITV to which some dirty-minded (!) people took exception. All he said was, 'The referee is now looking at his whistle!'

Jimmy Hill is credited with this gem – 'Over now to Nigel Starmer-Smith, who has had seven craps as scumhalf for England!'

I am never quite certain who was the originator of *this* remark – not much double entendre about it! Anyway, it was a cricket commentator who was talking about Cunis, the New Zealand fast bowler. 'Cunis,' he said, 'a funny sort of name. Neither one thing nor the other!' I promise you it wasn't me!

Incidentally, talking of names, Bill Frindall assures me that once when referring to Asif Mahsood the Pakistan bowler I called him by mistake: 'Masif *Ahsood*'!

And appropriately, in Jubilee Year, I was reminded recently of an occasion when Henry Riddell was the commentator on some royal procession or other. After describing the Queen's carriage and escorts as they passed his commentary position, the carriage turned a corner and went out of his sight. Said Henry: 'And now the Queen's gone round the bend'!

But one of the best gaffes of all was perpetrated recently by a lady journalist when writing about our world champion motorcyclist, Barry Sheene. She described him as the glamorous sportsman with that throbbing power between his legs! I think that caps anything which we broadcasters have said.

26 It's the Ashes! It's the Ashes!

IN FEBRUARY 1977 I suffered a great disappointment. Len Maddocks – the old Australian wicket-keeper and manager of their 1977 team to England – rang me from Australia to ask me to go out there for the Centenary Test at Melbourne in March. He wanted me to make a speech at the champagne breakfast, which was going to take place on the first morning of the match before play started. I couldn't really believe it. Many of my cricketing friends were already booked to go and here I was being asked to fly 13,000 miles just to make a speech. I dearly wanted to go, but, alas, the invitation came too late. I was already committed for *Down Your Way*, at least four dinners and the Boat Race, and could not cancel them all at such short notice.

I shall always be sorry that I was not able to be there at such a unique occasion – unique, because when again will there ever be such a gathering of past and present Test players spanning nearly sixty years of English and Australian Test cricket. What a fabulous opportunity it was for old and young players to meet and swap experiences. Everyone who went there was full of praise for the wonderful hospitality and organisation. Nothing seems to have gone wrong. Even the weather and the cricket matched the occasion. The gods must indeed have been on the side of the Australian organisers.

Fancy arranging for the Queen to visit the match on the *fifth day* and to find that when she arrived the game was building up to a dramatic climax. The betting must have been that the match would have already finished or be heading for a dull draw. And to think that England lost by 45 runs – exactly the same margin by which they had lost that first Test in 1877. And what about Derek Randall's brilliant and cheeky innings of 174? You can see why I was so disappointed – which reminds me of the difference between disappointment and despair. Disappointment is the first time you discover you can't do it twice. Despair is the second time you discover you can't do it once!

Over the past thirty-two years I have been extremely lucky in having a grandstand seat for all the big Royal occasions during that time – and incidentally I have always been *outside* somewhere, never *inside*. First in 1947 I was on the Victoria Memorial outside Buckingham Palace for the wedding of Princess Elizabeth and Prince Philip. Then I was at Hyde Park Corner for TV for King George VI's funeral and for the Coronation procession. I was with the TV cameras on Horse Guards Parade to describe Princess Margaret's wedding procession and I was there again, on radio, thirteen years later for Princess Anne's wedding. On all these occasions I have had superb close-up views of all the processions as they passed by, but never in my wildest dreams did I ever imagine that I would take part in one.

It happened on Jubilee Day – 7 June 1977 – which was the climax of a week of festivities to mark the Queen's twenty-five years on the throne. I was covering part of the celebrations for radio. My first position, which I reached by 8 am, was on Queen Anne's statue outside the steps of St Paul's Cathedral leading up to the west door. Scaffolding and a platform had been placed round the statue so that we could see right down Ludgate Hill to Ludgate Circus, or behind us up the twenty-eight steps into the Cathedral itself as the congregation took their seats.

It was cool, windy and cloudy, but not actually raining as we made our way through the crowds already five or six deep behind the barriers. Many had been there all night and we actually found a vicar from the Isle of Wight who, with his family, had been on the pavement since midnight on the Sunday. Everyone was in tremendous spirits and already at this early hour there was plenty for them to watch, with troops marching along the route to take up their positions. A dustman at the back of a cart, which had been sprinkling sand on the wet streets, acknowledged the cheers of the crowd in the Queen's best manner. There were wolf whistles from the teenage girls as some Scottish soldiers marched by, their kilts being blown up by the wind. I'm sure that at least some of the crowd now know the answer to that eternal question: 'Do they?' or 'Don't they?' An important-looking official in top hat and tails had a rather mincing gait and was greeted with cries of 'Are you free, Mr Humphries?' Some of the crowd kept singing *For She's a Jolly Good Sovereign* and others shouted the odds when a large picture hat blew off the head of a stately dowager and was pursued down Ludgate Hill by her top-hatted escort.

Between 9.30 and 10.30 am the official guests arrived, some like the Speaker and Lord Mayor in their own coaches. Then came the carriage processions with their escorts and the crowds were really getting their reward for their long wait. Princess Anne and Captain Mark Phillips came first, then the Queen Mother and her two grandsons Prince Andrew and Prince Edward. And what a cheer she got! As usual she looked superb.

And then the big moment with the clip-clop of the Household Cavalry coming slowly up the hill, followed by the eight Windsor Greys pulling the four-ton newly gilded Golden Coach with the Queen and the Duke of Edinburgh, waving to the crowds as the band of the Honourable Artillery Company played the National Anthem. I got a perfect view as the coach wheeled slowly round in front of the steps, and there was an anxious moment as one of the greys slipped and took fright.

Two days later I was in Goring on Thames for a *Down Your Way* and interviewed the Queen's saddler, who has a saddle and harness shop there. He told me he had been up at 4 am in the Royal Mews preparing and checking all the harness. He revealed something which I don't think anyone saw – I certainly didn't and I was only a few feet away. As the Golden Coach was swinging round to the right, the off-side back wheel knocked against one of the bollards outside the Cathedral. It not only shook the coach, but the wheel might well have come off. I expect the Queen and the Duke must have realised something had gone wrong when they felt the bump.

I was able to watch the Royal party greeted on the steps by the Archbishop of Canterbury and the Lord Mayor, and then see them disappear into the brilliantly lit interior of St Paul's before the big west doors were closed. The service was relayed to the crowds outside and I was able to listen to it from my perch on Queen Anne's statue.

At the end of the service the Royal party came down the steps and then the Queen and Duke of Edinburgh, accompanied only by the Lord and Lady Mayoress, started what was to be the Queen's happiest and most successful of all her many walk-abouts. It was certainly seen by more people than all the others put together because of the worldwide TV coverage of Jubilee Day.

I said just now that the Queen was accompanied by the Lord Mayor and Lady Mayoress. That's not quite true. By some means the BBC Radio had been given permission for me to follow closely behind the Queen with a small mobile transmitter. I just couldn't believe my luck, though I felt some slight trepidation at having to walk through so many thousands of cheering people. The Queen was used to it, but I definitely wasn't! Anyway, with my producer, Roger MacDonald, and our engineer, Cedric Johnson, we set off. We followed just a few yards behind the Queen and I gave the best commentary I could manage as I walked along. It was a really fantastic experience. The Queen stopped every few yards to talk to the crowd, and accepted dozens of little posies from small children all along the route. The

Lord Mayor, Sir Robin Gillett, did his best to act as a carrier bag!

Many people thrust their hands out for the Queen to shake, but I only saw her shake hands with one person – an old grey-haired soldier with a cluster of medals on his chest, and as she left him, there were tears pouring down his cheeks. A magnificent moment for him. We soon got a long way ahead of the Duke, who as usual had plenty to say to everyone and cracked jokes, which drew roars of laughter from the crowds. We walked through the gardens on the north side of St Paul's, then out into Cheapside through the lines of spectators. The noise was deafening and as you can imagine I got quite a bit of friendly barracking from the crowd. They must have been surprised to see me coming *Down 'Their' Way*, and amazed that I was following so closely behind the Queen apparently talking to myself.

I stopped and asked quite a few of them what the Queen had said to them and generally it seemed to be: 'Where do you come from?' and 'How long have you been waiting?' and so on. It was noticeable that when the Queen stopped to talk to someone, the cheering stopped, only to be renewed as soon as she went on her way. The Duke occasionally caught up with us and even remarked that I looked like a man from space, with my headphones and the aerial on our mobile transmitter.

When we turned into the narrow King Street with high buildings on either side the noise became deafening. I was getting a bit cocky by now and so far forgot myself as to ask the Duke whether he would say something to the listeners over my microphone. With a cheerful grin he shouted, 'I can't hear myself speak!'

We finally reached the Guildhall and the walk had taken about half an hour. Even the Queen, so used to these sorts of demonstrations of love and loyalty, must have been overwhelmed by the tremendous reception she received from everyone along the route. I certainly will never forget it and it was definitely one of the highlights of my broadcasting career.

After the glorious summer of 1976, England's victory in India, and all the euphoria of the Centenary Test, it was too much to hope that cricket could continue to be so lucky. Not only did the skies open for most of May, and much of the summer, but on 11 May 1977 the Packer affair burst upon the cricketing world.

It all started because Kerry Packer, of the Channel Nine television network in Sydney, was refused exclusive TV rights for Test matches in Australia by the Australian Cricket Board. Mr Packer – possibly out of pique, possibly to give himself a bargaining weapon – promptly set about signing up over fifty of the world's top players to play in a series of 'Super Tests', in direct opposition to the official Tests already arranged for Australia against India and England over the next two years.

He did this in complete secrecy and I think what stuck in the gullets of old squares like myself was the underhand way in which it was all carried out. That Tony Greig, captain of England, straight from the successful tour of India and the Centenary Test, could play a leading part in these signings, passed my comprehension.

Maybe because of the way it was done, the establishment overreacted. But if someone suddenly points a pistol at your head, your first instinct is to defend yourself and that is precisely what the ICC and TCCB set out to do when they threatened to ban the Packer players from playing for their countries and counties. In the thirty-one-day court case brought by Mr Packer, Mr Justice Slade declared this ban to be illegal and an incitement to the players to break their contracts with Mr Packer. Ironically if the cricket authorities had done absolutely nothing and then just not have picked the players all would apparently have been legal.

Personally I feel it is all so very sad. I am sure that

eventually there must be a compromise. But coming out of the blue as it did, the Packer affair has split cricket down the middle, put a severe strain on old friendships and introduced argument, resentment and rancour into the dressing-rooms.

As for the Australians, I cannot believe that it did not affect their morale and concentration during the Ashes series. Most of them had signed for Packer, but a few had not, and that must have caused some division. At any rate they never showed the fight and determination which Australian sides have always had.

They had too many players who lacked experience of playing under English conditions, and because of the terrible May weather, this weakness was never really overcome. Match after match played by the tourists was ruined by rain, so that by the time the first Prudential match took place at the beginning of June, the whole Australian team was woefully short of practice – especially the inexperienced newcomers.

For the first time, the three Prudential Trophy matches were to precede the five Tests, instead of coming immediately after the last Test at the Oval. This was an excellent innovation, as in the past there had been danger of anticlimax following so closely on the tensions and excitement of a five-day Test. These fifty-five-over games also served as useful pipe-openers, and an introduction to big match atmosphere for newcomers to international cricket on both sides.

England managed to win the first two matches at Old Trafford and Edgbaston, but not without the usual alarums and excursions. In the third and last match at the Oval, England made 242, of which Amiss and Mike Brearley put on 161 for the first wicket – a record for any wicket in the seventeen Prudential matches since 1972. But as in the earlier matches, the rest of the England batting looked brittle. Australia were going well at 181 for 1, thanks to a superb innings by Greg Chappell. However the match ended in farcical conditions, the game going on in torrential rain, which even made it impossible to identify the players from the commentary box.

I have never seen cricket *of any class* continue in such a deluge. But the next day was Jubilee Day, and neither the teams nor the authorities wanted to have to come back. In spite of the appalling light and pelting rain Chappell continued to play magnificently and his 125 not out was the highest individual score in any Prudential match so far. It enabled Australia to win by two wickets, although England won the series 2–1.

There was to be no respite from the terrible weather when the 1st Test match was played at Lord's in mid-June. It was one of the coldest Tests which I have ever attended and in addition most of the second day was lost because of rain and bad light. So the match was drawn, with Australia still needing 112 to win with only four wickets left at the finish.

Tony Greig, deposed as captain because of his involvement in the Packer affair, received a mixed reception from the crowd, but played one of his typical forcing innings which have so often saved England's bacon. His successor Mike Brearley, in his first Test as captain, acquitted himself well in his quiet and studious manner. He was the first to admit that his task was made easier by the team spirit already existing in the side he had taken over from Greig.

For the benefit of my Manchester friends who resent aspersions cast at their climate, I would like to record straight away that the 2nd Test at Old Trafford was played in gloriously hot sunny weather throughout. England's nine–wicket victory was their first success at home since 1974 and after it Brearley was made captain for the three remaining Tests. In his first innings Bob Woolmer followed his 120 at Lord's with his second successive Test hundred and confirmed his class. Then in England's second innings, to the disgust of Bill Frindall, Woolmer was sent in with just three more runs needed, which meant he lost the chance of scoring three Test hundreds in successive innings.

Amiss was 28 not out at the end but still looked unhappy against Thomson. With Geoff Boycott now lurking in the wings after declaring himself once again available for Test selection, it looked like curtains for Amiss, and that this would prove to be his fiftieth and final Test. And so it turned out – for the 3rd Test at Trent Bridge, Boycott came into the side in place of Amiss and a newcomer called Ian Botham was brought in to join England's attack.

The Test was similar to the one at Old Trafford in two ways – England again won – this time by seven wickets, and the weather was even more perfect over all five days. It was also a sort of fairy tale with Boycott, the old boy, and Botham, the new boy, getting the welcome touch from the fairy's wand. Boycott's return was unbelievable. He batted on all five days of the match and was on the field for all but one and a half hours. Botham, besides playing a useful innings of 25, took five wickets in the first innings he bowled for England, and proved that he really can swing the ball in the air, away from the batsmen, under any conditions.

It was a good performance by the England bowlers to get Australia out for 243 as the pitch was a typical Trent Bridge beauty. In reply, the new England opening partnership crawled slowly to 34 before Brearley was out. Then followed one of those collapses England supporters know all too well. Woolmer made 0 (so Bill Frindall needn't have worried) and then – horror of horrors – Derek Randall in front of his packed home crowd was run out for 13 by Boycott, who hid his head in his hands as the groans from the crowd made him realise what a crime he had perpetrated. Randall can do no wrong at Trent Bridge and it was a bitter disappointment to his thousands of supporters.

It was in fact Boycott's fault and he was genuinely upset. The whole affair must have made him even more determined to make a hundred – something I'm sure he had in mind at the start of the innings. Boycott made 107, greatly helped by Alan Knott, who encouraged and comforted him, and together they put on 215 for the sixth wicket.

In the end England won easily enough by seven wickets. To the joy of the crowd their hero Randall made the winning hit in a bright little innings of 19 not out, some slight reward to them for their wonderful behaviour throughout the match. And of course also among them were many Yorkshire supporters who had come to watch *their* hero's return to Test cricket, and had witnessed a unique display of determination and dedication.

Boycott had now made 98 hundreds, and even then people were saying that the fairies were saving up his final triumph for his home crowd at Headingley in the 4th Test. A hundredth hundred in a Test *by* a Yorkshireman, *before* Yorkshiremen *in* Yorkshire. Impossible surely, pure fantasy. But now read on.

In the one match which Boycott played for Yorkshire between the 3rd and 4th Tests he made the ninety-ninth first-class century he needed to set the stage for Headingley. The odds against scoring 3 hundreds in successive first-class matches are extremely high. The odds against a batsman reaching his hundredth first-class century with the third of these are even higher. But the odds of achieving this feat in a Test match before your own home crowd must be astronomical. And yet I am sure that the majority of that large Yorkshire crowd on the first day at Headingley *expected* Boycott to do it. He himself, in spite of all his self-confidence, must have been one of the few who felt it was virtually asking the impossible. But in spite of losing Brearley without a run scored, Boycott proceeded slowly towards his target.

Helped by some consistent England batting for a change, it took him over five hours on the first day. For the latter part of his innings the hundred began to look inevitable, and just a question of time. He finally reached it with a classic on-drive off a full pitch from Greg

Chappell. Even as the ball left his bat Boycott seemed to know that it would race down the hill towards the football stand for four. He raised both his arms above his head, waving his bat on high, and just had time to do a little war dance before he was swamped by invading spectators. Headingley erupted for several minutes. This was Boycott's moment and his alone. Remarkably, the fact that if England were to win this Test they would win back the Ashes seemed to fade into the background. Remembering how much had happened in the few weeks since his return to Test cricket after an absence of three years, I rank this as one of the most unlikely and emotional feats I have ever witnessed on a cricket field.

Boycott continued to dominate the match on the second day. Would he make 200, would he carry his bat? Well in the end he did neither and was out after tea for 191 from England's total of 436. The luck was all against Australia. In overcast weather they found the movement and swing of Mike Hendrick and Ian Botham practically unplayable. Only three batsmen reached double figures.

When they followed on, 333 runs behind, the weather was still against them and Hendrick and Bob Willis did most of the damage. Just before tea on the fourth day, Randall caught Marsh at mid-off off Hendrick and as he did so turned a super cartwheel to signify that England had won by an innings and 85 runs and so had regained the Ashes after two and a half years in Australia's possession.

This was a great day for Brearley and the England team and needless to say there was much revelry upstairs in the English dressing-room. Also being toasted was Alan Knott, who in his eighty-eighth Test had achieved his highest Test score of 135 and made his two hundred and fiftieth dismissal. But even as the celebrations went on inside, there outside on the balcony was Boycott savouring and acknowledging the cheers of his supporters – cheers, which in spite of the Ashes, seemed to be for him rather than for England. The prodigal son had returned in triumph. All was forgiven. In Yorkshire at least the 1977 Test at Headingley will always be remembered as Boycott's match.

Inevitably the final Test at the Oval was an anti-climax with the Ashes no longer at stake, and to make matters worse the wet weather *before* the match prevented any play on a perfectly fine first day. The match was drawn and England had won the series 3–0.

England were undoubtedly the better team. Well led by Brearley, they caught and fielded better than any England side I have ever seen. A special word of praise for young Botham, who took five wickets in his first Test innings and followed it with another five at Headingley. He is an enthusiastic cricketer who could become a great Test all-rounder. He has a prodigious out-swing, is a fine forcing batsman and a good fielder anywhere, including the slips.

Finally, of course, England won. That made a change and gave encouragement to the many hundreds of thousands of faithful lovers of cricket who either at the grounds, or through their TV, radio or papers, follow the fortunes of their country and enjoy nothing more than seeing Australia well and truly beaten.

After we had won the Ashes at Headingley, a lady sent me this splendid parody on the famous Crispin's Day speech by Henry V before the Battle of Agincourt from Shakespeare's *Henry V, Act 4, Scene 3*. I was able to read it out at the end of the 5th Test at the Oval, when we had some time to spare. I wish we had had Lord Olivier in the box with us so that he could have given it the rendering it deserved.

> *This day we won the Ashes*
> *He that lived this day and came safe home*
> *Will stand a tiptoe when this day is mentioned*
> *And rouse him at the word 'Ashes'.*
> *He that lived this day and sees old age*

Will yearly on the vigil feast his neighbours
And say 'Tomorrow is Ashes day'.
Old men forget, yet all shall be forgot
Then will he open Wisden *and show his record,*
And say 'These wickets I had on Ashes day'.
But he'll remember with advantages
What feats he did that day, then shall our names
Familiar in his mouth as household words
Brearley the Captain, Boycott and Willis
Hendrick and Botham, Randall and Greig
Be in their flowing cups freshly rememb'red
This story shall the good man teach his son
And Ashes day shall ne'er go by
From this day to the ending of the world
But we in it shall be remembered
We few, we happy few, we Band of brothers
For he today that won the Ashes with me
Shall be my brother
While others think themselves
Accurs'd they were not there
At Headingley on Ashes day.

27 In the box

THE SUMMER OF 1977 was certainly a vintage one for our Radio 3 *Test Match Special*. Over the years the Press and listeners have been most kind and generous in their appreciation of our efforts. The idea, which we always try to get across – namely that cricket is fun and something to be enjoyed – seems to have caught on in a big way. In 1977 the fulsome praise which we received was really quite staggering, but none the less welcome for all that! There were big spread feature articles about us in the national dailies, Sundays, and London and provincial evening papers. Some of the reporters and writers came and spent a whole day in the commentary box with us at one or two of the Tests to see exactly how it all works and what makes it tick.

The one thing which seemed to surprise them all was the friendly atmosphere, the lack of the alcoholic stimulants which cartoonists delight to show, and the apparent casualness of the whole operation. 'Just like a group of friends watching a match together and obviously enjoying themselves,' said one of the writers to me. And I think he hit the nail on the head. To start with we *are* all friends and it's incredible but true that I have never had a row with anyone in the commentary box over thirty-two years.[2] We all love cricket, enjoy watching it and talking about it – even living it. We are also all utterly different in voice, character and approach. By ringing the changes of the four

[2] Brian was still a member of the *Test Match Special* team when he died aged eighty-one in 1994. In all he was a cricket commentator on the BBC for an extraordinary 48 years – 24 years on television and a further 24 years on radio.

commentators three times every hour the listeners are given a complete contrast.

The various boxes at the six Test grounds are basically the same in size and shape. Except at Old Trafford and Headingley they are all situated in the pavilion at balcony height directly behind the bowler's arm. Possibly because we have to make instant judgements we have always been far luckier than the Press in this respect. In only three of the Test grounds are they directly behind the stumps. At Old Trafford and Headingley the pavilions are sideways on to the pitch. So at Headingley we are high up at the back of the football stand, and at Old Trafford our box – the smallest and most cramped – is in the block which houses the main scoreboard and seats for the official guests. The boxes have glass windows, which can be opened or not, and ideally there is room for five people to sit comfortably in a row at a baize-covered shelf, on which are four or five stand microphones.

The summarisers – either Trevor Bailey or Freddie Trueman, who change over every hour – sit in one corner, usually with a small TV set in front of them so as to be able to study the action replays if they wish. Next to them is the commentator, then a large space for the bearded wonder, Bill Frindall, with all his books, score sheets, calculators and coloured pens and pencils, plus a thermos flask or two. On his other side will be another commentator who is 'resting' and then in the other corner a spare seat and microphone. This is used by casual visitors to the box whom we often interview – people like the manager of the touring side, the chairman of the selectors, or the captains at the end of a match.

People often ask me about life in the box, its routine and what we do when not at the microphone or when it's raining. We all have our different ways of spending the day so I will only speak on my own behalf. I always try to get to the box at least an hour before play is due to start and can always rely on our producer being there already

– either Peter Baxter in London, Don Mosey in the North, or Dick Maddock in the Midlands. They will have stuck a roster up on the wall and by the commentator's mike, showing our commentary times during the day – normally one twenty-minute period every hour. They will also have sorted out into piles the large number of letters which arrive for us each day. If I can, I always try to open mine and give them a cursory glance, in case there is anything in them which I feel should be brought up during the day's play.

These letters are very welcome and reveal a faithful and seemingly ever-increasing band of *TMS* listeners. Some letters are just kind and say how much they enjoy the programmes. Some ask technical questions, others want information about records. Some disagree with something which we have said, or point out a mistake. But the great thing about them is that even when critical they are written in a friendly way without any of the abuse and rudeness so often posted to television commentators. Why this should be so I have never really discovered. But I do know that when I was doing television commentary I regularly received a small percentage of letters telling me to put a sock in it, or why couldn't I be like Peter West – or just simply telling me to get well and truly stuffed. Some of our radio listeners no doubt feel the same but they are either too polite to say so, or just don't bother to write. We each try to answer the more personal letters, some are answered from time to time during gaps in play, others get included in the listeners' letters session during the Monday lunch interval. The rest – as many as two thousand in 1977 – are acknowledged by Peter Baxter on behalf of the BBC.

One type of letter does create problems and that is the one asking us to get the autographs of the two teams and both commentary teams as well. Some even include autograph books or miniature bats. Others enclose treasured cuttings from old newspapers or photographs of past cricketers, which they want returned after we have seen them. If only they could see the piles of letters, small parcels and old envelopes littering the confined space of the boxes they would realise the folly of sending anything of any value which they want to be sure to get back. There is real danger of it being lost in the all inevitable chaos.

As for the autographs – well, many years ago we had to make it a rule not to bother the teams. We get so many requests that we would become an intolerable nuisance were we to grant them, even if we could spare the time to keep on trailing off to the dressing-rooms. We do, however, do our best to send our own autographs though we appreciate that they are only a very poor second best. And by the way a stamped addressed envelope is the most certain way of being successful.

A word about the parcels. People are very kind and send us a varied assortment of presents. A lady from Bournemouth regularly sends us our favourite pastilles, another from Maida Vale personally delivers a bottle of wine at the London grounds. There's a lovely lady who keeps a flower shop in Hounslow, who sends a beautiful bouquet at the end of each match. Other ladies send us cakes. One thing leads to another. After we had thanked someone for some sweets, the next day a dental centre sent us a toothbrush. When we thanked them for that, someone followed with some toothpaste. A big sweet manufacturer sent boxes and boxes of their particular confectionery – so many that we could not possibly consume them all, and the local children's hospital benefited.

On one occasion, for some reason, Greg Chappell lay on his back and kicked his legs in the air. I remarked that our Yorkshire Terrier, Mini, did this on our lawn as she had eczema on her back. Not only did this produce a shoal of letters, including two from Australia, but a chemical firm sent me some skin powder to put into her food. We really *are* spoilt and are most grateful to everyone for their thoughtfulness and kindness.

But I've digressed! Back to the day's routine. After looking at the letters and parcels, I usually read the day's papers to see what they have to say about the game and to check in case they have got hold of a story which we have missed. Then I usually watch the players practising and get the latest news on any team injuries. After a cup of coffee it's back to the box for the start of our day's broadcasting – fifteen minutes before play on the first day and five minutes before on the other four. Once we are on the air the microphones in the box are live so that those who are not commentating have to keep as quiet as possible. With about four or five extroverts this is not easy, and I'm afraid that the odd chuckle and whispered remark do sometimes come over the mike.

The lunchtime summary finishes at 1.35 pm and then we all go our separate ways. On some grounds we have a packed lunch or bring our own sandwiches. At Lord's I always picnic with my family on the lawn behind the Warner Stand. At Headingley I am lucky that Sidney Hainsworth, who sponsors the Fenner Trophy at Scarborough and also presented the Sutcliffe Gates to Headingley, gives me a slap-up lunch in the Taverners Tent. At Edgbaston the Warwickshire Committee generously entertains us, while at Trent Bridge we are royally looked after by the famous old Trent Bridge Inn. So we do pretty well but not, alas, on every day. As I've said, on Mondays we spend the lunch session answering listeners' letters, and on some Saturdays one or two of us are needed for the phone-in programme, *Call the Commentators*.

Most of the grounds provide us with a pot of tea and biscuits and these keep us going until close of play. Then after Tony Lewis has given his witty, expert and informative summary of the day's play, I think that most of us feel that we deserve a drink!

During play, when I am not commentating I usually sit

watching at the back of the box. I'm still rather like a small boy. I dread missing a ball. But occasionally I do go out to stretch my legs and get some air, as I must admit that Fred's cigars and Trevor's cigarettes do sometimes clog up the box a bit! It's also quite a good thing to watch play for a short time from a different angle and I find that by sitting sideways on I can get a better idea of the speed of the bowlers and the pace of the pitch. The others, some of whom are writing for newspapers, leave the box more often than I do. In fact John Arlott likes to come in only a minute or two before he is due on the air, and usually leaves immediately after it.

When it rains we do our best *not* to return to the studio for music. We realise that people have switched on to us because they want cricket. They can get music on at least two other channels. So we talk about some current cricket problem or topic, answer letters, tell stories – though these are not all about cricket! As for instance at the Oval, Freddie Trueman asked us out of the blue if we knew what was the fastest thing on two wheels. Naturally we didn't know. So he told us: 'An Arab riding a bicycle through Golders Green'. Last season during one long stoppage for rain we kept talking for almost the whole session about one thing or another. The trouble is some people write in to say that they enjoy the chit-chat more than the commentary! So we had better be careful or we shall do ourselves out of a job!

Only when we run out of puff or material do we hand back to the studio. But then, funnily enough, unlike the players, we never play cards. We either just gossip or tell some of the stories which were not suitable to tell on the air. When Don Mosey is one of the commentators he and I play a word game on paper which produces some ding-dong struggles and keeps us out of mischief.

Finally a word of praise for our producers and engineers, who get none of the limelight and work for very long hours with scarcely any break. As a reward we make sure they get their fair share of the sweets and cakes. There are two producers for each Test. One sits in a studio back at Broadcasting House. He opens up the transmission and is responsible for filling in with music during intervals of play and giving the lunch-time and tea-time county cricket scores. He has to listen to every ball (poor chap) and can let us know if we are off mike, not giving the score enough or making too much noise in the background. He also has a large coloured TV set and there are occasions when he can help us out by saying up the line what is happening out of our sight – such as the Queen arriving, or something going on in the pavilion below us, which *we* cannot see, but which one of the TV cameras can pick up.

In the box itself is the producer in charge of the outside broadcast at the ground. He prepares the roster and sees that we keep to it! He arranges for people to come into the box to be interviewed. He cues us with a card when we have to greet *World Service* or *Sport on Two*. He tells the summarisers how long they have got and places a stopwatch in front of them. He arranges our tea and coffee, and, as I've said, sorts out all the mail and parcels. He encourages us, reproves us gently, but always keeps us happy. He is the most indispensable person in the box, including Bill Frindall. Because at a pinch our producers can also score by the Frindall method. By the end of the day he must be exhausted, as he does not even get a break during the intervals, when he has to produce *Listeners' Letters*, *Call the Commentators* and so on.

I hope now that you have got some sort of picture of what goes on behind the scenes in the box. It may all sound a bit chaotic – and so at times perhaps it is. But so long as you enjoy your radio visit to the Test match as much as we enjoy being there, then we are all happy.

That is how I see a typical day in the box. But others see it differently! We were much amused by an article in *The Times* in which Michael Leapman gave *his* impression of the way we carry on.

Now over to Brian Johnston at Lord's:

Brian Good morning. I'm afraid the news from here isn't too good. Play has been delayed because of picketing outside the Grace Gate by dozens of the less successful county players, who are complaining that they haven't been made offers by Kerry Packer's cricket circus. It's fairly nasty out there. None of the Test players has yet crossed the picket line except Mike Brearley, the English captain, whose fetching crash helmet is standing him in good stead at last. Now you know I don't like to get involved in politics, but this unfortunate incident does reinforce my view that the game isn't what it was. What would some of the all-time greats have made of a picket line, I wonder? I remember old 'Goofy' Grunwick, that great Essex wicket-keeper/batsman – the greatest player of underarm full tosses of his generation I should say, wouldn't you Fred? Anyway, I remember a policeman once tried to stop him getting into Lord's on the grounds that it was three in the morning and he was trying to climb in over the Tavern roof. He happened to have his stainless steel groin protector on at the time, so he just thrust his midriff into the policeman's face and knocked him flying. The policeman was fined for indecent assault. Pickets, I don't think he would have given much time to them. But here's Trevor and he's panting, as though he's hot from the fray. Good morning, Trevor, what's the latest?

Trevor Good morning, Brian. Well it's looking pretty ugly out there. I was just on my way in when I happened to meet this old friend of mine that I hadn't seen since late last night and we decided to go to the Tavern for our first of the day. It was ugly, very ugly – that's the only word I can think of to describe it. It took us several minutes to fight our way through to the bar. 'Blacklegs!' they shouted at us, which was doubly unfortunate since my friend happened to be a West Indian. I think you know him – 'Fingers' St Paul, surely the fastest left-handed scoreboard operator of his generation. He and I were wondering what the old-timers would have made of all the fuss. Do you remember 'Goofy' Grunwick, the great Somerset leg-break bowler, who could make the ball turn on a sixpence, but lost his touch when they barred the use of coins on the field of play?

Brian Yes, we were just talking about him. Let's ask Bill if he can look through his record books to see if there's ever been a picket at a cricket match before. (Pause and sound of record books being riffled through). Ah, here we are. He says no, there's never been one, but there was once a strike at a cricket ball manufacturer's in Peshawar, where the workers were campaigning for bigger stumps to be used. This would have shortened each innings, so you could have matches of four innings each instead of two, doubling the number of balls you needed.

Trevor Never came off, did it Brian?

Brian It didn't, no. And now while we're waiting for the umpires to sort things out, I'd like to thank those listeners who've sent me little favours, as they always do. A listener in Glastonbury has sent me some wine gums packed in a pair of stout gumboots. She says I'm to suck the gums, wear the boots when rain stops play and fill them with champagne if England win. 'And if you're ever in Glastonbury,' she writes . . . no, I don't think I'll read that, but it does sound a lot more fun than sitting here droning away about cricket. And another young woman from Bayswater has sent me a pair of undergarments to warm myself during the cold spell we've been having, though I must say they don't look too practical. She's sent me a limerick to go with them, which again I can't read to a family audience but I'll tell you the last line. It goes: 'Oh no, they're not mine, they're the vicar's.' But let's get back to talking about the all-time greats. John has just struggled up here. What have you got to tell us, John?

John Well, Brian, you were talking just now about 'Goofy' Grunwick, that great Worcester opening bat who still, I think, holds the record for scoring the fastest single in Test matches against New Zealand. I was just wondering if you remembered how his brilliant career was ruined in that famous Lord's Test against Pakistan. He went off to get another sweater and when he hadn't come back after an hour they went looking for him and found him *in flagrante* . . .

Brian Really. I thought it was in the Long Room.

John Anyway, they caught him with the wife of one of the selectors and it was clear that he'd managed several times to get past her perhaps rather half-hearted defensive prods. Her husband did him a terrible injury with the groundsman's turf-cutting implement.

Brian Never played again did he, John? He took up female impersonation, I remember. In fact I saw him in action a year or so afterwards in a drag pub near the Oval, doing an amazingly intricate exotic dance with a bat and a set of stumps. Fred, you come in now, who was the greatest performer you ever came in contact with?

Fred Funny you should ask me that, Brian, because I once came up against the wife of that selector myself. It was at a charity game down at Little Filandering on behalf of Prince Charles' fund for arthritic coachmen.

Brian Marvellously worthwhile cause, that.

Fred Yes, but unfortunately it rained most of the day and I was sent to help this lady make the teas and the upshot was that nobody got any tea and I remember coming away thinking that maybe Grunwick wasn't as goofy as people thought.

Brian That wasn't quite what I meant, Fred. Who had the biggest feet of anyone you can remember?

Fred Funny you should ask that because the wife of that selector I was mentioning had the most colossal pair you've ever seen. She played once in a women's Test and was the only player ever to have been warned by the umpires for wearing down the pitch when she was fielding at slip.

Brian Well, while we've been rabbiting on here, play has actually got under way and the Australians have lost a couple of quick wickets. But, John, you were going to tell us something?

John Yes, Brian, it was about 'Goofy' Grunwick, the Surrey left-hander, who was certainly the finest extra cover of his generation . . .

Among the many hundreds of letters which we receive during a season, there is always a lot of poetry. I never knew there were so many budding poets and poetesses. A cricketing friend of mine once told me the difference between poetry and prose. He quoted the lines:

> *There was a young batsman called Walls*
> *Who was hit a terrible blow on the thigh.*

My friend explained that these two lines are prose. 'But,' he added, 'had the blow been four inches higher, that would have been poetry'!

One piece of poetry was sent to me in 1976 by Mr Alan Hamilton of Torquay. He called it *The Cricketer's 'If'* (with apologies to Rudyard Kipling). I think it sums up quite beautifully exactly what cricket is all about, and explains just why it means so much to so many of us. Mr Hamilton, who was eighty-five, sent a copy of the poem to his old school, Wellington, where it was hung up on the noticeboard of the pavilion. Alas he died in 1977 but his widow has kindly given me permission to use it.

THE CRICKETER'S 'IF'
(with apologies to the late Mr Rudyard Kipling)

If you can keep your head when bowlers skittle
Both opening batsmen with the score at three –
When, knowing that your later batting's brittle,
You grimly think 'It all depends on me!'
If you can play defensive, watchful cricket,
Leaving alone out-swingers on the off,
(Knowing full well that, if you grope, you'll snick it)
However much frustrated watchers scoff!

If you can overcome unsure beginnings,
And start to push the score along a bit –
If you can play a really sterling innings
And play your natural game, which is to HIT
If you can score a hundred, and be master,
Yet shield your partner while he settles in –
If you can wrest a triumph from disaster,
And lead your side to a noteworthy win.

Or, if outwitted by a paceman's terror,
You see your middle stump shot out for 'duck'
If, still unruffled, you can note your error
And not just put it down to rotten luck!
If you can bowl a 'long hop' and get pasted
Yet keep direction and your length as well –

If you can think 'That lesson won't be wasted –
I'll serve him up some teasers for a spell!'
If you can bear to hear, though sorely shaken
The umpire's 'No' to your assured appeal –
And realise you might have been mistaken
And show no outward sign of what you feel!

And if you can, when mid-off drops a sitter,
Curb your impatience and still play the game.
Reflecting that the poor chap's feeling bitter
And think 'Ah, well! I might have done the same'

And when, at length, you ache in every sinew
Your limbs feel leaden and your fingers sore.
If, when your Captain asks: 'Can you continue?'
You can still rise to just one over more.

If you can field with keen determination
Watching the stroke and ever on alert
Stopping the hard ones with anticipation
And never make complaint although it hurt.
If you, at slip, can hold an awkward flyer
Or run the batsman out from deep third man.
If in the deep, you catch a swirling skyer
And keep your head from swelling – if you can!

If you can mix with cricketers as brothers
And mingle with both teams at close of play –
And pass the spirit of the game to others
Wherever you may meet them day by day –
Although you hold no County Member's ticket,
And play your local matches just for fun:
You will have done a mighty lot for cricket
E'en though you never play for England, Son!

Alan F. Hamilton

I am well known for making terrible puns in the commentary box, but there was one I actually missed and I immediately received letters from two different people pointing out what I *should* have said.

It all started with a man who wrote in to say that he was in trouble. He said his Afghan hound had chewed up the inside of his *Wisden*, and eaten all the records! What should he do? I didn't really see what *I* was expected to do about it, but remember making one or two rather wet suggestions such as that he should build higher shelves or get a smaller dog.

But as my two correspondents so rightly pointed out the obvious reply I should have given was that the Afghan hound should have his 'Wisden' teeth taken out!

28 Horse d'oeuvres

TOWARDS THE END OF 1976 I had become slightly involved in a new sport for me – horse racing. I became part-owner of a flat racehorse. And for those of you, who like me, know very little about racing let me hasten to explain that flat is not the shape of the horse, but records the fact that he runs *on* the flat and not over hurdles or fences.

I had done something fairly similar about ten years earlier, when I owned one leg of a greyhound with Colin Cowdrey, John Woodcock and Michael Melford. As it was trained and ran in Kent and because of Colin's nickname, we called it Kentish Kipper. It used to run at Catford and won two or three races, though we were never there to see them. That's the trouble about owning a greyhound. It's not a very satisfying business. The owners have no say when it will run – that is arranged between the trainer and the stadium. They cannot see it *before* a race like you can a horse in the paddock, though they are very generously allowed to give it a gentle pat afterwards. We did once visit its training quarters but somewhat naturally the dog did not recognise us as his owners. We also went to watch it run once or twice, and it was amusing to see the way its price shortened when the bookies realised that we were there. They assumed we had come especially to back it – as if our measly £1 to win would make any difference to them. Another thing against greyhound racing is that the races are over so quickly you hardly have time to read the race, and even if your dog runs well, the pleasure is so fleeting.

So in the end we were quite pleased when Arthur Milton, the Gloucestershire cricketer and double England international at cricket and soccer, made an offer for Kentish Kipper. Arthur said that he knew of a lonely little old lady down in Bristol who wanted a greyhound as a pet. He said he would give us what we had paid for him. So thinking that we were doing both ourselves and the lonely little old lady a good turn, we sold Kentish Kipper to Arthur for £100. We thought no more about it for some time until a friend showed me a cutting from a Bristol newspaper, reporting the greyhound races down there. 'Kentish Kipper wins again!' was the headline. Arthur has always been a bit cagey about it and I still don't know how many races the dog won down in the West Country. But I strongly suspect that the lonely little old lady was none other than a stylish opening batsman, a brilliant close fielder and an England right-winger!

My entry into horse racing came about through David Brown, the England and Warwickshire fast bowler. I suppose it started in 1967 during the MCC tour of West Indies. David met and fell in love with a very attractive girl called Tricia Norman. They met in Kingston at some sportsmen's gathering when Tricia was in Jamaica with her father, a well-known gynaecologist. She had always been a good point-to-point rider in England and while in the West Indies rode as a jockette in flat races against men jockeys. In fact we saw her come in second in a race at Georgetown, Guyana. It was a case of love at first sight and Big Dave – as he's called – had definitely bowled a maiden over. And to continue with cricket jargon, he soon got *hooked* on horses after they were married.

For some years, the Browns lived just outside Worcester where they raised a family and bred ponies. Dave had always wanted a farm and in the winters when not on tour used to study pigs and their breeding, so after a very successful benefit in 1973 they began looking round for a farm, which they eventually found near Kidderminster. They turned it into a stud and sort of livery stable, with masses of loose-boxes transformed from the old cowsheds.

There they started to breed and break horses. They owned a mare called Santa Marta and sent her to a stallion called Grey Mirage. He was a class horse and among other races had won the Two Thousand Guineas trial at Kempton and had also broken the track record for two-year-olds over seven furlongs at Newbury.

The happy result was a strapping roan colt, which Tricia brought up and broke and was the first person to get on his back. Dave asked me whether I would like a share in him and for a bit of fun I said I would. I brought in my friend, Sir Martin Gilliat, racing manager and private secretary to the Queen Mother, and Dave already had the two Warwickshire cricketers Jack Bannister and 'Big' Jim Stewart, and three others. We started as eight partners, but one fell by the wayside, so now we each own one-seventh of the horse – though which part has never been specified! And now for his name – and I'm afraid you are in for a bit of PUNishment. In order to keep the Grey of Grey Mirage and the cricketing connection, I suggested that we might call him W. G. Greys, and surprisingly this was accepted by Wetherbys. He is trained by the well-known Midlands trainer, Reg Hollinshead, who had his best season ever in 1977 with fifty winners.

W.G. ran in six races – he had a few weeks off with a damaged muscle and a cough – and he finished 'in the frame' twice. The other four times he ran well and never let us down, usually finishing about sixth or seventh out of big two-year-old fields with over twenty runners, after leading for most of the race. He is a big colt and stands 16.2 and the experts say that he won't be fully developed until he's a three-year-old, and we then hope his distance will be a mile. In 1977 he ran one 5–furlong, three 6–furlong and two 7–furlong races. At York in October we had our first thrill, when he finished third in a 5–furlong race, and then came our first taste of victory in November during the last week of the flat racing season. He won a

6-furlong race at Teesside Park by a neck, but alas I was not able to see him win.

But Dave and Tricia were there to celebrate with Reg Hollinshead and his admirable stable jockey, Tony Ives, both of whom think highly of W.G. So do we all, and hope that he will prove to be as successful as the famous bearded 'Doctor' after whom he has been nearly named.[3] At this stage I am not quite sure what happens if he wins a really big race. Do we get a long leading rein so that all seven of us can lead him in?

Anyhow, it never pays to boast, as an American once found when visiting a small farm somewhere in England. The English farmer took him on a tour round the three hundred acres or so and when they returned to the farm after walking a couple of hours, the American said: 'You know, way back home in America it takes me two days in my car to go round my farm.' 'Yes,' replied the Englishman. 'I once had a car like that too!'

During the winter when not doing *Down Your Way* or writing books, much of my time is taken up by speaking at lunches, dinners, or even at business conferences. Besides bringing in some useful lolly, it satisfies my urge to stand up in front of an audience and tell stories and jokes. This all stems from my admiration of the old stand-up comics, whom I used to enjoy so much when I went to the music halls.

In the days before radio and TV, a comic would tour the country using virtually the same act, year in year out. He might occasionally add to it, give it a bit of polish, or adjust it slightly to suit a particular audience. But basically it didn't change and I do much the same with my speeches. I have about three, which I normally use. One completely on cricket, one based on my overall BBC experiences over thirty-two years, and the third just an after-dinner speech, with jokes and stories – some true, some not. I have this

[3] In fact W. G. Greys only won one more race.

absurd hankering to make people laugh, and get tremendous satisfaction from hearing the laughter after telling a tale.

There are virtually no new stories – just old ones in a different wrapping. It all depends on the way they are told and more or less everything depends on timing. I learnt a lot by studying the methods of the great stand-up comics like Max Miller, Ted Ray and Tommy Trinder. My wife Pauline often asks me how I can go on doing the same old speeches.

The answer is that each audience is different, and reacts differently to the same story. So that each performance is a new challenge. One thing I learnt from the comics was how important it is to win over your audience right from the word go. This is especially so with the Round Table dinners. The Tablers are a boisterous lot and very appreciative, but unless you do 'get' them at the start, they are inclined to barrack or interrupt. But another thing I learnt was to keep going at a good pace, so if one joke falls a bit flat, you are soon on to the next one, and hope for better luck!

I find the Tablers most stimulating and thoroughly enjoy my evenings with them. They are all under forty years of age, so are lively and quick to see a joke. They must be pretty near to what used to be a typical music-hall audience. I treasure the memory of one of their chairmen who announced after the loyal toast: 'You may smoke now the Queen's drunk!'

I was told of one Round Table who thought up a most ingenious idea, which amused me, though I know it shouldn't have done. During one of their more boisterous dinners it was reported to them that two Panda cars were waiting outside in the car park, obviously hoping to catch one or two of the diners with the breathalyser. So at the end of the evening their chairman found a teetotal Tabler (a rare bird!) and told him to go out into the car park and pretend to be roaring drunk, and then to get into his car and drive away. This the t.t. did, singing at the top of his voice, and swaying and lurching all over the place. He staggered into his car and drove off very, very slowly, as if he was having difficulty in seeing. Sure enough the Pandas, thinking that they had a certain victim, followed him slowly out on to the road. They let him go about a mile, then one of them passed him, and signalled for him to stop. They asked him to blow into the bag and were amazed when it did not turn green. Nor could they smell any drink on his breath. However, since he had done nothing wrong, they just asked him for his name and address and then let him drive off. They realised that they had been 'had', and were not surprised on returning to the car park, to find that, thanks to the decoy, it was empty.

I am also occasionally asked to propose the health of the bride and bridegroom at a wedding. Here I have quite a good tip for anyone asked to do the same thing. You inevitably have to start with a number of 'in' family jokes, but after that I recommend that you read out what the stars foretell for the young couple. You will find by just reading out what the astrologer has to say, that there are quite a few innocuous innuendos which should amuse the wedding guests – especially when they have had some champagne.

I recently had to do the honours at a wedding of the daughter of great friends of mine in Yorkshire. By scanning the London evening papers for a week or so I was able to read out one or two appropriate forecasts. Things like:

'You'll now be able to start on a job you've been too busy to deal with earlier in the week.'

'Probably the quietest day of the week – favours those of you who want to be left in seclusion to get on with what you want to do.'

'You'll be putting spare time this evening to practical purposes.'

And one especially for the bride:

'Be careful today if handling any electrical gadgets or tools.'

And for the bridegroom:

'There's nothing to be afraid of – it's just that you must be prepared to mark time and not burn up too much physical energy!'

Besides Jubilee Day I did quite a number of one-off broadcasts during 1977. There was my usual Boat Race commentary from Chiswick Bridge, with interviews with the crews afterwards. Then I did a programme called *It's a Funny Business*, produced by Mike Craig, an amusing Yorkshireman from Dewsbury, in which he talks to people about the funny side of their careers. He kindly did me the honour of including me among such stars as Morecambe and Wise, Ted Ray and Arthur Askey and used quite a few of my old recordings from *In Town Tonight* days.

Then came the *Archive Auction*, in which Phyllis Robinson invited me to choose about half a dozen records or tapes for which I might bid if ever there was an archive auction. It was a sort of *Desert Island Discs*, except that the choice was limited to material which had been recorded by the BBC since it started. Needless to say it is a fantastic and quite unique collection and one could have chosen enough records to make a hundred programmes. However I tried to make it as personal to my own tastes as possible and this was my selection:

1 *Tommy Handley, Jack Train (Colonel Chinstrap) and Diana Morrison (Miss Hotchkiss)* in an excerpt from *ITMA* recorded just after the end of the war. I chose it because Jack and Diana had been great friends of mine, and I have always considered Tommy Handley by far the greatest *radio* comedian, thanks to the brilliant way he could read a comedy script.

2 *A recording of the occasion in September 1938 when Neville Chamberlain left Heston Airport to go to meet Hitler in Munich.* At the time I was sharing rooms with William Douglas-Home and one evening his brother, Lord Home, rang up. He was then Lord Dunglass, parliamentary secretary to Mr Chamberlain, and had been told suddenly he, too, was to go to Munich. He wanted us to lend him a shirt as all his clothes were up in Scotland. He actually borrowed one of mine, so we thought we had better see them off.

I can still remember Mr Chamberlain with black homburg and umbrella standing by his (by modern standards) ridiculously small two-engined plane. He made the following little speech: 'When I was a boy I was always taught to be an optimist. When I return from seeing Herr Hitler I hope I shall be able to say – as Hotspur did in Shakespeare's *King Henry IV* – "Out of this nettle danger, we pluck this flower safety." ' This received a sympathetic cheer from the small crowd who had gathered to see him.

On listening to the recording it is amusing to see how broadcasting has improved. Before he makes his little speech you can hear Mr Chamberlain say in a hoarse whisper: 'Let me know when to start,' and then the engineer's voice saying: 'OK, go ahead.' Imagine that happening at London Airport today.

3 *Peter Bromley's commentary on the finish of the 1977 Grand National, when Red Rum created a record by winning for the third time.* Red Rum has always been one of my heroes and I think he is a fabulous horse. But I really wanted to pay tribute to what is, in my opinion, the most difficult of all forms of commentating. And I chose Peter Bromley because I think he is the best of them all. A racing commentator has to know and remember so many things, and be able to produce these facts while giving the fastest commentary of any sport, with the possible exception of ice hockey.

Often at places like Newmarket there may be a field of thirty comparatively unknown horses charging straight towards him in a line, and often to make it even more difficult, with the field split, half on one side of the course, half on the other. The commentator has to know the colours, owner, jockey, trainer of each horse and put the right name of the horse to them, and at the same time read the race and make sure to call the first three horses home in the right order. How racing commentators do it I don't know except that it does involve endless hours of homework, juggling the colours and the names around until you get them right. So far as I know, Peter himself has never called the wrong horse home, and what's more, if a photo finish is asked for by the judges, Peter is always prepared to stick his neck out and say who *he* thinks has won. I take off my hat to the racing commentators.

4 Next came a nostalgic pre-war memory of *Harry Roy and his Band from the Mayfair Hotel*. In the thirties after a visit to the Palladium or Holborn Empire we often used to go along to hear them, sitting at a table close to the band so that we got to know them well. The piece I chose was *Somebody Stole my Gal* with clarinet and a touch of singing from Harry himself, and plenty of that magnificent pair at two pianos – Ivor Moreton who did the twiddly bits in the treble, and Dave Kaye who provided the vital rhythm and accompaniment.

5 *The famous speech by Gerard Hoffnung, which the BBC recorded at the Oxford Union after the war.* It describes his adventures with a bucket on a pulley at a building site, and with his high-pitched voice, gives me hysterics every time I hear it.

6 *Alan Gibson's commentary on the last over of the 1963 Test match at Lord's between England and the West Indies.* I had to have something to do with cricket and this was one of the most exciting Tests I have ever watched, not just

because of the finish, but because throughout the five days, fortunes had swung first one way, then the other. I was doing the TV commentary during the exciting last moments, when with two balls left of the match to be bowled by Wes Hall, England needed six runs to win, with only one wicket to fall. David Allen was the batsman and he had just been joined by Colin Cowdrey, whose broken left arm was in plaster. If he had to bat he was going to stand as a left-hander and play with his sound right arm. But luckily David Allen resisted the temptation to hit a six for victory and kept out the last two balls safely. A draw was the fairest result to both teams.

7 'Scorn Not His Simplicity' – sung by Adrian Hardy. When Down Your Way visited Kilkeel in County Down during the summer of 1977 I interviewed a young teenage student artist, who not only painted but also sang in a group. His name was Adrian Hardy and at the end of the interview, instead of choosing a piece of music for us to play later, we recorded him there and then. The song he chose to sing was a haunting ballad composed by Phil Coulter, who among other things had composed Puppet on a String for Sandie Shaw when she won the Eurovision Song Contest. Phil has a mentally-handicapped son and the title of the song explains exactly what it is about. I, for very personal reasons, found it terribly moving, and just had to include it for my final choice.

My appearances on TV are practically nil these days, but for the last six years I have done the TV commentary on the Lord Mayor's Show. As in 1976 we were part of the Saturday morning TV programme, Multi-Coloured Swap Shop, and before the procession started I was persuaded to offer a miniature cricket bat as a swap. The Lord Mayor was again wired up under his robes with a small transmitter and microphone so that he could give a message to viewers as the coach passed our cameras opposite St Paul's.

When he had made his little speech, the Lord Mayor, Air Commodore the Hon. Sir Peter Vanneck, thought he would make a professional handback to me, but unfortunately cued back to Raymond instead of Brian! Raymond Baxter had helped him at his Press conference about the show, and he must somehow have got Raymond's name stuck in his mind. But he immediately realised his mistake because our sound engineers heard him say as he sat back in his coach – 'Blast it! I should have said Brian.' Luckily, though, they had already switched back to my microphone, so his remark did not go out over the air.

The one other TV appearance I made was in *The Generation Game* with Bruce Forsyth. This was a tremendous *tour de force* by Bruce and I can think of no one else who could anywhere near match his bubbling audience-winning personality. He makes wonderful use of the camera, and his various facial expressions after cracking a corny gag, which has either gone well or flopped, are real television. But no matter how great an artiste he is, much of his success is due to his professional preparation beforehand and all the hard work which goes with it.

It was fascinating to watch the rehearsal, with Bruce putting stand-in contestants through the various games. He even read through the cards about each contestant and as he did so I kept thinking of what gags I would make about the various items on the cards. For instance, one man had just been promoted to be superintendent of a cemetery. I thought my comment might have been: 'Well, you're *dead* lucky, aren't you?' As it turned out, during the actual show Bruce remarked 'Oh, so you've got a lot of people under you!' His great skill is in making these gags appear to be spontaneous, though of course with the help of a scriptwriter, they have been worked out carefully beforehand.

After a day-long rehearsal Bruce had a two-hour break before the show. Then he went out to warm up the audience just before the recording started. The show was recorded on the Thursday evening before the Saturday it went out, and ideally many of the audience were in parties and Bruce gained an immediate rapport with them. Incidentally, he did not meet the real contestants until they appeared in the show, nor did they have any idea of what the various games would be.

My small part was in No. 3 game called *Name the Commentator*. Five of us: John Snagge, Dan Maskell, Peter Alliss, John Motson and myself, each in turn read out a bit of doggerel giving clues about the game on which we usually commentate. The contestants had then to write down who they thought each commentator was. One team guessed me, the other said 'Robertson of *Down Your Way*'; the male partner apologised afterwards and said his mind went blank. John Snagge and John Motson were each guessed by one team, but Peter Alliss and Dan Maskell stumped everyone. Remarkable really, when you consider how regularly they are on TV, commentating on golf and tennis during the summer. One team in fact gave the hilarious answer of Virginia Wade when trying to guess Dan!

Anyhow, it was all a lot of fun, and meeting the contestants afterwards cleared away any doubts I might have had about them being made to look fools. They had all thoroughly enjoyed themselves and would not have missed it for the world.

29 Who's been a lucky boy?

I T WAS IN 1977 that I became an OAP and the day before my sixty-fifth birthday – 23 June – produced one of the happiest surprises of my life. It all started way back in March when I received a letter from my old friend Edward Halliday, the famous portrait painter, who lives just down the road from us in Hamilton Terrace. He wrote that he had always wanted to paint me and would consider it a great honour if I would allow him to do so for his own enjoyment. I was naturally very surprised but thrilled. Ted is president of the Royal Society of Portrait Painters and numbers among his past sitters the Queen (goodness knows how many times), the Queen Mother, Prince Philip, Prince Charles and countless heads of state and VIPs from all walks of life. So I sat down immediately to write and say how honoured and delighted I was to join this galaxy of stars.

I imagined that he would show my portrait at the Royal Society of Portrait Painters' annual exhibition. I had to restrain myself from running as I went along to pop the letter through his letterbox. We had half a dozen sittings of about two hours a time and we thoroughly enjoyed ourselves gossiping and talking about every subject under the sun – refreshed every now and again by a glass of sherry. Ted and I had known each other from the old Television Newsreel days at Alexandra Palace. He had been the commentator and I used to go down there to do voice-overs on the cricket films. He likes cricket and knows everybody in all walks of life. So we were not short of conversation!

After the last sitting, Ted expressed himself satisfied, except for the background, which he was going to make the Grandstand at Lord's with Father Time on the weather-vane on top of it. At this point I hadn't even had one glance at the picture, though Ted asked Pauline to come along and give her opinion. I was putting off the shock for as long as possible.

With the cricket season in full swing I thought no more about it, presuming that Ted would tell me when it was finished. I had heard nothing by the middle of June, when Barry and Clare told me that they were going to take me out to dinner on the night before my birthday. The rendezvous would be secret, but I was to be ready in a dinner jacket by 7.15 pm when they would pick me up.

This is what I did, and at the appointed time on the day they turned up to find Pauline and me all dressed up and waiting to go. Then the doorbell began to ring, and in streamed twenty of my closest friends, all dolled up in evening dress. Bottles of champagne and glasses soon appeared from some secret hiding place and we all went into the garden and had a splendid party.

Then came another surprise. We were all summoned indoors and there was Ted Halliday with the completed picture – a present, I was told, from Pauline, with the children providing the frame. Needless to say I was very touched, but pleased beyond belief. The whole party and the picture had been such a wonderfully kept secret. It had all been Pauline's idea and she had organised everything, starting her planning in January, so as to make sure my friends could reserve the date. She had also contacted Tony Smith of *Down Your Way*, Peter Baxter of *Test Match Special*, and Paddy Davis, the marvellous lady who arranges all my speaking engagements. Pauline asked them all to make sure they didn't ask me to do any job on that day and sure enough it remained blank in my diary. It was certainly one of the best-kept secrets of my life and I had no inkling of what was up.

But there was still more to come. After we had consumed quite a bit of champagne, I was blindfolded, put in a car, and driven off to an unknown destination. I had no idea where we were going and didn't guess even when we stopped and I was led into a building, across a thickly carpeted entrance hall and down some stairs. Then I guessed it, as I heard the tinkling piano, which could be no one else except Ian Stewart. So it was the Savoy Hotel, where all my friends had already arrived and we had two tables of twelve in the restaurant. We had a wonderful evening and danced into the early hours with a huge birthday cake with a cricket match being played on top, plus of course *Happy Birthday to You* from the band.

Oh, I had almost forgotten about the picture. I must admit that as many people hate the sound of their own voice when they hear it recorded, so do I dislike looking at pictures of myself. But Ted had certainly got a wonderful likeness, whether *I* liked what I saw or not. One of my 'friends' said charmingly that he could tell which was me, as Father Time was holding a scythe!

One of the bonuses of becoming an OAP in London is the free bus pass to which one becomes entitled. I went to collect mine from the City Hall in Victoria Street, and returned by bus for my first free ride. It was quite an exciting moment as the bus conductor came along saying: 'Fares, please.' It was, however, slightly deflating that as I reached for my brand new pass, the conductor looked at me and murmured, 'That's all right guv'nor, don't bother,' and continued along the bus without waiting to see my pass. Did I look *that* old?

I began reflecting on my past – always a dangerous occupation. But I am glad that I did so, because once again it was brought home to me how very lucky I have been all through my life. The last two months especially have constantly reminded me of the variety of my life, and the different cross-sections of people whom I have met and been able to call my friends.

There was an evening reception for the official opening of the Lord's Cricket School by Gubby Allen. As the gossip writers would say 'anyone who is anyone in cricket' was there to see Derek Shackleton bowl the first ball to Colin Cowdrey. It is quite easily the best cricket school I have ever seen. It has superb lighting and six nets with varying degrees of pace and spin. And vital in our search for fast bowlers, there is a long run-up for the bowlers of at least seventeen yards, which many people would consider to be the maximum necessary for *any* fast bowler even in a Test match.

The school was paid for by members of MCC with some help from commerce and a magnificent contribution from that lover and patron of cricket, Jack Hayward. In recognition of this the playing area is known as the Hayward Hall. Jack told me he was off that week back to his home in the Bahamas to rehearse for the annual pantomime out there. He was going to play one of the Ugly Sisters in *Cinderella* and I was able to give him two gags to use in the 'dressing for the ball' scene. One ugly sister to the other:

'How do you like my religious dress?'

'Religious dress?'

'Yes – lo(w) and behold!'

'Well, I call *mine* a barbed-wire dress – it protects the property without obscuring the view.'

I wonder if he used them!

The biggest occasion during the autumn was a theatrical one – the lunch for one thousand guests given by the theatre producer, Peter Saunders, at the Savoy to celebrate the twenty-fifth year of *The Mousetrap*. It was a marvellous opportunity to meet again so many of the stage personalities with whom I have worked from time to time in the last thirty-two years, such as Donald Sinden, Leslie Phillips, Vera Lynn, Michael Denison and Dulcie Gray, Celia Johnson and Tommy Trinder. Pauline and I gave a lift home to Evelyn Laye and Anna Neagle – how's that for three beautiful ladies in one taxi?

Many of those in the theatrical profession also love cricket and perhaps it is not so surprising, as they are both forms of the arts requiring great skill and technique, utter dedication and hard work. At the same time they both offer the individual the chance of showing off his talents, while remaining the member of a team. Peter Saunders is another cricket enthusiast and a kind, generous person, completely unspoilt by his great success. He is the only one of my friends who has a telephone in his car. But unlike the impresario, Lew Grade, he only has *one*. So if you ring him up you can't be asked to hold on 'as he is on the *other* line'!

In November 1977 I was asked to go back to my old private school, Temple Grove, to open a new gymnasium. The school used to be at Eastbourne when I was there in the twenties, but it moved to Uckfield during the thirties, and has been there ever since. There was a big audience of parents and boys, as after the opening the boys were going off for their half term. I remember the speech days which we used to have, when an Old Boy, who usually seemed to be a general or admiral, got up and waffled away for about twenty minutes. They normally boasted complacently that they had been no good at work or exams, and implied that it did not seem to have handicapped them in after life.

I hope I did not fall into the same trap. I kept my speech as short as possible and included a few jokes, which were so old that they were fresh to this new generation of boys. The headmaster did a great job in introducing me to the parents, masters and boys, and never seemed stuck for a name.

This was unlike a headmaster I once knew who was getting on in years, and becoming more and more absent-minded. At one speech day he was going round talking to the old boys, and said to one of them with a note of triumph in his voice: 'Ah, it's Smith major, isn't it?'

'Yes sir,' replied Smith.

'Well, tell me Smith,' said the headmaster, 'I can never

remember. Was it you or your brother who was killed in the war?'!

Luckily I did not have to give away any prizes, or I might have had an embarrassing experience such as the actor Gerald Harper once had. He was presenting the prizes at the speech day of a girls' day-school and shook hands with all the winners as they came up to receive their books. Each time he murmured some innocuous remark like 'Well done', 'Congratulations', or 'I hope you'll enjoy this book'. After a while he got a bit fed up with this, and thought he would try something different, and more interesting. So when the next girl – an attractive blonde aged about fifteen – stepped up on to the dais, he shook her by the hand, gave her the book and said confidentially: 'And what are you going to do when you leave school?' 'Oh,' replied the girl somewhat taken aback, 'I *was* going straight back home to have tea with Mum.'!

My post has also brought back some memories, including an invitation to dinner with the Junior Common Room at New College, Oxford, where I had spent three such happy years in the thirties. So far as I know I still hold two records there. First, I am the only rugger player to have scored a try for the college in a macintosh, which a spectator had lent me to cover my confusion when my shorts had been ripped off. And secondly, I must still be the only person to have had his trousers removed and thrown through the window of the senior common room, where they landed on a table round which the dons were sitting drinking port.

And of course there is the wonderful variety of Christmas cards. Like those from some of my old Grenadier staff when I was Technical Adjutant in the 2nd Battalion Grenadiers from 1941 to 1945. The nice thing is that they still sign themselves with the nicknames which I bestowed on them. My scout car driver 'Hengist', my chief clerk 'Honest' Joe, the driver of the store truck 'Tremble' – so called because it was the name of a decrepit old butler, whom he played in a sketch in one of our battalion revues. And my soldier servant (as the Brigade of Guards called a batman) 'Pasha' whose surname was Ruston. One ex-guardsman sent me an old programme of the revue we did at Seigburg in Germany in the autumn of 1945. It was called *What About It Then?*, and to show you the standard of its humour, here is one of the jokes which I remember:

'What's the difference between funny and fanny?'

'Well you can feel funny without feeling fanny, but you can't feel fanny without feeling funny.'

And a card from an old friend Frank Copping took me back to my few years as a city gent, disguised in a bowler-hat, with a rolled umbrella, and in a pin-stripe suit too tight under the armpits. Frank ran the cable department where I started when I joined our family coffee business in 1934. He nursed me and tried to teach me business methods without, I fear, a great deal of success. But I did enjoy ringing him up from the next office and pretending to be an irate Italian agent of ours called Enrico Colombino; not that my Italian accent was all that hot.

And always most welcome are the cards from all the friends I have made in the cricketing countries round the world, including this year one from Mike Brearley in Pakistan. I got to know Brearlers well when he toured South Africa with Mike Smith's MCC team in 1964, straight from his triumphs on the Fenners pitch at Cambridge. For some strange reason he hardly made a run on the tour and indeed looked a complete novice. But I shall always remember how well he took it, and never showed the terrific disappointment which he must have felt – fortified perhaps by his triumphs at the bridge table with Charles Fortune, David Brown and myself.

The BBC always have lots of parties at Christmas time and this year in December the Director-General, Ian Trethowan, gave a delightful dinner party at the Television

Centre in honour of Antony Craxton, who was retiring from the Corporation.

'Crackers' was brought up near Lord's in a musical family, but his first love was always cricket. We used to play a lot in charity matches and for all I know he may have been a very good leg-spinner. Unfortunately the ball never pitched, so I shall never find out! For years he was our TV cricket producer and we had much fun and enjoyment. Like me he thinks there is more to cricket than what goes on out in the middle, and he was always on the lookout for the unusual shot of off-the-field activities.

When he left cricket, Crackers became the Royal Producer, culminating in his triumphant broadcast of the Jubilee Service in St Paul's, which by coincidence was his two-hundredth Royal TV occasion. Many of his friends were at the dinner: John Snagge, Michael Standing, Peter West, Cliff Morgan, Richard Baker, Robert Hudson and myself all representing the commentators. As you can imagine there was much reminiscing and Crackers actually told an announcer's gaffe which I had not heard before – I thought I knew them all!

Here it is: An announcer was introducing a concert. 'Tonight's concert,' he said, 'will be given by the Ceffield Shity Police Band . . .' After he had finished the rest of the announcement his producer told him what he had said, and that listeners were already ringing up to complain. The producer advised him not to apologise as it would only draw attention to his mistake. But he ordered the poor announcer to be sure to get the name of the band right in the closing announcement. So when the end of the programme arrived the announcer – now a bag of nerves – steeled himself and came out with: 'You have just been listening to a concert given by the Sheffield City Police Band. The concert was broadcast from the Ceffield Shity Hall!'

But, in spite of all my friends, the true foundation of my happiness has been my wife, my family and my home.

Pauline and I will soon be celebrating our Pearl wedding. I would just like to thank her for her continued love and understanding. Also for her patience with my jokes, my many absences from home, and my possible over-indulgence in work. My family, thank goodness, have given me few problems, only boundless joy and amusement. Barry and Clare live in their own homes in London, and Andrew is still working in Sydney, so that Ian and Joanna are the only ones still at home. But almost every weekend we have a family reunion for Sunday lunch when we laugh, quarrel, play cards and table tennis, and tuck in to roast beef and Yorkshire pudding (when the housekeeping account is not too heavily overdrawn). So thanks too to them for making me so happy and I forgive them for trying to get their own back on me – they now tell *me* far worse jokes than I ever told *them*.

It is interesting that my way of life and connections with the entertainment world have obviously influenced their choice of jobs and careers. Not one of them is a member of any of the professions. Nor do any of them do nine-to-five humdrum office jobs.

Barry's pop group, Design, broke up amicably in 1976. He still composes songs full of melody and now has a small music publishing business. He also does a first-class cabaret act which includes all the well-known Noël Coward songs, which he delivers crisply and clearly just like the Master.

Clare after three years in Australia now works as a PR executive in London, and one of her accounts is a famous TV and recording company. She is much travelled and she and I have a 'visited the most countries' contest. Since her return from Australia via South, Central and North America she has edged ahead and her total is now fifty-three against my forty-four.

Andrew worked in Foyles Book Shop over here and then three years ago left for Sydney where he now works for a worldwide English publishing firm. And to keep up the entertainment theme, Ian – after a year's varied experience in Australia as a messenger for ABC, a jackaroo on an estate, a 'showie' on bumper cars and a researcher for a mining firm – now has a job with a large group of record shops. The nice thing about all their jobs is that they got them on their own merits without any help or influence from Dad. Incidentally, whenever she has time off from running the house, looking after Joanna or her charities like the Life-Boats and the Mentally Handicapped Children, Pauline does a spot of photography at which she is highly trained and expert.

And finally our home in St John's Wood, where we are so marvellously looked after by our wonderful housekeeper Cally. What we would do without her I don't know. She and Pauline between them continue to look after Joanna with loving care and devotion. As a result Joanna – now aged twelve – is a happy pupil at the Gatehouse Learning Centre in Bethnal Green.

We have been in St John's Wood now for thirty years and I could wish for no more friendly nor delightful place in which to live – remarkably peaceful and still with a village atmosphere, although only ten minutes away from Piccadilly Circus by car. The large garden is an added joy, not just for us but also for our Yorkshire terrier, Mini, who spends her life chasing (but never catching) grey squirrels. I am the destroyer in the garden – I weed, mow and light the bonfire. Pauline and our faithful friend Mr Webber do the creative work. The colourful result of their labours is enjoyed as much by our neighbours as by ourselves.

So there we are. I hope you have stayed with me until close of play, and have enjoyed, or at least tolerated, the meanderings of a remarkably happy and lucky person, to whom life – like cricket – is a funny game and still A LOT OF FUN.

St John's Wood
Christmas 1977

PART III:
RAIN STOPS PLAY

30 Slips

W HEN PEOPLE ASK ME where I work, I sometimes reply: 'In a box.' Actually I don't *really* work, anyway. I just go to a match with some friends who love cricket as much as I do. Together we try to tell hundreds of thousands of other cricket lovers about the game which we are watching.

There's a relaxed, friendly atmosphere on *Test Match Special* and, I must admit, a certain amount of schoolboy humour. This is partly explained by the fact that we all think that cricket is fun. So we *have* fun. We are delighted to know that some of this manages to come through the microphone into people's homes, cars or wherever they may be listening. It is because we know that we have this enthusiastic and apparently appreciative band of faithful followers, that we try to do our best never to return to the studio when play is interrupted for some reason or other. We chat away amongst ourselves and many people – especially the ladies – have told me that they think it far better when it is raining than when cricket is being played!

Now, for the first time under one heading, here are some of the most amusing incidents which have happened to us in the Box. Here are the gaffes made by the TV and radio commentators during actual commentary, the leg-pulls and funny happenings which have taken place behind the scenes, and the cricket stories which have been told during our many conversations when Rain Stops Play.

We start with some of the gaffes, slips of the tongue or innuendos which have been made on radio or TV over the last thirty years or so. As the chief gaffer myself, I can only assure you that I never do them on purpose and that all of them are perfectly genuine. Funnily enough, although some of them may appear rather rude, no one ever seems to write in and complain. This may be due to the fact that we have all been taught never to stop and apologise. Just go straight on and the listener won't believe that he or she has heard right!

At Leicester two years ago I am told I welcomed listeners with: 'You've come over at a very appropriate time. Ray Illingworth has just relieved himself at the Pavilion End'!

At Hove in a match between Sussex and Hampshire, Henry Horton of Hampshire was batting and I thought I should tell the radio listeners about his funny stance at the wicket – he stuck his bottom out in a most peculiar way. So I *meant* to say, 'Henry Horton has got a funny sort of stance – it looks as if he's sitting on a shooting stick' – BUT I got it the wrong way round!

I may say that my scorer, Michael Fordham, gave a loud snort and collapsed with laughter. Luckily for me I managed to control myself and carried straight on as if nothing had happened.

In 1976 Northants were playing Worcestershire at Northampton where spectators can drive their cars in and sit in them to watch the play around the ground. It was quite an important match as Northants were in with a chance of drawing level with Middlesex at the head of the County Championship table. In spite of this there was a disappointingly small crowd. So I said, to introduce the game, 'There's a small crowd here to watch this important game – in fact I would say that there are more cars here than people!' Just work that one out – did the cars drive themselves in?

On one occasion I said that Freddie Titmus was bowling and that he had two short legs – one of them square. A listener wrote in to say that he was travelling in a car in Belgium listening to our commentary, and trying to explain cricket to two Belgian friends. When the Belgian lady heard my remark she asked why it was necessary to draw attention to a player's physical disabilities!

At Lord's in 1969. England v New Zealand. Ward is bowling very fast from the Pavilion End to Glenn Turner.

Off the fifth ball of one of his overs he hit Turner a terrible blow in the box. Turner collapses, bat going one way, his gloves another. TV camera pans in. I have to pretend he's been hit everywhere except where he has been! (Nowadays one *would* say!) Turner writhes in pain in the crease for a minute or so, then slowly gets to his feet. Someone hands him his bat, someone else his gloves. I say, 'Turner looks a bit shaky and unsteady, but I think he's going to bat on – one ball left!'

At Worcester on one occasion I greeted the listeners with: 'Welcome to Worcester, where you've just missed seeing Barry Richards hitting one of Basil D'Oliveira's balls clean out of the ground!'

One of my most famous gaffes was made during England v Australia at Headingley in 1961. The Australians were fielding and Neil Harvey was at leg-slip. Suddenly without warning the camera panned in on him so that he filled the screen. I had to think of something quickly to say. 'There's Neil Harvey,' I said, 'standing at leg-slip with his legs wide apart waiting for a tickle.'

I realised immediately what I had said and wished the earth would open and swallow me up. The Australian commentator, Jack Fingleton, made matters worse by drawing attention to it, saying, 'I beg your pardon. I presume you mean waiting for a catch.' I did not answer. For once I did not dare to speak!

I was at Southampton one Saturday to commentate on a match between Hampshire and Surrey. Rex Alston was up at Edgbaston covering one of Warwickshire's matches and close of play there was not until 7 pm.

At 6.30 pm at Southampton, as the players left the field, I said something like: 'Well, that's close of play here with Hampshire 301 all out. But they go on playing till 7 o'clock at Edgbaston, so over there now for some more balls from Rex Alston.'

Rex himself is reputed to have once said: 'Over now to Old John Arlott at Trafford!'

On another occasion Ken Barrington had made a hundred and I said that he was playing well now, but was a bit lucky, as he was *dropped when two*. Believe it or not a letter came in from a listener complaining about the carelessness of mothers!

Roy Lawrence during the 3rd Test West Indies v England at Sabina Park in 1960: 'It's another wonderful day here at Sabina Park – the wind shining and the sun blowing gently across the field.'

At the Oval in 1976 England were playing the West Indies and after the match a lady wrote to me saying how much she had enjoyed our commentaries but that I ought to be more careful, as we had a lot of young listeners. She asked if I realised what I said when they came to me as Michael Holding was bowling to Peter Willey. She told me that I had said: 'The bowler's holding the batsman's willy!'

John Snagge was once reading the latest cricket scores. He said: 'Yorkshire 232 all out – Hutton ill – no I'm sorry – Hutton 111.'

I was once doing a commentary on the annual Whitsun

match between Middlesex and Sussex, when John Warr was captain of Middlesex. Middlesex were batting and making a big score when I had to hand back to the studio for another programme. After a while they handed back to me at Lord's for the latest news and I began, 'Well the latest news here is that Warr's declared.' The duty officer at the time in Broadcasting House told me later that an old lady had switched on as I said this and rang up the duty officer to see whom it was against!

One unknown commentator is reported to have said: 'He was bowled by a ball which he should have left alone!'

Robert Hudson during England v New Zealand at Lord's in 1969. The two teams are being presented to the Queen and Prince Philip during the tea interval . . . 'It's obviously a great occasion for all of them. It's a moment they will always forget.'

Surprisingly I never heard John Arlott make a gaffe. So let's reward him by printing one of the best of his many bons mots. He was describing the Pakistan fast bowler Asif Mahsood's action. You may remember that he used to run up with bent knees. John described him perfectly: 'He reminds me,' he said, 'of Groucho Marx chasing a pretty waitress!'

At Lord's during a Middlesex match Rex Alston once said, 'No runs from that over bowled by Jack Young, which means that he has now had four maidens on the trot!'

Rex also once said that one of the Captains had asked for 'the medium pace roller.'

Another commentator on England's tour of Australia in 1978/79 said: 'John Emburey is bowling with three short legs – one of them wearing a helmet!'

31 On the air

THE EXPERT IS A vital ingredient to a cricket commentary team. He is almost always an ex-Test player who can interpret the finer points of the game because he has been out in the middle himself. On television, nowadays, ex-Test players provide both the commentary and the summaries. On radio the commentary is almost always done by broadcasters and the summaries by ex-Test players. Their guidance and expertise make our job so much easier and we value their presence in the Box more than we can say. But that does not mean that they are not human like the rest of us – as one or two of these stories will show.

One Saturday, Robert Hudson was the commentator in our old commentary box in the Warner Stand at Lord's. Bill Frindall was the scorer and Freddie Brown the 'expert' summariser. At the end of one particular over he was giving his summary when listeners must have been amazed to hear him suddenly let out a yelp – rather like a puppy which has had its toe trodden on. What had happened was this. Robert was always a tremendous fiddler whilst commentating. He used his hands the whole time to pick up pencils or rubbers, bits of paper or books and so on. In those days Bill used to secure his score sheets to wooden boards with large rubber bands. These were special favourites of Robert's, who used to pull them out and stretch them to their utmost limits.

He had just finished describing a particularly exciting over, during which he had been fiddling away with one of the rubber bands. As Freddie started his summary Robert fiddled once too often, and one of the bands came off the board. As if catapulted it shot across the box and hit Freddie a stinging blow in the left ear. But apart from the yelp – a natural reaction – and a nervous glance over his left shoulder, Freddie continued talking, not sure whether he had been stung by a wasp or struck by a poisoned dart! It is not surprising that during his MCC tour of Australia in 1950/51 they said that Freddie Brown had a heart the size of October cabbages.

I have this habit of sometimes addressing my colleagues in the box as Sir – especially Freddie Trueman, whom I often address as Sir Frederick. When my previous book – *It's a Funny Game* – came out, I sent off copies to all the commentators and cricket writers. I wrote something in each one, and my publishers, W. H. Allen, then posted them off for me. In Freddie's I put something like: 'To Sir Frederick. With happy memories of days together in the commentary box . . .'

I thought no more about it until I heard from Don Mosey that Fred was very annoyed with me. Evidently his friend the regular postman came rushing up the path one morning shouting, 'Congratulations Freddie – you've got it at last – you've got it.' He handed a surprised Fred a parcel obviously containing a book and addressed to Sir Frederick Trueman!

Later I discovered what had happened. The girl who dispatched all the books from W. H. Allen had looked inside the book and seeing my message to 'Sir Frederick' really thought he *was* a Knight!

Once when televising at Lord's, I noticed John Warr sitting with his fiancée, Valerie, in the Grandstand. We quickly got the cameras on to them and I introduced them to the viewing public as 'Warr and Piece'.

One incident in 1953 which concerned Jim Swanton still remains a mystery to this day. Jim was commentating on

TV at the Headingley Test v Australia when a man walked past our commentary point. He was carrying a ladder over his shoulder, and round his neck – like a giant collar – was a lavatory seat. As you can imagine, he caused quite a commotion in the crowd, as he disappeared under the football stand. But Jim with his usual sang-froid (and good taste!) completely ignored the man, even though he had been picked up by our cameras. Instead, Jim drew the viewers' attention to Lindwall's beautiful action out in the middle.

Almost ten minutes later the man reappeared from under the stand and walked back past our commentary box still with the ladder *but minus the seat*. What *had* he done with it, and if he'd had to fix it, why did he need a ladder? Jim again ignored him and offered no solution to this mysterious happening. I only wished that I had been doing the commentary at the time! But perhaps it is just as well that I wasn't.

Once I was commentating for radio on a county match at Clacton on Sea. Essex were fielding and Trevor Bailey – unusually for him – had placed himself in the deep. One or two balls came to him and although he stopped them he didn't look too lively. Finally he did let one through for a boundary and I commented that he didn't look too energetic and possibly he had had too good a party the night before. As I said it I was watching him and he turned round to my commentary box and shook his fist at me! I hadn't realised that he could hear my commentary from a portable radio belonging to someone sitting in a deck-chair on the boundary. A salutary lesson to be careful what one says over the air!

In the summer of 1978 at the Oval I registered a 'first' in the *Test Match Special* box. We had two policemen up on our balcony at the top of the pavilion, and as it was a hot day they took off their helmets. As I was commentating, someone – I'm not sure who – took one of the helmets and put it on my head. I now have a certificate to register that I am the first BBC commentator to give a live cricket commentary wearing a policeman's helmet – belonging to PC 418 Barry Brown.

On the Saturday of the Oval Test between England and Australia in 1977 we all got a shock when we first entered the commentary box before play started. There, sitting in Bill Frindall's usual corner, was an Arab in full white Arab dress and head-dress. He was a bearded figure who kept his head down, apparently absorbed in Bill's score sheets and record books. None of us knew what to do except to mutter 'Good Morning', to which the Arab murmured something into his beard without looking up. We, of course, suspected it might be a leg-pull, but on the other hand it could be someone from the BBC Arab Service, who was to be attached to us for the day. Anyhow, none of us dared to be the first to challenge the stranger.

However, just before we went on the air it became obvious that it must be Bill Frindall, since he had not yet appeared in the box – at least as himself. On being challenged he pleaded guilty, but it was still difficult to believe that it was not a genuine Arab, with Bill's big black beard and authentic white Arab dress. All that was missing was a camel tied up outside the box!

During the morning we explained to listeners what had happened and questioned him about it. Evidently the night before he had been at a party and had been introduced to an Arab in Arab dress. This Arab thought that Bill was also an Arab – from his dark, swarthy appearance – and started to speak to him in Arabic. Bill's hostess hurriedly explained the mistake, but there and then bet Bill that he would not spend a whole day at the Oval Test dressed as an Arab. Her Arab friend promised to lend his clothes and so Bill said he would do it for charity. Sponsorship for £62 was soon guaranteed, the proceeds to go to Cancer Research if Bill succeeded.

Next morning when he drove his car up to the Oval gates the attendant was surprised to see an Arab driving a car with the Official Car Park label stuck on the windscreen. However, he let the car through and Bill immediately drove to the usual space which was always reserved for him near the back door to the pavilion. Another worried official ran up: 'Hey, you can't park there. It's always reserved for Mr Bill Frindall as he has so many briefcases to carry.' Bill muttered through his beard that he couldn't care less for Mr Frindall. 'I have just bought up the Oval,' he said, 'and I shall park where I like.' Then, to spare the astonished official – an old friend – any more embarrassment, Bill revealed who he was. He made his way through the crowd in the pavilion up to the commentary box. He somehow managed to keep a straight face as we all muttered our tentative greetings.

He stayed in his Arab dress all day and so won his bet for charity. The white robes, he told us on the air, were called 'Dish Dash' and had once belonged to King Hussein, who had given them away to a friend. 'I don't blame him,' said Fred Trueman, 'I would have done the same thing to get rid of them!'

Nowadays television commentary boxes are far more accessible than they were when we first started. They used to be on a high platform supported by scaffolding, and could only be reached by climbing an ordinary builders' ladder. This was terrifying for the likes of me who are scared of heights. But it also used to produce some good laughs for the crowds. I remember well the barracking and shouts of encouragement which they used to give to Roy Webber and Jim Swanton – at that time the bulkiest of the commentators – as they made their perilous climbs. Actually on a windy day, when the scaffolding swayed dangerously, we were very pleased to have them with us up there as ballast.

Once at the Oval the crowd had an extra bonus so far as ladder-climbing entertainment went. The cameramen, riggers and sound engineers used to come up to our balcony on top of the pavilion via an iron ladder fixed against a stone wall. It was a short cut and saved them going through the pavilion. At one Test match a *very* high BBC executive had lunched somewhere rather well with a lady. After lunch they decided they would like to watch the Test at the Oval. The executive had no ticket to the pavilion but paid at the gates to gain admittance to the ground. He walked round to where the TV scanners were parked and saw some of the TV crew climbing the iron ladder up to our commentary position on the balcony. So he decided that he in his black homburg, and his lady friend – who was dressed in a thin summer dress and wearing a big picture hat – should follow them.

They started their climb amidst roars of laughter and shouts of encouragement from the members in the stand at the side of the pavilion. The ladder went up a long way above this stand and as the intrepid climbers slowly passed the members, there were loud gasps from the men, and some squeals of delight from the ladies. What the executive had not realised was that there was a strong wind blowing and that the skirt of his lady friend, who was following him up the ladder, was billowing around her neck revealing (luckily!) a pair of very snazzy knickers!

32 Pulls to leg

EARLIER ON I stressed that the atmosphere in the Box is friendly, relaxed and spiced with a certain amount of schoolboy humour. Here now are some of the leg-pulls which we have perpetrated from time to time on an unsuspecting colleague.

At Port of Spain during Colin Cowdrey's successful MCC tour in 1967, I played a dirty trick on Tony Cozier. Rain had stopped play and he had gone across to the Press box on the other side of the ground. I stayed in the box to give an occasional up-to-date report on the weather. I saw him returning after a time, so as he entered the box I pretended that we were on the air, and that I was broadcasting. 'Well,' I began, 'those were the statistics of the MCC team, with their exact batting and bowling figures, plus their ages and dates of their birthdays. Ah, I see that Tony Cozier has just rejoined us, so I will ask him to give exactly the same details of the whole West Indian side. Tony . . .'

I have rarely seen a greater look of horror on anyone's face. He sat down at the mike and began to stammer, making frantic signals to our scorer to hand him *Wisden* or any other book which would give him the necessary information. 'Well, Brian,' he said, 'I'll try to tell the listeners in a minute, but as I've just seen the pitch perhaps you would like to hear about its state first.' 'No, sorry, Tony,' I said, 'we've just talked about it whilst you were away. All we want – and straight away please – is the information about the West Indian statistics.'

At this point I couldn't go on any further, he looked so miserable and desperate, so I said: 'Well, if Tony won't give us the details I suppose we had better return to the studio.'

There was a deathly hush for about five seconds and then I broke the news to him that we had *not* been on the air! It took him quite a time to get over the shock, and I sometimes wonder if he has ever forgiven me!

For many years Jim Swanton, Peter West, Denis Compton and I did the television commentaries and we found that Jim was a perfect target for leg-pulls. Here are a couple:

At Lord's in 1963 we were televising that magnificent Test match between England and the West Indies which ended in such an exciting draw. On the Friday, while we were commentating, the Sacred College of Cardinals were in conclave in the Vatican to elect a new Pope to succeed the late Pope John XXIII. The crowds were assembled in St Peter's Square awaiting the puff of white smoke to come from the chimney in the Vatican, which would announce that a new Pope had been elected. I suddenly spotted that one of the chimneys in the old Tavern had caught fire and that black smoke was belching out of it. With the help of producer Antony Craxton the cameras were quickly directed onto it and I was able to say, 'Ah, I see that Jim Swanton has been elected Pope!'

In 1963 we were televising the August Bank Holiday match between Kent and Hampshire at Canterbury. Jim was one of the commentators and Colin Cowdrey was in our box as an expert, after breaking his wrist in the Lord's Test. Before play, we got together with that arch leg-puller Peter Richardson, who was captain of Kent, and Bill Copson, one of the umpires. Kent were batting and we laid our plans which were to start as soon as a handkerchief was waved from our TV box as a signal that Jim Swanton was commentating.

As soon as he saw the signal, Peter – who was one of the batsmen – had an earnest mid-wicket conference with his partner, ostentatiously gesticulating in our direction.

He then went over to Copson and spoke gravely to him, still pointing to us. Antony Craxton zoomed one of his cameras in on the pitch and said to him, 'I wonder what's going on? What's the conference all about? Comment on it please.'

At this point Copson began walking towards our commentary box. 'Ah,' said Jim, 'obviously some small boys are playing about below us here and putting the batsmen off – or perhaps it's the sun shining on the windscreen of a car . . .' Copson stopped when twenty yards short of our box, cupped his hands and shouted so that the millions of viewers could hear: 'Will you stop that booming noise up there. It's putting the batsmen off. Please stop it.' Colin, just to rub it in, pretended not to have heard and shouted down to Copson: 'Sorry, can you repeat that?' Copson did so, twice as loud, and there was a roar of laughter from the crowd, and Jim soon realised that his leg had been well and truly pulled.

Rex Alston was commentating at Lord's with Jim Swanton as his summariser. Rex tended to hold his head between his hands when broadcasting – so that he looked straight ahead – rather like a horse in blinkers. A batsman snicked a ball which fell just in front of the second slip. 'I don't think that was a chance but as it's the end of the over, let's ask Jim Swanton what he thought.' He turned round, and to his horror found an empty seat beside him and on the desk a short note which read: 'Have gone to spend a penny. Back in a minute. Jim.'

With one exception I have very happy memories of commentating on any match in which India has been playing. The exception was one Sunday in 1967 when India was playing Lancashire at Southport in a 40-over-a-side game. I was working for television, but instead of commentating I was doing in-vision interviews with the batsmen as they returned to the pavilion. It's not a particularly easy job as most batsmen are not in a very good mood after being dismissed – especially as nowadays no one ever seems to think that they are out.

I was sitting with my microphone in a deck-chair in front of the pavilion when I saw that Ajit Wadekar was out. So I got up and went to meet him. We had become good friends on the tour and I always called him 'Wadders' and he called me 'Johnners'. So it was with some confidence that I approached him and in front of the camera asked him:

'What happened, Wadders?' Instead of the smile I was expecting, I noticed that his face was completely blank. Thinking he had not heard me over the applause of the crowd I repeated the question. To my utter astonishment he said in broken English: 'Sorry – I no speak English. I do not understand,' and continued on his way to the pavilion. 'But Wadders,' I gasped, 'we've often talked together during the tour – surely you understand? How did you get out?' But it was no good. He brushed me aside murmuring: 'Me no speak English – sorry,' and disappeared into the pavilion.

Was my face red as I turned to face the camera! I tried to laugh it off – not very successfully – before I hurriedly handed over to the commentator.

I discovered afterwards that Wadekar had got permission from his captain, the Nawab of Pataudi, to pull my leg. I must admit that he succeeded in a big way!

In 1960 England won the first three Tests to beat South Africa 3–0 in the series and there was no real tension when we came to the Oval for the last Test. On the last morning, play was particularly dull, with light rain falling and England batting drearily. In the television box we were becoming a bit bored, so we thought that we would liven things up a bit.

We had one of those very rude seaside postcards and put it inside an envelope from one of the telegrams which we had received. We addressed it to Neil Adcock and persuaded the South African twelfth man, Griffin, to take it out on to the field at the end of an over. He did so and Neil stuffed it into his pocket until he had bowled another over. He then opened the 'telegram', saw the postcard and burst out laughing. He signalled to the rest of his team to have a look and even the two umpires, Charlie Elliott and Eddie Phillipson, could not resist taking a peep.

Soon everyone on the field was laughing and all we said on TV was that Adcock had obviously had some very good news from home. We heard our colleagues in the radio box next to us speculating. Had Adcock's wife had twins or had he won the pools or what? At the lunch interval Neil had to make a statement in the press but though he now knew who had sent it, he didn't give us away, but admitted it was a practical joke. At any rate, it had cheered things up a bit!

In 1974 on the Saturday of the 2nd Test at Lord's v Pakistan it rained most of the day and there were constant interruptions. We were doing our best to fill in with talk so that we did not have to return to the studio for music. At 2.30 pm we were all sitting in the box having a general discussion, when Henry Blofeld got stuck into some topic in which he was especially interested. When he gets excited Henry talks very fast and hardly draws breath. On this occasion he looked straight into the microphone and gabbled away at a great pace for about three or four minutes, completely ignoring the rest of us.

We got a bit fed up, so all quietly left our seats and went out of the box. We then got Peter Baxter, our producer, to slip a note in front of Henry as he was in full spate. The note simply read: 'Keep going till 6.30 pm.' It momentarily stopped Henry in his tracks, as he looked round the box and saw that he was alone and had to keep talking by himself for at least four hours. But he carried on bravely and after a few minutes we had mercy on him, and slipped back into our seats . . .

As I have said, people are very kind and send all sorts of gifts to the commentary box – sweets, chocolates, biscuits – even wine. At Lord's in 1977 some kind lady sent me a gorgeous sticky chocolate cake. I cut it into slices and during a rather dull bit of play I noticed Alan McGilvray standing chatting at the back of the box. So whilst commentating I turned round and offered him a piece of the cake, which he gratefully took. I saw him take a good mouthful and as soon as the next ball had been bowled I said, 'I'll now ask Alan McGilvray what he thought of that particular delivery – Alan come up to the mike and give your opinion.' The result was hysterical. Alan tried desperately to speak and crumbs spattered all over the box. He managed to gulp down some of the cake and spoke a few incoherent words. But by that time it didn't matter. Everyone in the box was laughing out loud.

33 Batting

LASTLY, THE STORIES which have been told to fill in
time when Rain Stops Play. We all have our special
favourites among the great characters which cricket
has always produced. I suspect that John Arlott's favourites are George Gunn, Bomber Wells or anyone from
Hampshire. My own is certainly the one and only Patsy
Hendren. Everyone's favourite seems to be Freddie
Trueman himself. I hope that you will find yours among
this sample of stories which have been told in the Box.

Dr W. G. Grace had just packed his bag one morning and
was ready to go off to play for Gloucestershire, when a
lady rushed up to his door and said: 'Can you come
quickly, Doctor, I think my twins have got the measles.'
'I'm sorry, Ma'am,' said the Doctor, 'I am just going off to
Gloucester to play cricket and can't stop. But contact
me at the ground if their temperatures reach 210 for two.'

George Gunn, when playing for Nottinghamshire against
Glamorgan, started to walk off the field at half-past one
with the impression that it was time for lunch. However,
under the conditions for that match, lunch was not due
to be taken until 2.00 pm and Gunn was recalled to
continue his innings. He lifted his bat away from the
next ball, was comprehensibly bowled – making no
attempt to play the ball – and as he retired to the
pavilion, said, 'You can have your lunch, gentlemen,
when you like, but I always take mine at 1.30 pm'

During Len Hutton's tour of Australia, Frank Tyson's
tremendous speed caused dismay and destruction

amongst batsmen, wherever he bowled. On one occasion when he was at his fastest, he had run through a side until it was the turn of the No. 11 batsman to come in. Looking pale and apprehensive he came down the pavilion steps, but was so nervous that he couldn't close the catch of the pavilion gate. A voice from the crowd shouted: 'Leave it open, you won't be long!'

A batsman had played and missed a number of times. Yabba, the famous Sydney Hill-barracker, shouted out to the bowler: 'Send him down a grand piano, and see if he can play *that*!'

When 'Bomber' Wells came in to bat for Nottinghamshire against the Australians at Trent Bridge in 1964, Neil Hawke was in devastating form. The umpire, ready to give him guard, said: 'What do you want, Bomber?' To which Bomber replied: 'Help!'

Arthur Wood, to a batsman who had played and missed at three successive balls, each of which just grazed the stumps without disturbing the bails: 'Have you ever tried walking on water?'

And to Hedley Verity at Bramall Lane in 1935, after H. B. Cameron had just hit Verity for thirty in one over, Wood offered this advice: 'Keep 'em there Hedley. Thou hast him in two minds – he don't know whether t'smack thee for four or six.'

It appears that when 'Bomber' Wells was playing for Gloucestershire he was batting one day with Sam Cooke.

They got into a terrible tangle over a short single, with Sam just making the crease by hurling himself flat on the ground. As he lay there panting he shouted out to Bomber, 'Call!', and Bomber shouted back, 'Tails!'

Alf Gover, of Surrey and England, as a young 19-year-old, arrived at Lord's for his first Middlesex v Surrey match. When he got to the old 'Pro's' dressing-room, only one other person was there – the great Patsy Hendren. 'Hello, young chap,' he called out, 'what's your name?'

'Alf Gover, Sir.'

'What do you do?'

'I bowl.'

'Quick?' said Patsy.

'Very quick,' he answered proudly.

Patsy looked round the room to make sure that he was not overheard, came over to him and said, very confidentially: 'Look son, I don't mind quick bowling, you can push it down at me as fast as you like, only...' – another conspiratorial glance round – 'only I don't like 'em if they are pitched short. You know this is my home ground and they like me to get a few. My peepers aren't as good as they were and I can't pick up the ball as fast as I used to, so keep them well up to me, won't you?'

Alf pondered on this self-admitted fear of the great England and Middlesex batsman and decided that there was a great chance for him to make his name.

He happened to be bowling from the pavilion end when Patsy came in, and said to himself: 'Ah, here's that old man who can't see and doesn't like short-pitched balls – so here goes.' His first ball to him was very short, just outside the leg stump and as fast as he could bowl it. It was promptly hooked for six into the Tavern. 'Fluke,' he said to himself and sent him down a similar short ball, only this time on the middle stump. Patsy took two steps back and cut it for four past third man. 'I've got him scared now – he's running away,' he said to himself as he walked back to his mark. Down came his third ball, just the same as the other two, and it went sailing away for six into the Mound Stand.

At the end of the over, Jack Hobbs went across to him

from cover. 'What are you bowling short at Mr Hendren for, son?'

'He's afraid of them,' Alf replied.

The 'Master' stared in amazement. 'Who told you that?' he asked.

'He did, Mr Hobbs,' said Alf.

'Young man. Never do it again,' said Hobbs. 'Patsy is still the best hooker of fast bowling in the world. May I remind you that he's an Irishman, and every night he kisses the Blarney Stone!'

On one occasion Patsy Hendren was fielding on the boundary by the famous Hill on the Sydney Cricket Ground. The batsman hit the ball high in the air towards him. As it soared higher and higher into the air, a raucous voice from the Hill shouted, 'Patsy, if you miss the catch you can sleep with my sister.'

Later Patsy was asked what he had done. 'Oh,' he replied, 'as I hadn't seen his sister, I caught the ball.'

Just before Patsy retired he was batting against Derbyshire on a wet pitch that was slippery with mud. Walter Robins was his partner and was batting against the leg-breaks of T. B. Mitchell. Robins, who always used his feet to attack slow bowlers, had got into the habit of dancing down the pitch and if he missed the ball, walking straight on to the pavilion without looking round at the wicket-keeper.

Mitchell was bowling from the pavilion end and as usual Robins danced down the pitch, missed the ball and continued walking towards the pavilion without so much as a backward glance. Patsy immediately shouted, 'He's missed it' – so Robins turned quickly round and flung himself on the ground, bat stretched out towards the stumps.

There was a roar of laughter from the players and the crowd, as Robins slowly got up, shirt, flannels and pads covered in mud. He looked up to see the bails lying on the ground and Harry Elliott the wicket-keeper chatting to the slip, having obviously brought off a neat stumping!

When I asked Patsy how Robins had taken it, he said that he hadn't been too pleased! Knowing R. W. V. R. that was putting it mildly.

Leicestershire were playing Nottinghamshire and Harold Larwood was bowling at his fastest and was in his most frightening mood. The light was very bad and he had taken four quick wickets when it was Alec Skelding's turn to bat. He came down the pavilion steps very slowly, then groped his way along the railings in front of the pavilion, shouting to the members: 'Can anyone tell me where this match is being played . . .?'

A similar story is told about Jack Newman when he came out to bat with Lord Tennyson, and his Lordship called down the wicket to Newman, 'Why don't you appeal against the light, Jack? They won't listen to me.'

'I can hear you, my Lord,' replied Newman, 'but I can't see you . . . where are you?'

And what about the unorthodox batsman who, like Brian Close, could play equally well either right- or left-handed. His opponents never knew which it would be until he took up his stance at the crease. One of them asked him how he decided which way he would play. He replied that if, when he woke up in the morning, his wife was lying on her right side, then he would bat right-handed. If she was lying on her left side, then he batted left-handed. 'But what happens if she is lying on her back?' asked the opponent. 'In that case,' said the man, 'I ring up the club to say I will be an hour late!'

34 Bowling and fielding

EACH YEAR AT THE beginning of the season, Yorkshire used to play some one-day matches against clubs around the county. The idea was to give the team some practice out in the middle before starting their championship matches. One year they were playing against a club just outside York. Yorkshire fielded first and Freddie Trueman soon got among the wickets, bowling with surprising speed and ferocity for so early in the season. He had taken the first five wickets and the next batsman emerged from the pavilion.

He was an upright military figure, with bristling white moustache and an old-fashioned I Zingari cap on his head, complete with button on the top. The sleeves of his cream shirt were buttoned down to the wrist and he had on a pair of those skeleton pads, which used to be fashionable in the days of W.G. He was an imposing figure, but understandably enough he looked a trifle apprehensive at what he had to face.

Norman Yardley, the Yorkshire captain, saw him coming and, realising the county were doing a bit too well, went up to Freddie and said: 'This is Brigadier X. He is an important member of the county. Let him get a few.' So Freddie, in his most affable and friendly manner, went up to the Brigadier as he approached the wicket and said: 'Good morning, Brigadier, don't worry. With my first ball I'll give you one to get off the mark.'

The Brigadier looked greatly relieved, but his expression changed as Freddie went on: 'Aye, and with my second I'll pin thee against flippin' sightscreen!'

Harold Larwood was once staying with a friend in the

West Country, and visited a village cricket match on the Saturday afternoon. The visiting side were one short and Larwood was pressed to play without anyone knowing who he was. As both umpires came from the home side, who were batting, it proved difficult to get them out.

In desperation the captain asked Larwood if he could bowl. He said that he would have a try and, taking a short run, sent down an off-spinner, which the batsman missed. It hit him in the middle of both legs, which were right in front of the wicket. To the appeal – 'Not out' was the reply. The next one, a leg-break, was snicked into the wicket-keeper's hands. Again 'Not out' was the reply.

Larwood then took his usual run of over twenty yards and sent down a thunderbolt, which knocked all three stumps out of the ground. Turning to the umpire he said, 'We very nearly had him that time, didn't we?'

When Harold Larwood played against Wilfred Rhodes for the first time he noticed that the Yorkshire batsman when taking his stance had the front of his left foot cocked off the ground. 'What's he doing that for?' said Lol to umpire Bill Reeves.

'Oh, he always stands like that,' said Bill.

'He won't to me,' said Larwood, and rushing up to the wicket bowled a full toss which landed with a mighty crack on Rhodes' toes. 'How's that?' yelled Larwood.

'Bloody painful I should think,' said Reeves.

Arthur Mailey was bowling for New South Wales in the famous match in which Victoria scored 1,107 against them. Mailey's figures were 4 for 362. He said afterwards, 'I should have had an even better analysis if a bloke in a brown trilby hat sitting in the sixth row of the pavilion roof hadn't dropped two sitters!'

On another occasion, after suffering from a surfeit of dropped catches in the slips off his bowling, Alf Gover was having a drink with some of the offenders after close of play. After a while one of them said: 'Well, so long Alf, I must be off. I've got a train to catch.' Alf replied: 'So long. Hope you have better luck – with the train!'

Joe Hardstaff said of Roly Thompson of Warwickshire, who used to take an unnecessarily long run: 'He takes such a long run that you're out of form by the time he reaches the stumps.'

In 1937, against Yorkshire, Fred Price, the Middlesex wicket-keeper, caught seven catches in an innings – a record at that time. He was having a drink in the Tavern after the game, when a lady came up to him and said, 'Oh, Mr Price, I did admire your wicket-keeping today. I was so excited, I nearly fell off the balcony.'

'If you had done so, madam,' he replied, 'on today's form I would have caught you too!'

Whilst in Australia with the 1962/3 MCC team, poor David Sheppard came in for more than his fair share of dropped catches. The story was going around that a young English couple, who had settled in Australia, were due to have their first-born christened. The husband suggested that it would be nice if they got David Sheppard to do it for them. 'Oh no,' said the horrified wife, 'not likely, he would only drop it!'

Cecil Parkin once suggested to his captain, Johnny Douglas, whose bowling figures were nought for plenty on the score-board, yet still kept himself on, 'Why not go on at t'other end – maybe tha'll see scoreboard better from there.'

E. J. (Tiger) Smith said once, 'I never missed a catch in my life. They just dropped out!'

In a match against Gloucestershire, Brian Close was fielding at forward short leg with Freddie Trueman bowling. Martin Young received a short ball, which he hit right in the middle of the bat. It hit Close on the right side of the head and rebounded to first slip who caught it!

Close seemed none the worse, but when he returned to the pavilion at the next interval a member asked him: 'That was a terrible blow; aren't you worried standing so near? What *would* have happened if the ball had hit you slap between the eyes?'

'He'd have been caught at cover,' replied the indomitable Yorkshire captain!

It was a Sunday in Australia, and Percy Chapman and Patsy Hendren decided to get away from it all and borrowed a car for a run into the country. After a few miles they went round a corner and saw a cricket match about to start in a field adjoining the road. As all cricketers are wont to do – they stopped the car with the intention of watching the game for a few minutes. The car no sooner stopped than an Australian strolled over to the car and said, 'Do either of you chaps play cricket?'

Chapman pointed to Patsy and said, 'He plays a little.'

'Good oh,' said the fellow, 'we are a man short. Will you make up for us?'

Although it was Patsy's day off, he obliged, and as his adopted side were fielding, the captain sent him out to long-on. Patsy went to the allotted position, and as the field was on a slope he was out of sight of the pitch. He had nothing to do except throw the ball in occasionally. He was lost to sight for a long time when at last a towering hit was sent in his direction. Patsy caught the ball and ran up the hill shouting, 'I caught it, I caught it.'

The batsman looked at him with daggers drawn – it was *his* captain. 'You lunatic – *they* were out twenty minutes ago. *We* are batting now!'

Godfrey Evans, of Kent and England, made a particularly good stumping on the leg-side when playing in an up-country match on one of his tours of Australia. As he whipped off the bails he shouted to the umpire, 'How's that?' and the umpire replied, 'Bloody marvellous!'

In a Lancashire match a fast bowler was bowling on a bad wicket, and the opening batsman – who shall be nameless – had to face a number of terrifying deliveries. The first whizzed past his left ear – the second nearly knocked his cap off – and the third struck him an awful blow over the heart. He collapsed and lay on the ground – then after a minute or two got up and prepared to take strike again. The umpire asked him if he was ready – he replied, 'Yes, but I would like the sightscreen moved.'

'Certainly,' said the umpire. 'Where would you like it?'

The batsman replied, 'About halfway down the wicket between me and the bowler!'

35 Umpires

MY FAVOURITE CRICKET STORY occurred at the Duke of Norfolk's lovely ground at Arundel. His team were playing the Sussex Martlets, but just before the start they found they had only one umpire. The Duke said he would go and get his butler, Meadows, who was cleaning the silver down at the Castle. He did not know much about cricket but would be better than nothing.

So Meadows was fetched, put into a white coat and the game began with the Duke's side batting. They did not do too well and with seven wickets down the Duke himself came into bat. He was at the non-strikers' end and Meadows was standing at square leg. The batsman thought he had better give the Duke the strike, so pushed the ball to cover and called, 'Come on, your Grace.'

Unfortunately the Duke slipped and landed flat on his face in the middle of the pitch. Cover point threw the ball over the top of the stumps to the wicket-keeper, who whipped off the bails with the Duke yards short of the crease. 'How's that?' everyone roared, and looked at Meadows at square leg.

There was a pregnant silence. What would he do? Would he give his master out? After a second or two's pause Meadows drew himself up to his full height and with his two hands in front of his chest in a way butlers have, he gave his verdict: 'His Grace is not in!'

Ray Robinson tells of the occasion when umpire George Borwick was signalling to an attendant, who was moving the sightscreen at the batsman's request. Borwick was holding his arm aloft for quite a long time as a signal to the attendant to keep on pushing. Yabba, the famous Sydney barracker, noticed the upstretched arm and shouted: 'It's no use, umpire, you can't leave the ground – you'll have to wait till the lunch interval, like the rest of us!'

In a Middlesex match at Lord's before the war Walter Robins had just completed a very productive over as far as the batsmen were concerned, and decided that it was time to make a change. He called over to a Middlesex fast bowler, 'Take the next over at this end, Jim.' Umpire Bill Reeves walked across to the retiring Robins and said, 'Do you want your sweater, Sir?' As it was a hot and perspiring day, Robins rather grumpily said to Reeves, 'Keep the b . . . sweater – and you know what you can do with it.'

'What, Sir,' said Reeves, 'swords and all?'

Charlie Knott of Hampshire was bowling to Dusty Rhodes of Derbyshire and roared out a terrific appeal for a catch at the wicket: 'Howizee?' To which Alec Skelding replied: 'Oh, he's not at all well and he was even worse last night.'

Skelding, after an appeal for a run-out, which was a very close thing: 'Gentlemen – it's a photo finish – and I haven't got time to develop the photo. NOT OUT.'

At Cheltenham when Surrey were playing Gloucestershire, Alf Gover was asked by Bill Reeves whether he wanted guard. 'No, thanks,' he replied, 'I've played here before.'

Johnny Wardle enquired of an umpire (who shall be nameless): 'You know, I think that ball would have hit the wicket. Where do you think it would have hit?' 'How should I know,' retorted the umpire, 'the gentleman's leg was in the way!'

Alec Skelding was umpiring a match on a hot, dusty day. One of the bowlers had a full set of false teeth, and as he ran up to deliver a particularly fast ball all his teeth fell out on to the ground. The ball hit the batsman on the pad and the bowler turned round and mouthed unintelligible noises. Alec, quick to see what had happened, said, 'I beg your pardon. I cannot tell what you say.' The bowler tried again, but Alec still pretended he could not decipher his words. So the bowler stooped down, recovered his dentures covered in dust and replaced them. Turning round, he said rather grittily: 'How's that?'

'Not out!'

Surrey were playing Middlesex at the Oval and Bill Reeves was one of the umpires. Nigel Haig opened the bowling and Andrew Sandham went in first for Surrey. Not being very tall, a ball from Haig hit him in the navel and there was a loud appeal. 'Not out,' said Reeves. 'Why not?' asked Haig. 'Too high,' said Reeves.

Haig went back to his mark muttering, possibly thinking that even if a ball hit a little chap like him on the head it couldn't be too high. A few balls later a beautiful ball beat him all ends up and hit Sandham on the pads. 'What about that one then?' yelled Haig. 'Not out,' said Reeves. 'Why not?' said Haig. 'Too low!' said Reeves – and that ended all arguments for that day!

When he was at school Gilbert Harding hated cricket. The headmaster, appreciating this, excused him playing on condition that he took some other exercise such as walking or tennis. But the games master was always very annoyed about this and got his own back one day (so he thought) by making Gilbert Harding umpire in the annual match of the Masters v the Boys.

The Masters batted first and the games master, resplendent in his Oxford Authentic cap, batted superbly and was 99 not out when a bowler from the end at which Gilbert Harding was umpiring hit him high up on the left thigh. 'How's that?' said the bowler.

'Out!' said Gilbert. The games master was furious and

as he passed Gilbert on his way back to the pavilion said, 'Harding, you weren't paying attention. I wasn't out.'

Gilbert replied, 'On the contrary, sir, I *was* paying attention and you weren't out!'

In a village match a visiting batsman was hit high on the chest by the local fast bowler – the village blacksmith.

To his surprise the bowler appealed for lbw, and to his even greater surprise the umpire gave him out. As he passed the umpire on his way back to the pavilion, the batsman said, 'I couldn't possibly have been out, it hit me in the chest.'

'Well,' said the umpire, 'you look in the local *Gazette* next Thursday, and you'll see you were out right enough.'

'*You* look,' snorted the batsman, 'I am the Editor!'

In a Central Lancashire League match a batsman snicked the ball hard on to his pads, from where it went down towards long leg. He ran one run, but was amazed on approaching the other end, to hear the bowler appealing for lbw. To his horror the umpire then put his finger up. Unable to contain himself the batsman blurted out, 'I can't be out lbw, I hit it.'

'I know you did,' said the umpire, thinking quickly. 'I'm only signalling byes.'

W. G. Grace was batting on a very windy day, and a fast bowler succeeded in getting one past him which just flicked the bails off. The Doctor stood his ground and said to the umpire, 'Windy day today, umpire.'

Whereupon the umpire replied, 'Very windy indeed, Doctor – mind it doesn't blow your cap off on the way back to the pavilion!'

And finally a couple of the jokes with which we have regaled the poor listeners when rain has stopped play.

Don't judge them too harshly. Remember they were made 'at a stroke'!

Before the start of a needle village match, the home captain found he was one short. In desperation he was looking round the ground for someone he could rope in to play when he spotted an old horse grazing quietly in the field next door. So he went up to him and asked him if he would like to make up the side. The horse stopped eating and said: 'Well, I haven't played for some time and am a bit out of practice but if you're pushed, I'll certainly help you out,' and so saying jumped over the fence and sat down in a deck-chair in front of the pavilion.

The visitors lost the toss and the home side batted first, the horse being put in last. They were soon 23 for 9 and the horse made his way to the wicket wearing those sort of leather shoes horses have on when they are pulling a roller or a mower. He soon showed his eye was well in and hit the bowling all over the field. When he wasn't hitting sixes he was galloping for quick singles and never once said 'Neigh' when his partner called him for a run. Finally he was out hoof before wicket for a brilliant 68, and the home side had made 99.

When the visitors batted the home captain put the horse in the deep and he saved many runs by galloping round the boundary and hoofing the ball back to the wicket-keeper. However the visitors were not losing any wickets and were soon 50 for 0. The home captain had tried all his regular bowlers in vain when he suddenly thought of the horse. He had batted brilliantly and now was fielding better than anyone. At least he could do no worse than the other bowlers. So he called out to him: 'Horse, would you like to take the next over at the vicarage end?'

The horse looked surprised, 'Of course I wouldn't,' he replied. 'Whoever heard of a horse who could BOWL!'

A man, whose wife was in hospital expecting a baby, telephoned one afternoon to see what the news was. By mistake he got the local cricket ground. When he asked what was the latest position the reply came back: 'There are seven out already – and the last two were ducks!'

Index